HUMBLE   ADVENTUROUS   FAMILY   LEARNING

WEIRDNESS   CHANGE   POSITIVE

DELIVER   CREATE   OPEN-MINDED   SERVICE

TEAM   **Zappos.com**   **ZiP**

6pm.com   RELATIONSHIP

HONEST   WOW   OPEN

COMMUNICATION   SPIRIT   DRIVE   EMBRACE   GROWTH   **Z** RETAIL

DETERMINED

 FUN   PASSIONATE

AS DEFINED BY
OUR EMPLOYEES,
PARTNERS
AND CUSTOMERS

OPE
POSITIVE
DRIVE
ADVENTUROUS
OPEN
FAMILY
DETERMINED
SERVICE
LEA
EMBRA

2010
CULTURE
BOOK

WEIRDNESS
CREATE
HONEST
COMMUNICATION
N-MINDED
GROWTH
FUN
TEAM
WOW
DELIVER
SPIRIT
RELATIONSHIP
RNING
HUMBLE
CE CHANGE
PASSIONATE

©2010

by
Zappos IP, Inc.
and its affiliates

Design and production by
JENN LIM @jennlim | facebook.com/byjennlim
and
FADHLY BEY @fadhlybey | facebook.com/fadhlybey

CONTENTS

10
CORE
VALUES

1. Deliver WOW through Service

6. Build Open And Honest Relationships With Communication

8. Do More With Less

7. Build A Positive Team And Family Spirit

10. Be Humble

Embrace and Drive Change

4. Be Adventurous, Creative And Open-Minded

5. Pursue Growth And Learning

3. Create Fun And A Little Weirdness

9. Be Passionate And Determined

2. Embrace and Drive Change

FORE WORD

Welcome to the 2010 edition of the Zappos Family Culture Book!

The culture book is an annual tradition for the Zappos Family. Every year, I send an email to our employees asking people to write a few paragraphs about what the Zappos culture means to them. Except for typos, it's unedited, because one of our core values is to Build Open and Honest Relationships With Communication.

For us, our #1 priority is company culture. Our belief is that if we get the culture right, most of the other stuff -- like delivering great customer service, or building a long-term enduring brand and business -- will happen naturally on its own.

In my book "Delivering Happiness: A Path to Profits, Passion, and Purpose", I write about how a company's culture and a company's brand are really just two sides of the same coin. The brand is simply a lagging indicator of the culture.

Over the past 11 years, we've continuously experienced rapid growth. As we continue to grow and hire new people, we need to make sure that they understand and become a part of our culture. That is the purpose of this culture book -- to provide a glimpse of what the Zappos culture is all about to new hires, prospective new hires, our vendors and partners, and anyone else who might be interested.

So what is the Zappos culture? To me, the Zappos culture embodies many different elements. It's about always looking for new ways to WOW everyone we come in contact with. It's about building relationships where we treat each other like family. It's about teamwork and having fun and not taking ourselves too seriously. It's about growth, both personal and professional. It's about achieving the impossible with fewer people. It's about openness, taking risks, and not being afraid to make mistakes. But most of all, it's about having faith that if we do the right thing, then in the long run we will succeed and build something great.

Our culture is based on our **10 CORE VALUES:**

1) Deliver WOW Through Service
2) Embrace and Drive Change
3) Create Fun and A Little Weirdness
4) Be Adventurous, Creative, and Open-Minded
5) Pursue Growth and Learning
6) Build Open and Honest Relationships With Communication
7) Build a Positive Team and Family Spirit
8) Do More With Less
9) Be Passionate and Determined
10) Be Humble

Unlike most companies, where core values are just a plaque on the wall, our core values play a big part in how we hire, train, and develop our employees.

In addition to trying to WOW our customers, we also try to WOW our employees and the vendors and business partners that we work with. We believe that it creates a virtuous cycle, and in our own way, we're making the world a better place and improving people's lives. It's all part of our long term vision to deliver happiness to the world.

Of course, the Zappos culture means different things to different people, so I thought the best way for people to learn what the Zappos culture was all about was to hear from our employees directly. Below is the email that I sent to our employees in early 2010:

From: Tony Hsieh
To: All Zappos Employees
Subject: Zappos Culture Book

It's time to put together a new edition of the Zappos Culture Book, to be distributed to employees, prospective employees, business partners, and even some customers.

Our culture is the combination of all of our employees' ideas about the culture, so we would like to include everyone's thoughts in this book.

Please email me a few sentences about what the Zappos culture means to you. (What is the Zappos culture? What's different about it compared to other company cultures? What do you like about our culture?) We will compile everyone's contribution into the book.

When writing your response, please do not refer to any previous culture books, any training/orientation material, the company handbook, or any other company-published material. We want to hear YOUR thoughts about the company culture.

Also, please do not talk to anyone about what you will be writing or what anyone else wrote. And finally, if you contributed to last year's Culture Book, please do not look at what you wrote last year until after you've written and submitted this year's entry.

Remember, there are no wrong answers. We want to know what the Zappos culture means to you specifically at this point in time, and we expect different responses from different people.

FORE WORD

We hope you enjoy
the 2010 edition of the
Zappos Culture Book!

Tony Hsieh
CEO - Zappos.com, Inc.
ceo@zappos.com
twitter.com/zappos

the wow!

Tony Hsieh

PS: If you'd like to learn more about our culture, check out our blogs at:

   http://blogs.zappos.com

You can also learn more about the Zappos Family at:

   http://about.zappos.com

Our job openings are available online at:

   http://jobs.zappos.com

Also, we offer free tours of our offices in Las Vegas. You can schedule a tour at:

   http://tours.zappos.com

what makes Zappos one of Fortune's Best Companies to work for?
in one word, CULTURE.

what is Zappos Culture?
in the words of our employees, partners and vendors...ready to find out?

OPEN

DETERMINED

DELIVER ADVENTUROUS

SERVICE

EMBRACE

H

PASSIO

TEAM
SPIRIT
NEST
HUMBLE
POSITIVE
CHANGE
OPEN-MINDED
REATE
DRIVE
COMMUNICATION
LEARNING
WEIRDNESS
WOW
OWTH
FUN
ATE
RELATIONSHIP
FAMILY

ABBIE "ABSTER" M.
employee since 2005

At Zappos, we live and breathe our Ten Core Values, which I'm sure are all over this book, but I felt that one stood out when writing my entry: "Embrace and Drive Change." It really blows me away to sit back and think about the dynamic of our values because they all support each other. We've had a lot of change over the last year, from our marriage to Amazon (YAY!), to smaller-scale changes in our department. What is remarkable to me is that throughout so much change, our other nine Core Values remain the same. In the real world (not where we live :), a person could be easily overwhelmed by the fast pace of these changes and be unable to deliver WOW through service or build a positive team. However, because we are Zapponians, we couldn't imagine NOT delivering the exceptional service that we do and not being super-positive throughout each and every day. I would honestly be caught off guard if I said hello to someone who didn't say "Hi," back. If I asked someone for help, and they told me to take a long walk off a short pier, I think I would faint. A lot of people might say that Zappos employees work in an un-realistic environment, where everyday frustrations don't occur and cupcakes grow from rainbows in our break room. While I've yet to see the cup-cake- producing rainbow, I can say that we do have all of the same daily pet peeves as everyone else, but because of our Zappos Culture, we rise above it and over come. These are the types of things that we Zapponians have become accus-tomed to, and we should be, because that's our culture. Maybe we don't live in the real world, but that's ok because we like it here. :)

ABBY N.
employee since 2007

The Zappos Culture is like no other.... I am thankful that I have been able to work here for three years and have WAY TOO MUCH fun! To me, Zappos culture is like jumping into a chilly pool on a super-hot day. It is a bit shocking when you first experience it, but then it becomes refreshing, glorious and just plain AWESOME. I thank God every day that I can walk in this building and see my extended family. It is the best feeling in the world!!

ADRIAN M.
employee since 2009

Zappos is more than another retail company. We care about our co-workers, customers and community. In my short time here, I have been amazed, day-by-day, by the incredible acts that this company and its employees do. (Too many to list!) I am grateful (especially for the happy hours) every day that I work for such an great place and wouldn't have it any other way

AIMEE M.
employee since 2009

I am so lucky to have a job where I get to be myself all day! I get to wear what I like, decorate my desk and answer the phone with a greeting I like! I love everything about the Zappos culture. I love getting to know the people around me. Every other job I have had frowns down on adding a personal touch to things, Zappos encourages it. I am always excited to meet new co-workers because I can actually get to know who they truly are. I also love that I get to work with my dad every day — most people would be annoyed. I am very lucky to be working for Zappos.

ALAN O.
employee since 2007

Zappos Culture means diversity and allows everyone to be themselves, yet at the same time, to be a member of a group with a higher purpose. Our culture is different from most businesses I have worked for because everything is not as structured or cut-and-dry; you are allowed to bend the rules if needed. There are always exceptions, there are always new things to try and if they don't work, we will try something else. That is part of the allure here. Jump in and try, if it works that's great, if not, there will be a plan B or C... we try until we get it right... we "work" on delivering happiness.

ALEXIS H.
employee since 2008

Zappos Culture is very special to me. It is welcoming, understanding, personal and enduring. I hope one day all who work will look forward to arriving at work as much as I do. It is so simple and so enjoyable that all workplaces should adapt a more blissful culture, such as ours.

ALICIA A.
employee since 2007

The Zappos Culture means so much to me. It means being my crazy, outgoing self. It means building meaningful connections. It means being happy to come to work every day. It means being proud of my company, my co-workers and myself. It means feeling like everything I do, every day really makes a difference. It means knowing that I have a home away from home and a family away from my family. I love Zappos!

ALICIA J.
employee since 2009

The Zappos Culture is born from Ten Core Values that are key to living life, not just to working here. So many companies talk about core values and mission statements at orientation, but few follow through. Zappos lives and breathes its core values.

I had always hoped for a job that I would genuinely be happy to go to every day, but never thought it was possible. Now I have that job. It took a lot of research, a few emails and some trepidation, but I knew then, as I know now, that I couldn't have made a better choice. My original career was making people happy with desserts — pastry and cakes. I still do that on the side, but now I make people happy with service (and great shoes!). I'm surrounded by positive people who want to see me succeed and it helps me keep my positive outlook. Who could ask for anything more?

The culture here is unique — but it shouldn't be. We all could use more positivism at work, after all, it is where we spend most of our time! And even though this is my first Culture Book entry, it won't be the last. I can't wait to see what happens next at this crazy, wonderful, exciting company that I call family!

AMANDA K.
employee since 2006

I was talking to a few friends the other day and I realized just how out of place I was among them. It started when I complimented one of them on the new purple streaks in her hair. Her response was, "Thanks, but I have to figure out how to hide them since our dress code was just released today." This started a huge discussion about having to hide piercings and roll down sleeves to cover tattoos, and having to duck when managers and supervisors are present either, because the employees were breaking rules or they were just intimidated by their chain of command. My friends started to chat about various things that need to be changed and how they have left suggestion after suggestion in that little box and nothing ever changes. The common belief was that those suggestions were being used as toilet paper.

After about 45 minutes of this, one of them turned to me and said "Wow, you're kinda quiet tonight, what's wrong?"

"What's wrong?" I said. "Nothing's wrong. "I just have nothing to contribute to this conversation."

The unanimous response was "Yeah, right! You can't tell us that your supervisors actually care about what you think!"

"Well actually, they not only care, but there's a monthly survey to gather that exact information. We're also encouraged to make suggestions whenever we have them. One of my suggestions resulted in a second nap room, two days later."

"Wait, a SECOND nap room? You mean there's a first?"

"Yeah! Zappos realizes that if we're not happy and feeling well, we can't give the customers the service that they deserve!" I told her. "It's the same reason that we are encouraged to be ourselves. As long as we're not offending anyone, we can wear what makes us happy and we don't have to cover our colored hair, piercings and tattoos. I mean, do you really give your customers great service when you're so unhappy that you commiserate with others, even in your off time? "

With this, I pulled out the netbook and played a selection of Zappos YouTube posts. By the time they were finished watching them, they all wanted to switch jobs. I explained to them that I know there are a million things that I would like to try, but at this point none of them are worth giving up a place like Zappos. I like who I am here, and that's something I know few people aside from v can say!

AMBER W.
employee since 2008

After being unemployed for a few months, I got a part-time job and was hanging on there by a string when Zappos called me in for an interview. I was so excited, because I knew everything would change if I got this job. I did get hired and I was right — everything in my life has changed for the better! I have benefits, too many snacks to munch on and a full-time paycheck to help me catch up with bills! Sometimes I look around the call center (at the endless decorations and amazing individuals answering the phones) and I feel total gratitude for this place. I just can't express enough how happy it makes me to be a part of it! Viva Zappos!

ANA S.
employee since 2009

To me, the Zappos Culture means excellence, acceptance and FUN. I have never ever worked for a company that is so conducive to my goofy personality and, for that matter, encourages it. When I first moved to Las Vegas in February of 2009, my brother-in-law mentioned Zappos because he had seen a feature on "this guy who prides himself on customer service and he's the owner of the company and he sits in a cubicle like the rest of the people. This is right up your alley." Of course, the cynic that I am, I said, "Yeah, yeah, yeah, I will look into it" because, at the risk of sounding like a cliché, experience has taught us all anything that sounds too good to be true, isn't.

Well, it's a good thing I didn't bet any money on that one. I was already unemployed and broke and would have further contributed to my financial woes. There are several things I love about our Zappos Culture; coming from a big, close-knit family, I love how the family spirit is captured, cultivated and nurtured here. I am grateful that the last company I worked for decided to minimize their staff; yes, you read that right. While I enjoyed my short tenure with them, I am trying to figure out how I can thank them without sounding smug and ungrateful because I am truly grateful that I was afforded an opportunity to form friendships there as well. I've met some great friends from past jobs and still have maintained the friends but again, never, ever have I met a GROUP of people that I can honestly call my family — especially "My Zangstas."

ANDI R.
employee since 2009

There is something fulfilling in knowing that my day job is not just a paycheck, or a place for me to kill time. I come to a place that is fueled by the very things other companies fear... Change and Diversity. I'm able to show up in my own clothes and with my own ideas, plan team-building events and dress up in costumes. Every day, I'm happier for it. Zappos doesn't TRY to be an amazing and liberating workplace, it just is.

ANDRE N.
employee since 2008

The Zappos Culture is absolutely amazing. I never would have imagined working for a company that is so inspiring. It is so encouraging to see all of the employees learn and grow as much as possible. Looking back, it is amazing to see how much I have grown during my time here (about two years), not only as an employee, but also as a human being. The Zappos Culture is definitely something that I cherish, and it has helped me in all aspects of my life.

ANDREA B.
employee since 2008

The Zappos Culture runs deep in all the Zappos employees. It's a way of life for most of us, with principles and beliefs that we all apply to daily life, not just work. It's almost like an infectious disease. For example, once you walk in the building you're greeted by genuine smiles and next thing you know, you're smiling at everyone — and maybe even everything — that you walk past. (lol)

Zappos is definitely one of the best places to work for. I almost feel like I'm at home when I come to work, and its not because of the numerous PJ days we have. It's because the people here are almost as awesome as those people who are super close to my heart.

ANDREA R.
employee since 2007

Zappos Culture is something that makes you smile when you talk about it. It's a culture like no other and can't be explained in just one sentence. The culture at Zappos makes you happy, it's supportive, it's family oriented and it builds long-lasting friendships. I am only a couple weeks away from my three-year anniversary here and the culture has been the same ever since I started! I have never worked at a place like Zappos! I am truly blessed to be a part of such a wonderful environment that has such an awesome culture. It's hard not to be happy when you're here! I love it!

ANDREW T.
employee since 2008

I love the Zappos Culture. It provides us all with opportunities to be the best that we can be and the support that we need to attain these goals. It's hard to believe that I've already been here at Zappos two years and yet I am still on the road to discovery. I think I haven't even scratched the surface!

Also, the great Zappos Culture maps out the road to happiness and fulfillment. I have experienced the world in Zappos from good times and through some challenges. One thing that is clear to me: whatever or however the Zappos life is presented to you, it is up to you to take it to the next level. The trick is to find your balance.

The Zappos Culture has changed my perspective in so many ways ... I am looking forward to more good things to come.

ANGELA W.
employee since 2010

First off let me say I love working at Zappos!! I am still in training, and up to this point everything that I have gone through has exceeded my expectations, especially the Zappos Culture and how everyone treats one another! I mean, everyone is so nice and helpful, it's amazing! I feel that there is no comparison to any other company in the world!

ANITA B.
employee since 2009

What can I say about working at Zappos other than WOW!? It's been a wonderful experience since day one and the people I have met through Zappos are some of the nicest and funniest people I have ever met. I don't know of any other place where you can go to work, have fun and get paid to do it.

ANONYMOUS

When I first started working at Zappos, I was amazed at the culture; it's so diverse and so accepting. It is great to work for a company that has so much respect for its employees regardless of their background. I feel honored and blessed to be part of a young company that doesn't seem so young anymore. It would seem that a company that is so well known would have been around for a while, slowly building its reputation while getting employees to b7elieve in their system. What makes Zappos so well known and successful, not only as a business, but as a positive workplace as well? The Zappos Culture, and our very important Ten Core Values. Zappos Rocks!

ANONYMOUS

The Zappos Culture, to me, is about building strong relationships, being passionate about your job, working hard, and having a lot of fun while you do it!

ANONYMOUS

What makes Zappos different than other companies? It's the Zappos Culture. What I appreciate most and love about this job is how the management and leaders of this company care and actually value your opinion, taking it into consideration when brought to their attention.

ANTHONY "TONY" F.
employee since 2009

Thanks for the opportunity to add my feedback to the Zappos Culture Book. As a fairly new employee, I have been so impressed with the amount of time and effort that went into the training and incubation process. I am also impressed with the amount of feedback that management requests from us … they ask about our ideas and opinions regarding everything, from attendance policies to the new CLT team and how it should refine the QA process. It's a rare company, in my experience, that actually listens to its employees' ideas and opinions, whether they are positive or negative, and then molds company-wide policy while taking these opinions into consideration. Thanks for considering us as a vital part of the Zappos Culture!

ASHLEE E.
employee since 2007

Zappos to me means family. Our culture embraces everyone who walks through these doors, no matter what they're here for. Our culture is a family feeling of warmth, and I honestly don't know what I would have done without this company. At my baby shower, everyone was a Zappos employee. At my wedding, everyone was a Zappos employee. When I go out for girls' night out, or for a night of bowling, or a movie, everyone is a Zappos employee. Our culture gives everyone here a sense of a second home and family. Every other company I've worked at hasn't given me this second home or family, making it feel like a regular 9-5 without feeling or emotion. I love working at Zappos and I wouldn't trade it for working anywhere else. Everyone here is my family and I love everything this culture has to offer.

ASHLEY T.
employee since 2009

Since I've been working for Zappos, I have come to realize that I am now excited to come to work, even at 3 a.m. I am myself and can be myself. Every employee is allowed to be themselves and speak their minds without being looked down upon. In the last week, I have also realized how much love and support there is here. I have had the hardest week of my life and was able to take time off at the last minute AND was also told I could take personal time. NO questions. That to me, is truly amazing. I can say thank you a hundred times but it still would not be enough. I also was welcomed back with arms wide open, and more love and support then ever — and trust me, I needed it. I will be at Zappos as long as I can be. This is my new home. I wake up every day happy and go home happy because I love my life, and Zappos has made that possible for me. Everyone is treated equal, no matter if they are CLT or a manager. Thank you Tony for everything, I am truly blessed and will always be thankful!

ASHOTTA W.
employee since 2007

They say, "Knowledge is the Antidote to Fear." If that's true, then Zappos is the antidote to the retail industry. Zappos is like me, one of a kind, and I am very proud to be a part of this growing family.

In order for Zappos to evolve over the last decade, many of us have been driven and continued to make the experience better for our customers. This has all happened because we learn how to deal with change and embrace it openly.

ATRELL J.
employee since 2005

Zappos is a blessing! There's no other way to describe our culture and family than inviting. From the moment you walk in the door to the time you leave, you feel an overwhelming presence of happy people. "Is there something in the water... are these people drunk?" Well not exactly (hehe), but one could say we are drunk with excitement and passion for our company and our Zappos brand which exudes in every facial expression and conversation. Five years ago, I stumbled upon this "place" without any idea of its value. Today, I stand as an ever-changing seed that continues to grow with "my family."

AUGUSTA S.
employee since 2007

Zappos Culture. What is it? What does it mean to me?

I have asked myself these questions many times and I come up with the same answers. I am the Zappos Culture, and it means EVERYTHING to me.

It hit me early on while I was in my training class almost three years ago. The happiness I feel every day when I come to work, or when I think about Zappos is truly the current of the Culture running through me. It's a feeling that makes me feel really good. I feel like I am part of something that most employees at other companies don't know about and have not experienced yet. I love the fact that we are so diverse and free to express ourselves in our own way. We are responsible for taking care of the Zappos Culture and not letting it change — except to get better. I love seeing people happy, especially my co-workers. Our Ten Core Values are the foundation, our "declaration," if you will, that we will respect, protect, and cherish our Culture.

I talk about the Zappos Culture to anyone who will listen, at work and outside of work. And usually I get the same response — an awareness and sense of WOW! It confirms to those of us who work here how special and fortunate we are, and for those who do not work here, they always say, "Wow, I wish I worked there!"

I hope one day, other companies will emulate our culture so that their employees can get that feeling of happiness I experience so much here at Zappos! If I can contribute to that happening in any way, I will!

BEATRIZ "BETTY" L.
employee since 2004

Working at Zappos has been one of the best things that has happened to me and my family. I enjoy every part of it. Coming to work has never been this easy. Having the opportunity to choose the career path that works best for me is awesome. There are many areas where you can pursue growth and learning. Not all will be good for everyone but at least we have the opportunity to try it and it won't go against you if it doesn't work out. Being at work here is like being surrounded by your direct family. I have never worked in a place that does really care about its employees and customers. It feels good to know that your opinions really do count. The open and honest communication that we share with in the company really makes a difference. Just like Zappos WOWs its customers, it has WOWed me in many different ways.

BETH M.
employee since 2009

Wow, where do I begin? The first time I walked through the doors at Zappos, I knew I was at home. Everyone was friendly, you could see different personalities shine, and there was an obvious team/family environment. The Zappos Culture is like nothing I have ever experienced. Be myself? Weirdness is encouraged and embraced. Make customers happy — do whatever it takes? What a concept! I know I have changed for the better. I am the happiest I have ever been. I look forward to coming to work every single day!

I can remember wondering how my life would have been different had I started working for a company like this 20 years ago... then I realized I had done my time and this was a blessing! This IS the last job I ever want to have, and I look forward to all of the new opportunities that Zappos has to o offer me. I love me some Zappos!

BOBBY C.
employee since 2007

Freedom... to be better than average, to do what's right, to want to be responsible, to have fun, to be yourself.

BRITNEE B.
employee since 2008

Culture is being a VIP at Zappos and participating in the Zappos experience
I <3 Zappos!!

BROOKE T.
employee since 2009

I have been working at Zappos now for three months. Before I started to work here I never really knew what it was or what the company did. Fortunately for me, I met someone who worked here. She came up to me and said, "You need to work at Zappos, you are the perfect fit." After that comment, I started to look into what the company actually did. I was hired two months later. I then went through the training process and thought, "Where's the catch?" There never was one. Everyone was wonderful, real, they all joked, played pranks and laughed. That was the catch — you had to know how to have fun.

Over the last three months I have fallen in love with this company. It is remarkable what Zappos people do for the company, customers, vendors, and how they are always willing to lend a helping hand. Zappos is not just about talk, it's about action! I strongly believe in the Ten Core Values and work at achieving more of them every day. Zappos is definitely the best place to work. As they say, " WELCOME TO YOUR LAST JOB!" I know it will be mine.

THANK YOU, ZAPPOS, for changing my life.

BRYAN B.
employee since 2009

When I first heard of Zappos.com I honestly thought to myself that it functioned like a cult. I would hear stories from friends that worked there, not going to throw out any names, and was worried that it was going to end up being one of those Ponzi scheme companies that profess to have culture so they can suck you in. Thankfully I was enlightened on what truly made Zappos what it is and that some things are not "too good to be true." My first experience with my now-fellow Zapponians was a Halloween party back in 2008 that was amazing… not only was the party, in general, fun, but I couldn't believe that everyone was being so amazingly nice to me, someone that wasn't even part of their "Zappos crew." Once I actually started working here I realized that the humility, the friendliness… that whole familial vibe that Zappos exudes… was one of the key aspects of the company. It's one of many values that truly make Zappos unique and a wonderful "cult" to join.

CAMILLA B.
employee since 2009

What I love about our culture is the family spirit within the people. There is a genuine concern for your fellow co-workers. People here will go out of their way for you. You can be standing outside waiting on your ride, and someone will ask you if you're okay and if you have a ride home. When you tell them that your ride is on the way, they tell you "Come on, I'll take you home." All I can say is that people who work here CARE!!!

CANDACE C.
employee since 2008

I had never given company culture a lot of thought until I started working at Zappos. I guess I always thought that fun, learning and good work ethics could be a way of life, without branding my habits and accumulated experiences as "culture."

I became aware of workplace culture for the first time when I was introduced to Zappos. It makes such a difference when you are consciously aware of the blending of everybody's life experiences and what they contribute to all aspects of life, including the work environment. Because Zappos is open-minded and encourages culture amongst us, it broadens views and opens us to new ideas that, without this culture, would be overlooked or entirely neglected at any other place.

It is great to work where you are appreciated for what you bring to the table, and where differences of opinions are not only welcomed, but also learned from, whether you agree with them or not! You come away being a better person as your views are broadened. Our culture is the Zappos experience, and I embrace it and am thankful for the understanding and knowledge it has given me. Our culture, not only gives you an open mind, it enables you to open your heart!

CANDACE S.
employee since 2006

I am into my fourth year at Zappos and I have to say I love the fact that every day there is something new. There is never time to get bored and it's about stepping out of your comfort zone and learning and experiencing new exciting things. This is the part of the culture I love the most. I love the feeling of family and friends.

CARA C.
employee since 2007

I have been at Zappos for over two years now and have seen the Zappos Culture grow and change. In that time, it has only gotten better. As with any company, there are hurdles to jump, the important thing is how you land. I believe we have landed strong and I foresee many more amazing years for Zappos!

CAROL T.
employee since 2008

The Zappos Culture means that I am able to work in a fun and friendly environment with people who are not just co-workers, but friends. It encourages me to become a better version of myself.

CATHERINE M.
employee since 2009

I have only been here at Zappos for a short time and can not tell you how awesome it is to come to work! Just when you think you are amazed by the people and culture, something else happens that totally blows me away. I am blessed that Zappos has included me in their family. I hope to spend many many years being a Zapponian.

CELINA E.
employee since 2009

Simply put, Zappos feels like home and I feel ever so grateful to work here.

CHASE S.
employee since 2006

Working at Zappos, you get asked many questions. One that appears more often than not, is why I like working at Zappos. Any person could tell you that the Zappos Culture is what makes the job. Although I cannot really disagree, I would like to take it a step further. Happiness is what makes our culture.

I once was told, "You will never be happy if you continue to search for what happiness consists of. You will never live if you are looking for the meaning of life." This is how Zappos is different from other cultures. Ultimately, Zappos listens. It is easy to believe when you live it every single day.

I guess the best way I can sum it up is by saying, "Success is not the key to happiness. Happiness is the key to success. If you love what you are doing, you will be successful."

CHELSEA S.
employee since 2007

The Zappos Culture has allowed me grow at my own pace as well as to be myself. Within a little over two years, I have learned various skill sets, been a Specialist on a specialty team, and have been given the opportunity to be a Senior Rep. I don't know of any companies that allow you to step into the role of a lead position to see if it's something you would want to pursue in the future. Zappos Culture has not only helped me grow professionally but personally as well. I have made some good friends here; at other jobs I barely knew the people I worked with for several years.

CHEREE H.
employee since 2004

I can't believe how time flies! I'm proud to say that I've been with Zappos for nearly five and a half years now. Since I started at Zappos I have grown so much, both personally and professionally. Over the years, I've met so many great people and developed a lot of close friendships with my co-workers. The Zappos Culture is a culture of its own; a culture that no other company can compare to. It's a family-like atmosphere where the focus is happiness for all our customers, internal and external. I'm honored to be a part of the many achievements Zappos has made, and will continue to make. My experience with Zappos has been nothing less than wonderful and it's exciting to be a part of something so great!!

CHERYL D.
employee since 2009

What does the Zappos Culture mean to me? It has helped inspire me to look at life with a more positive outlook. Many corporations have mission statements. Their mission statements are vague and some just do not make sense. Working for Zappos is such an honor because I have always had a saying, "Say what you mean and mean what you say." Here at Zappos, we are very passionate about our culture. Our Ten Core Values are simple and straight to the point. That is what I absolutely love. No fluff, it is what it is! This is my very first job that I can absolutely say I love and feel like this is where I belong.

CHRISTINA C.
employee since 2007

We serve therefore we are.

CHRISTINA L.
employee since 2008

I have been blessed to be part of an amazing company! A company filled with culture! I believe the culture at Zappos is what makes our companythrive. The culture is what makes us a true family!

CHRISTOPHER L.
employee since 2010

While all the Core Values are essential to the Zappos Culture, the value that sets Zappos apart from the rest, in my opinion, is "Create Fun and a Little Weirdness." While companies often restrict creativity and individuality, Zappos encourages you to express that individuality. When I decided to wear my new aviators indoors the entire day in hopes of resembling a young Tom Cruise (pre-Oprah couch fiasco) this was not scorned. My endeavors to find a mature flight instructor to woo with my charms were actually encouraged by fellow workers.

I find myself to be just one of many crazy people at this place, and I, for one, find this quite refreshing. This kind of zaniness is truly what makes Zappos unique. To sum it all up, Zappos is a place like none other that you will ever experience. All that is asked is that you be yourself, and enjoy yourself while getting paid. You really can't ask for much more than that in a workplace.

CHRISTOPHER N.
employee since 2009

It is a difficult task to define what the culture of Zappos is. You can watch all of our zany video blogs and read every article in existence written about us and still not gain a full appreciation of how unique the culture that has been developed here is. It truly is a breath of fresh air in comparison to typical corporate structure. Everybody here seems to be truly working towards a common goal: to grow, not only professionally, but personally.

The atmosphere is one of constant encouragement, friendliness and, of course, a little craziness! It truly has made all the difference in how I approach not only my work, but also my life in general. I'm very appreciative of the fact that I get to come into such an uplifting atmosphere everyday!

CRYSTAL S.
employee since 2009

From the first moment I began interviewing for Zappos, I was amazed, and I can't think of any other word to say it better. I couldn't believe that I actually had an opportunity to work for a company full of so much potential for growth, amazing people, awesome benefits, and of course, FUN! That is Zappos Culture. The connections we make with people go beyond just making acquaintances with co-workers, and it's a really great feeling when you know you belong. A lot of people go through life hating the daily grind; they spend their lives half miserable, just making a living, working toward retirement, all in all, trying to make their way in this crazy world. Zappos is like a fun detour along the way, except it also is the way too! How awesome to be part of a company — to have a lifelong career — that encourages fun and a little weirdness?!?! A place that encourages me to have fun with my co-workers, get to know them, and to build that family spirit. Zappos Culture, to me, is all about having fun and making connections that last a lifetime. :)

CHRISTY M.
employee since 2009

Zappos Culture is unique. I have not been with Zappos long, but I feel I can be myself here. The Ten Core Values drive the company and each one of us to strive for excellence. Other companies I have been with do not encourage originality. They do not work with you to advance professionally and personally. They do not treat you as family. Zappos does all of this and more. I am grateful to have come to work here and look forward to where the culture will guide us in the future.

CLARENCE R.
employee since 2008

Zappos Culture is the culmination of a diverse workforce coming together to achieve a common goal. It stands apart from other company cultures in that everyone's uniqueness is not just tolerated but embraced. The best part of the culture is that everyone strives to create fun and a little weirdness. After ten years, things have gotten very fun and very weird.

CLARISSA R.
employee since 2008

I have been with Zappos for almost two years. Time flies when you're having fun! This is not just a saying, but true in reality. I have had many jobs in my life and they all try to bend you to be the way they want you to be within their organization. Zappos allows you to be yourself and also provides you with the resources to become a better person. The Ten Core Values are either within you or they are not. My favorite is "Be Humble." The reading material is outstanding. After reading about each Core Value, your mind is open, you think differently and believe it or not, you begin to change within, for the better.

Everyone, no matter what their position, is kind, willing to offer assistance, helps you to achieve your goals, helps you to make goals ... like a family member. Speaking of families, I sometimes prefer to be at work than to be at home with my family. I am guaranteed to laugh, learn and grow daily. Just when you think it can't get any better, it does!! WOW!

I love talking with the customers, learning about the products, searching the internet, being creative and having fun. Where else could I do all this and get paid for it? Thank you, Zappos for allowing me to be part of such a great company!

CODY B.
employee since 2007

For every day that goes by I tend to feel closer and closer to the people I work with. I can't explain just how much it means to me. The culture forms an overwhelming sense of family. And once you find your niche within this company, in whatever form it comes, you feel even closer. People who have common goals, dreams and ambitions find each other. It is almost like a survival technique. Once we find each other, we are unstoppable. That is the company and its culture. It's an immovable force created by a strong sense of family. It's unlike anything I've ever experienced in a workplace. In fact it's not even like work. It's just where I happen to see my family and do my part in reaching a common goal. I love this place, it's culture and its drive.

COREY S.
employee since 2008

To me, the Zappos Culture is a code of ethics that apply not only to work, but to life as well. It is a guide to help us through the hard times, and carry us through the good times.

CORINA C.
employee since 2008

Family. That's what I think of when I come to work in the morning. When somebody is sad or happy, you feel that with them. You become so wrapped up in who they are as a person that you forget that you aren't really related. Our culture makes us who we are inside and outside of work. When you go home on your day off and find yourself hanging out with the people you work with, coming back to work doesn't feel that different. Our Core Values, to me, sum up family. You can't build a family and a relationship without feeling 100% comfortable around someone. We're already family.....Our values just make our family that much closer.

CRISTETA W.
employee since 2009

Before I worked at Zappos, I worked for a company that did not like people to even speak to each other during the day unless it had something to do with business. I felt like I always had to watch myself and was even uncomfortable saying "hi," to someone during the workday.

Can you imagine what it felt like when I walked into Zappos for the first time? I felt like a kid let loose in a candy store. People smiled at me, they said "hi," and they looked happy! What was this world that I had walked into? It was so foreign to me that when I went home at night I could not stop talking about it. I had a permanent smile on my face because I had reached work nirvana.

Zappos certainly changed my attitude about work and it also carries over into my personal life. Thank you so much, Zappos!!!

CRYSTAL D.
employee since 2008

There once was a girl from Rhode Island,
Who needed shoes and clothes to be stylin',
But with the high price,
The discount is nice,
Thus, Zappos always keeps me smiling!

CRYSTAL M.
employee since 2005

This is my fifth year giving my thoughts on Zappos Culture. Every year it gets better and better and it is hard to put into words. This time I decided to not be so wordy. Zappos employees live by the Ten Core Values. We love and support one another and are always there for each other. To sum it all up in one statement, here at Zappos. com "WE ARE FAMILY."

CRYSTAL S.
employee since 2009

From the first moment I began interviewing for Zappos, I was amazed, and I can't think of any other word to say it better. I couldn't believe that I actually had an opportunity to work for a company full of so much potential for growth, amazing people, awesome benefits, and of course, FUN! That is Zappos Culture. The connections we make with people go beyond just making acquaintances with co-workers, and it's a really great feeling when you know you belong. A lot of people go through life hating the daily grind; they spend their lives half miserable, just making a living, working toward retirement, all in all, trying to make their way in this crazy world. Zappos is like a fun detour along the way, except it also is the way too! How awesome to be part of a company — to have a lifelong career — that encourages fun and a little weirdness?!?! A place that encourages me to have fun with my co-workers, get to know them, and to build that family spirit. Zappos Culture, to me, is all about having fun and making connections that last a lifetime. :)

DAIL T.
employee since 2007

I recently had to visit an ENT specialist and when I told the doctor I worked for Zappos he told me that he had met you several times and thought very highly of you. The one thing he said that specifically stood out was, "Tony really cares about his employees." I think this not only says a lot about you but also explains why our culture is so much better than that of other call centers. In this economy, it is not only great to work for such a fun company, but offering in health benefits at no cost to the employee is amazing.

DANA C.
employee since 2007

I "heart" Zappos!

DANIEL H.
employee since 2007

I continue to enjoy when I get to speak with a customer who really seems to "get" how we're different. They are, in some cases, taken aback by the trust and respect that things like an advanced exchange demonstrate. People who sound like they would never bother offering feedback to a company end up effusively thanking me for quick fulfillment and shipping. It's nice to know we really are making a difference in customer's lives.

DANIEL S.
employee since 2009

I started with Zappos during the holiday season of this past year. Amidst the Christmas-time bustle, I was pleasantly surprised with the camaraderie of my team. It's an awesome feeling to have the Ten Core Values hold strong even during a hectic time. Coming right out of training and being new to the call center floor, it was a welcoming feeling to have my entire team take me in with open arms. Honest and open relationships via communication helped build a positive team and family spirit for me. It's one thing to have our Ten Core Values on banners, but it's an entirely different ball game to have them in practice. I'm honored that I am part of an amazing family like Zappos.

DANIELLE B.
employee since 2005

I think the Zappos Culture is the best thing about the company. I've been with the company since 2005 and I still enjoy coming to work every day, because of the people. The culture allows for employees to be more than just co-workers; it allows us to be friends and extended family. While most companies discourage employees from being more than co-workers, at Zappos we are urged to get to know each other so that we WANT to work together and help one another. The friendships and bonds that our culture forms are what make Zappos such a unique and great place to work.

DANIKA J.
employee since 2008

Has anyone ever heard of another company where employees consider their co-workers as their "second family," or as much a part of their family as they do their parents and siblings? Zappos IS that company, and always will be. I never thought I would ever work for a company where you can become so close with your co-workers that they become extended family members. This is the true spirit of the Zappos Culture. Our epic holiday parties, CLT happy hours, team building — I can't think of anywhere else that would have events like these to give Zapponians a chance to get to know each other on not just a professional level, but also a personal level. I think I enjoy this part of our culture the most, because it reminds me of the best thing about Zappos — we are not just employees, we are human beings who provide support, encouragement and compassion in the best and worst of times.

DAREESA W.
employee since 2009

My Zappos experience started well before my actual employment started. Backing up two years, I worked right across the street from Zappos' corporate office and had the pleasure of having MOST of the Zappos employees as customers. I realized then that there was something different about the people who worked here. They were always friendly, never in a "lunch rush" and they were the only ones who seemed to call their orders in when they had large orders that needed to be filled (which made my life easier and my staff happy). I was in love! As time passed, I switched companies only to find I disliked my new job. In the back of my mind I wondered if the Zappos employees were still as happy as they seemed a few years ago. I checked the website and figured, what the heck? I applied, interviewed and started training shortly thereafter. To my surprise, there are still smiling faces walking around. My first thoughts, were what's the catch? Why is everyone smiling? Can they all enjoy what they do that much to have such big grins? Did that guy just hold the door for me?

In the first week of working I ran home to my visiting mother and my best friend and told them all the exciting things that happened at Zappos. Every day it was something new... so much so that my best friend was a bit jealous to see that I had a job I love already. My mom told me if I ever leave she will kick me.

I have never worked for a company that cares so much about its employees. I love that we have a wide variety of employees and personalities. I remember working for companies where I have walked outside just to clear my head, and sometimes to cry, because I knew there was something much better for me out there. My family has never seen me so happy about a job... although I feel that working at Zappos is more than a job, it is a career. We are encouraged to learn all that we want and to make decisions that we feel will best benefit the customers and you can just be yourself.

I truly love what I do now!

DARLENE K.
employee since 2008

Where to start?? Well, Zappos culture, to me, seems to fit under only one thing that comes to my mind: family. If you are treated with respect, you will get it back a thousand times over. Family really means a lot to Zappos and I always feel very comfortable discussing daily activities there just like you would when you're with your immediate family. And I always think of this as not just another ordinary 9-to-5 "going nowhere" job. You have the opportunity to blossom and show your talents, and those talents will be recognized!! Just like your family at home, you have your ups and downs, but at least you know you will be forgiven in the end and it's all good. I always embrace the Ten Core Values in my daily life at work as well as in my home. And with so many tours that I see on a daily basis, we are definitely what people want to see and learn; they want take this great working atmosphere back with them to their companies and have it work for them too. Happy workers make happy customers, which makes customers come back to us time and time again. I look forward to greatness in 2010, and as Buzz Lightyear would say: To infinity and beyond!!!

DARREN F.
employee since 2009

When I first started at Zappos, I couldn't believe how helpful and courteous everyone was to me. Although I was new, I felt as if I had been with the company for years. As I learned more about the Zappos Culture and our Ten Core Values, I began to see how unique and essential they really are. I'm really grateful to be working for such an awesome company!

DARREN R.
employee since 2007

To me, Zappos Culture is about bringing together many disparate personalities and backgrounds into one amalgamated whole. We try to incorporate everyone's input, rather than trying to force people to fit into something that's already in place. It's always changing, always evolving, as we bring in new people and new ideas. The Culture Books themselves are the perfect expression of this!

DAVID J.
employee since 2006

When I think of culture, the first thing I think of is Zappos. I have been here for a few years now and every day gets better and better. I feel the culture at Zappos is what you make of it. There are so many unique people and ideas always flowing through the office. We embrace anything that comes our way with a smile. I enjoy waking up and knowing my job isn't just a 9-to-5 job but more of a home. I enjoy all the big and little moments I have experienced while working here.

DAWN E.
employee since 2009

I was referred to Zappos by a current employee. Every time I saw her, she was always happy, and I was always stressed out from my previous job. She told me that I should come to work at Zappos because it was such a great place to work. I must admit, I was a little hesitant, because I just didn't think jobs like that existed anymore. I provided her with my resume, then got a phone call to come in for testing. When I did come in, I was floored. Everyone was friendly and I knew right then and there that I wanted to be a part of the Zappos family. Green I have never worked for a company that cares so much about its employees and customers. I love the fact that they provide you with all the resources to be able to move to other departments. The sky is the limit here at Zappos. You can be whatever you want to be at Zappos, as long as you have the willingness to learn. I LOVE coming to work in the morning. This is so much more than a job; it's a career. I am a Zapponian for life! This is indeed the last job I will ever have!

DAWN H.
employee since 2009

I love the culture here! I come from big corporations and they are in need of some of our Zappos Culture! It's a refreshing and very freeing place here at Zappos. Actually it was a struggle for me when I first arrived here. The freedom, the enthusiasm, the fun, etc... I was not used it to because of my past jobs. I want to be able to come to work and have fun and be treated like an adult, not a number. Or to have someone looking over my shoulder telling me I am replaceable. Who likes going to work under a gray cloud everyday? I don't. I am so happy to have this opportunity to embrace and express myself in a safe place. I look forward to work every day and to what the future holds for me here at Zappos!

DEBORAH H.
employee since 2006

The Zappos Culture is a conscious effort to bring Happiness :-)... to one customer, one vendor, one fellow employee at a time. It's a conscious effort to bring happiness to the world, you can call it what you want ... great customer service or a personal emotional connection. It can be a simple act of kindness like holding a door, offering to carry a package or maybe just a smile to recognize a person passing in the hallway. When you treat someone with respect and kindness, they are happy and that happiness becomes part of them. Hopefully, it will happen enough so that the happiness builds and changes the person they are, causing them to pass happiness on to one family member, one co-worker, one stranger... it seems so simple.

DELORES M.
employee since 2006

The culture exemplified here at Zappos is unique for each Zapponian and together as a family we have a mixture of weirdness, fun, great opportunities for advancement in the company, doing many creative projects, parades, singing, learning and more. All of these and more make up a family culture with the instilled passion to deliver the "WOW" to our customers.

DENISE M.
employee since 2009

For the first time in my life, I am proud (instead of embarrassed) to tell people where I work. I have only been here for four months, and so far, every step toward the job has been just as much fun as the work here…from the application questions to the interview, through training, and now, on the phones. People thought I was crazy to be excited about working in a call center. But this is not your typical call center — this is Zappos! I am happy to be here, mainly because of four personal favorite Core Values (and that is narrowing it down):

"Create fun and a little weirdness."
I am weirdness. Finally I work in a place where that is okay. No one looks at me oddly because of my dorkiness (is that a word?) or my silly jokes or my random bursts of singing or dancing or whatever I feel moved to do in the moment. In fact, they do it with me. Yesterday half our team burst into an impromptu singing of "Brick House." It was awesome!

"Build open and honest relationships with communication."
Really?? This amazes me. I can talk to my lead or supervisor openly and freely with no fear of being looked down on, being in trouble, or anything. This took a bit of getting used to. I would send emails that would get the response "You know, it's okay to come talk to me." I was really not used to that; at my other jobs, I was always afraid to talk to my supervisors. It is amazing how much stress leaves you when you realize it is fine to go openly talk to your supervisor… and you know that he or she will help you, answer your questions and not just belittle or patronize you. It's a beautiful thing! I don't have to be scared of bosses anymore.

"Pursue growth and learning."
Zappos actually wants us to learn and grow. They give us the opportunity to learn what other departments do, to spend time with them and see if we would like to learn more. We can transfer from one department to another. They don't just tell us that when they hire us… we really can. They encourage us to. Other places leave you stuck in one position, and hire new people for upper-level jobs. Here they want us to learn the upper- level jobs and do them. We have classes all the time, and we can learn about everything from history and happiness to public speaking and Power Point. I've signed up for almost all of them!

"Build a positive team & family spirit."
I am all about being positive, bringing positive energy into my life and to the people around me. That vibe continues here. Which is great, because we all have moments of weakness. I have moments when I am not 100% positive, and when that happens, there is always someone here to cheer me up. We are a family. We celebrate birthdays, holidays, and births together, and we support each other during tough times. If ever I have a question, anyone within earshot is not just willing and able, but also happy to help.

I'm going to stop typing now because this started as my two favorite Core Values, then went to three, now it's at four and I keep thinking about the others. Thank you to everybody for being awesome co-workers, friends and family. Keep Rocking!

DEREK C.
employee since 2007

Zappos continues to be my extended family and I appreciate each and every person I work with. To our continued success, growth, and prosperity as we move on to the next step for Zappos!

DIAN C.
employee since 2010

Zappo's culture can't be explained in words, it needs to be lived.

DIANA A.
employee since 2007

I can't believe on how fast time is flying by. It's already been two years and I still love coming to work. I've built some great friendships in the amount of time that I've worked at Zappos. The Zappos Culture isn't like a culture you can find anywhere else. How many companies can you say give their employees carnivals, parades, happy hours, free lunches and pay employees-in-training to quit if they aren't culture fit??? Most of all, how many companies can say their CEO sits in the office among them?!

Wishing Zappos many prosperous years to come! Let's keep the culture alive and strong!

DIANA O.
employee since 2005

The Zappos Culture, to me, is the best culture in the world. It's a culture that brings us all together and allows us to grow, as individuals and as a group. It's what brings us a family and friends forever. It gives the ability to be honest with one another … to laugh, to cry, to learn, to joke with each other, and so much more.

Our culture is unique and interesting, in a wonderful way. Words cannot describe in detail what our culture is and what it all means, to me and to others. In order to somewhat understand our crazy selves and our culture, hang around us and you will definitely see people coming together and working as one, with a great attitude, honesty and so much pride for our company.

They say a picture is worth a million words. Our picture will have a million words to say and we hope you can carry that with you and be part of it forever. Our culture, to me, is definitely one in a million and has the ability to change us for the better. It's our glue and without it we wouldn't be who we are today… a company powered by happiness, laughter, memories, and friends. :-)

DIANE H.
employee since 2009

Well, where do I start? The Zappos Culture instills an entire variety of items. The Culture itself is beyond words, it's the way we live here at Zappos. It is the most phenomenal organization to work with. Where else can you come to work happy every day? Have you ever worked with people who smile constantly? If not, you need to be at Zappos.

Not only does Zappos care about its employees, management really wants feedback from them in regards to so many issues. They also provide the tools to grow within the "team", providing all that is necessary to ensure that you reach your full potential and they truly want you to succeed with your goals. It is the definitely the best environment to work in.

Never in my life have I been so truly blessed with my job and the opportunity to work here amongst the truly most wonderful people EVER!

DIANE M.
employee since 2004

I'm currently working on my sixth year with Zappos and I couldn't even consider leaving. I think of fun and family as a definition for our Zappos Culture. Our culture is unique and cannot even compare with other companies.

DONNA G.
employee since 2004

As an employee of five years, I have had the privilege of watching and contributing to the growth of this phenomenal company. Our Ten Core Values not only define our culture and company, but help us continue to grow as individuals. I love this culture because it is so positive! It is a pleasure to come to work each day.

DONNA H.
employee since 2005

What do I love about being here? The empowerment to make decisions on my own, the support and feedback to help me grow not only as a Zappos team member but also as a person, the encouragement to take risks and learn from my mistakes and the freedom to share ideas, dreams and vision for the future.

DREW G.
employee since 2008

I've had the opportunity to work for a few companies that have interesting and awesome cultures, but of course, Zappos takes the cake! Although I'm not a huge fan of Las Vegas in general, I'm here indefinitely because my passion for this company trumps whatever complaints I might have about the city we live in. I have never worked for a company that I wake up excited to arrive at every day. As I've progressed here in my career and taken on new responsibilities, I've continually been challenged to grow and contribute to our Zappos Culture. It's a challenge that I take very seriously, I strive to excel at, and that I take a lot of pride in when I am successful. Our Culture is what differentiates Zappos from what might be a simple, basic job, and instead, makes it a career.

What I love about our Zappos Culture is how organic it is. Everyone has the chance to contribute, they can be spontaneous when contributing, and everyone's heart seems to come through in our final product (although there never really is a final product :-)). Our Culture is constantly being rethought, revamped, improved upon, redefined, and evaluated. Our Culture is our heart, our soul, our brand, our compass, and our thermometer. Its the most difficult aspect of this job, yet its also what comes most naturally to us as a company. Our Culture will never be perfect, but at the same time, its what in the end will make our employees/customers the most loyal in the industry, and it will be what earns us our highest grade at the end of the day.

Thanks, Tony, for allowing us the chance to be a part of this beautiful company/family. It's my home more than my house is at times, and I'm very thankful for that.

DUKE C.
employee since 2006

Another year has gone by and it seems our culture is just getting stronger. The growth of our company is tremendous and is only matched by our goals and ambitions. Where one can expect the culture to diminish as a byproduct of this growth, I am amazed by our company's resilience to push through the adversities and keep our culture at the forefront of our minds. I'm looking forward to another remarkable year!

DURON P.
employee since 2007

Three years down and this place is still AMAZING!

A – Always ready to WOW!

M – My Zappos family is definitely one of a kind!

A – ACTION PACKED!!! (cheesy) lol... couldn't really think of anything for this one.

Z – Zappos!... what more needs to be said?

I – It's the 15th best company to work for according to Fortune... but, it's #1 in my book!

N – Never a dull moment!

G – Grateful to be working at such a wonderful company!

See ya in 2011.

DYLAN M.
employee since 2007

Our culture here is so special and it has helped me become the person that I've always wanted to be. The Zappos Culture is defined by our Ten Core Values; living up to them is not easy because our culture is not self-sustaining. To live and breathe the core values, day in and day out, we must be dedicated to the belief that by doing so, we improve the lives of everyone around us. That is a task that requires constant effort because it is too easy to fall in to the trap of complacency. I find myself constantly finding new ways to improve and the support structure here gives me new insight through open and honest feedback. They support me when they see me succeed and even more so when they see me struggle. I cannot encapsulate in words the awe I have for this place, the people, the opportunities, and the happiness that permeates everything here. Our Zappos Culture means holding ourselves to the highest standard and being open to our potential to positively affect everyone and everything around us.

EBONIQUE H.
employee since 2007

Zappos ... after three years, I'm still happy, thankful, and fortunate to have met such great people. No other job will ever compare.

EBONY M.
employee since 2007

This will be my third year at Zappos and, boy, can I say that time sure does fly. I can truly say I had no idea what Zappos was before my trip with a friend to the Job Fair in 2007. I hate job fairs — they are all boring and put you to sleep. That was no way near what I got when I walked through the Zappos' doors for the first time, and I am glad that I came that day!

Over the past three years, I have never woken up in the morning with a bad feeling of not wanting to come to work, because I don't hate my job. This place is the BEST place to work! My kids love to come visit when they can, and want to be included in everything Zappos does. Our favorite Zappos party is the company picnic because it is the entire company resting, relaxing, and having fun, with family, friends and co-workers who are also like my family. People say that I sound like a Zappos cheerleader and sometime it gets that way and I have to stop myself ... I don't want my friends to think I am crazy since, of course, every work place is not like Zappos.

Our Ten Core Values are SO, SO different from those at other companies and it is really hard to just narrow it down to just one so I will mention my three favorite values.

1. Deliver WOW through Service:
This is easy because most people are not used to the kind of Customer Service that Zappos provides. I can simply place an order for a customer or keep a customer company while they place the order online and they are so happy that they have just completed an online order without any help but simply loved that the offer was made to stay online in case they had a question.

2. Embrace Drive and Change:
Zappos is ever changing and keeps me on my toes. Nothing is ever boring.

3. Build a Positive Team and Family Spirit:
Zappos.com is a BIG family that truly cares about everyone and our customers.

To sum it all up, I love Zappos and hope to be a part of this family for years to come. Well, I could go on and on about Zappos. so I will say goodbye for now.

P.S. Tony rocks! Thank you for taking the chance on this venture.

EDRIC B.
employee since 2007

What I like about the Zappos Culture is that it's open to new ideas. It allows its employees to be creative and express themselves in unconventional ways. When I first came to the company, it was completely different from any other call center I'd worked at. Lately, we've been taking some steps backwards and beginning to look like all the rest. If we can get everyone in the company to follow our Ten Core Values, then the sky's the limit, but as of now there is still work to be done.

EILEEN S.
employee since 2009

I feel very fortunate to be a part of the Zappos family for many reasons. It is so refreshing to be a part of an organization that doesn't just talk about its principles and values, but actually stands behind them. I remember being blown away when, after emailing my feedback on the P and A system, I got a response from two different managers addressing my specific comments. No auto response. No form email. I couldn't believe it. It really shows that Zappos isn't just paying lip service to us as employees, but truly does make decisions that are based, at least partially, on what we as individuals think and feel.

I am also amazed by all of the relationships I have forged here. I know that I now have an extended family and friends that will be mine for life. When I walked in on my first day of training, I really did not expect anything like that to happen, but I will always be thankful that it did.

ELIA L.
employee since 2009

The Zappos Culture is something that is unique. Our culture is what separates us from the norm. It allows us the flexibility to learn, grow and expand in ways that are unique. I am so grateful to be part of something so special and rare. It is a privilege to be working with others toward a common goal. Our culture makes me want to go above and beyond what others would expect.

ELISA N.
employee since 2009

Zappos Culture, to me, is something that can only be created by the people I work with, where each individual has contributed their sense of self and personality into our work environment. There is no need to hold back here and you are free to express yourself. Tattoos, piercings, hair color, pajamas, capes, and Leprechaun costumes are welcome! We work hard and play hard, and that is what makes it so much fun. I would like to think of a cool quote right now, but can only think about the raffle tickets I just won at our Valentine's Day Carnival... YES! I heart Zappos.

ELISSA S.
employee since 2007

Word: Zappos

Definition: A rare art form that is a purposeful recreation of a new and special reality within the workplace, stemming from a strong connection to people, life and happiness that can never be copied.

ELIZABETH S.
employee since 2009

Zappos Culture, to me, simply means always having a good day at work, interacting with our Zapptastic customers and sharing smiles with my colleagues. It is such a wonderful feeling to be able to be yourself in a positive and family-oriented work environment. I am extremely grateful to be a part of this great company and am looking forward to more Culture Book write-ups in the future. Thank you.

ELSIE F.
employee since 2005

To work at Zappos is to have fun while having the freedom to be yourself! We all have an equal opportunity to grow and try different areas with one goal in mind: To provide absolutely the best customer service experience for both our external and internal customers. Any feedback is always welcome and appreciated. We are always having a great time while at work, from parades, potlucks, bingo, games, seminars, etc. We are always evolving and changing while growing. That is what makes Zappos so different from other companies. I truly love my job. There is no other place like Zappos!

EMILY B.
employee since 2009

Since I have been here, which has been since September 2009, I continually become more and more blown away by the way Zappos and our employees live and breathe the Zappos Culture. At first, I was a little hesitant to believe Zappos truly lived by the Ten Core Value and culture; other companies I had worked for before always had these values they spoke of on orientation day, but I never saw any of them put into action on a daily basis. This is why I was a little standoffish at first, but I quickly learned that each and every person at Zappos truly believes in our mission. Being lucky enough to work in CLT, I can see the way our culture spreads to our customers.

The Zappos Culture has taught me things about myself that I don't believe I ever would have learned without coming here. Our core values are so vital to the way I live my personal life and the way I help our awesome customers at work. The #1 Core Value, "Deliver WOW Through Service", is the one I think of during each call I take because I want to give every customer top-level service. Core Value #6, "Build Open and Honest Relationships with Communication," is very true because there are no lines of communication that cut off top management from me. I believe this is what allows Zappos to be so successful and it gives all employees a great sense of empowerment. Also, Core Value #3, "Create Fun and a Little Weirdness", reminds me to break out of my shell sometimes and really be myself, since I can be pretty weird! Our culture ROCKS because it drives me to pursue growth, be adventurous, embrace and drive change, and most importantly to me, be passionate and determined!

ERIC P.
employee since 2007

Fifteen. Quinze. Fünfzehn. Quindici. Petnaest. Vijftien. Pietnascie. Femton.

The number 15 has a very special meaning to Zappos this year, as it represents our placement on Forbes' "Top 100 Places to Work" (up from #23 last year). Although our unique culture has been featured on several TV segments and in magazine articles, it's not the reason we placed so high on the Forbes list. We're #15 because we have all been spoiled rotten by Tony! Ha! We're spoiled and you're not! Nanee nanee naaaanee! See what I mean? Sorry, I couldn't help it. Ok, relax. Ooooommmmmmmm. Time to remember our core value #10: "Be humble."

When a company has a CEO who does so much for his people, they're going to also find themselves placing high on the Forbes list of best places to work. We even go so far as to offer insights to other companies about how they, too, can create their own unique culture. Sure, we have all the amenities of a Holiday Inn, but it's the intangibles that really WOW us. From life-changing motivational speakers to pipeline classes focused on development to incredible holiday gifts to New Year's pencil holders personally delivered by the man himself, it truly is a privilege to be part of the Zappos family.

ERIC S.
employee since 2007

Zappos Culture has been 11 years in the making. Defined by Ten Core Values, but always being fine tuned. The rest of the business world is just now starting to understand it and is slowly modeling their practices around it. It's about making good choices — not just business decisions. Zappos Culture encourages the pursuit of happiness in our lives. In a society where humility is often forgotten, our tenth Core Value is "Be Humble."

40

ERICA R.
employee since 2009

What Zappos culture means to me is that it is a sense of family. A family that accepts you as you are and you don't have to change to fit in. That is exactly what Zappos does, with no questions asked. I not only come home to family but I come in to work and spend time with my family, which makes work so much more enjoyable.

ERIKA M.
employee since 2007

The Zappos Culture is about humanizing the potentials and visions of individuals from different walks of life, to develop a character for a company that was not born to fit in, but was born to stand out.

ERNIE L.
employee since 2007

When you first get to Zappos, you cannot help but notice how open and friendly this place is and see the willingness of everyone around you to do whatever they can do for you. It is truly a great feeling. It is the kind of feeling that makes you want to come to work each day.

Now that I have been here a bit, that feeling has changed. It has grown, and now that great feeling I have comes from the things I can do for those around me.

This really is a special place and I am glad that I am here.

FRANCES M.
employee since 2010

I LOVE ZAPPOS and here is why. Those at Zappos are striving to make the people around them HAPPIER. Sure, the customer always comes first at other companies, but often those people are just another wallet. Here at Zappos, our customers are our friends. They know that even if they're just lonely and want to talk, they can call us and we ADORE spending our time with them. We create connections that allow each customer to be seen as a unique individual rather than a bank account.

By doing this, Zappos has found the secret to making the world a better place. By being honest, positive, never shutting out change, accepting differences, and finally, ALWAYS thinking of our friends, we spread LOVE. That is what we're all after, right? Finding a little bit of love in the world?

Well, regardless of whether it is or isn't what he or she or you or me are looking for, we're more than happy to share. That's what makes Zappos more than just a shoe store. We're in the Business of Selling Happy.

GEORGE R.
employee since 2009

I am pretty fresh with the company (since September 2009). I admit, I was pretty skeptical about the culture and was waiting for everything to kind of come to a head after training. I am pleasantly surprised to see that things have progressed as I was anticipating. The Zappos Culture is absolutely infectious. Not only has my work environment changed for the better, but my personal life has changed as well. This truly unique culture really defines Zappos and I am looking forward to the many years ahead here at Zappos! WOW!

GEORGINA P.
employee since 2006

So, what does the Zappos Culture mean to me? Wow, where to start? For the past three-plus years, in such a huge company, I have actually felt like a person. For once I am not just a employee making numbers happen. It does not matter what department you are in — we are all one big extended family. In the past couple of years we have gone through some major stuff, but one of the reasons we came out fine was because of our culture. It has taught me so much. Even though we all have priorities and a life outside of Zappos it is nice to feel that we have an extended family to support us through the good, the bad, and the ugly things that life throws at us. I cannot wait to see what the future has in store for all of us — employees, customers and all.

GERALD M.
employee since 2008

As Zappos goes from being a relatively small company to becoming a big company, under the Amazon umbrella, all things are possible! Preserving the core values and keeping the unique and fun environment that has made us different from other corporate cultures will be more difficult as we grow and morph into what Zappos will become in the next decade, but somehow we will find a way. The first decade saw so many amazing dreams realized and it's very exciting to be involved with what's coming next!

GINA C.
employee since 2008

I truly believe that the Zappos Culture is what keeps this company strong and vital. The people here are so welcoming and understanding. It definitely keeps me going when I have had a rough day. I am very grateful to be working in such a positive, upbeat environment. :-)

GINA W.
employee since 2007

To me, the Zappos culture means the freedom to be an individual and to be respected for it. Being in the workforce for the last 16 years, I've worked for many different companies. However, none of them even compare to Zappos. Zappos is the only corporate office that I've ever heard of where employees are allowed to come to work as we are, brandishing piercings, with multi-colored or wildly styled hair and proudly displaying our tattoos. The kindness, empathy and humility that Zapponians display are truly unmatched. It's the only place I've ever worked where your co-workers go out of their way to make sure you're doing okay or to help you out when you need it. I also LOVE the fact that we're afforded so many opportunities to pursue growth and learning here, as I have an infinite thirst for knowledge because I believe that knowledge is power. To sum it up, I love me some Zappos! =)

GIOVANNA W.
employee since 2007

My definition of "culture" is something that gets inside the psyche of an individual, molding and shaping the very behavior of that individual. It is the thread that binds a community together in its traditions, beliefs and goals toward — hopefully — the betterment of that society and each individual within that society.

Zappos is a community with its own specific culture. The Zappos Culture has infiltrated my world by helping me on a daily basis to solidify a healthy mindset of helping and giving with a whole lot of fun thrown in! The Zappos Culture has created a "vibe" inside my world of "Yes, I absolutely can!" instead of "I can't" or "Maybe I'll try later."

I've had three years of practice in how to take my inter-personal relationships to much higher levels, and I have a sense of fearlessness when communicating with people — a personal goal I've wanted to accomplish for many years. Now, because of what I do here on a daily basis, I'm happy to say that it's difficult for me to imagine certain fears I used to have when it comes to people!

I don't know how long my road will parallel that of Zappos, but I do know that the time I'm having and had with them has given me the ability to make some wonderful personal accomplishments and has brought me closer by leaps and bounds to fruition of all the goals I've had in life within the past 25 years. I look around and take a gander at where I am when I come to work and try to rise above any feeling of the mundane I may feel from time to time, well, because we're all human. But when I snap back into reality, I know that being a Zappos employee definitely does not equate to, or necessarily lead to, a mundane existence just by virtue of what we do and how we do it!

I'm thankful I can use what I learn here at Zappos by working among the best to help me reach my own success. Thank you Tony, Alfred, Fred et al!

GRACE K.
employee since 2008

Zappos Culture to me, is a Family. You take a humongous group of people from different locations, cultures, religions, personalities, and put them together to learn the Zappos Way. "Deliver WOW Through Service."

As with any family, you are going to have some bumps in the road, but with our culture we are going to "Embrace and Drive Change" through those bumps! Just walking through our office you can tell how we "Create Fun and A Little Weirdness" to make every day better than the next! Every day as a family we will "Be Adventurous, Creative & Open Minded" to keep our Zappos way of living going. It doesn't stop there. As a family we "Pursue Growth & Learning" among each other and outside of our Zappos family to spread the Zappos Way. We "Build Open and Honest Relationships With Communication" with everyone around us to "Build a Positive Team and Family Spirit" in our work environment. Nothing can stop us as a family. We will always "Do More With Less" and "Be Passionate an Determined" to reach our goals no matter how small or big they are. The best part of our Zappos Family is we will always "Be Humble." No one in our family is better than any other. We are equal!

You can't really compare our Culture to that of any other companies because, in the end, we want everybody to have the Zappos Culture. All we can do is to spread the Zappos Way!

Thank you for your time and having me as a part of the Zappos Family! :]

GRAHAM K.
employee since 2009

In this world of customer-first customer service, Kindle reading, Cape Thursdays, Zappos Idol, All Hands, Vendor Parties, Holiday Parties, Connect Four Championships, Zuttles, Cows, Pandys, R-tenders, OVers, CLTers, Livestrong Weeks, potlucks, Spoken Word, Wow Teamers, TLCers, ITers, Take Your Kids to Work Days, Zappettes, Zollar Store, All You Can Eat Bistro, nap rooms, headshaving, team building, carnivals, llamas, backpack filling, raffles, Pipeline classes, Team Canadians, paintbrush holders, employee discounts, tie-dying, corporate challenging, Bald and Blew, Haunted Houses, Insights, Touring, Parades, book clubbing, Star Wars mailing lists, non-sponsored events, rubber duckies, Flook meetings, Mardi Gras celebrations, Zappos Games, Zappos Classic funerals, Zappos picnics, Toga parties, Cute and Funny Kitties, Zappos Peep Contests, Zappos Furry Friends, Monopoly games and 700 of your best friends, it's hard to narrow our culture down to just one thing.

GREGORY R.
employee since 2008

Zappos has been a huge blessing to my family and me. Zappos has not only given me the opportunity to take care of my family, but has really taught me the real meaning of customer service, to both customers and colleagues alike. I'd never really known how to relax, but learning to apply our Ten Core Values has taught me how to have fun and take care of business. I would like to say to everyone who has helped in this transformation, thank you.

HAWANDA A.
employee since 2008

The Culture at Zappos is the most amazing thing ever! Each day, it feels like I'm coming to see family rather than just another day at work. Family takes care of one another, and that's what it feels like here. Whether it is Zappos related or not, there is always someone willing to help out whenever possible. There's always feedback and never criticism, which makes it feel it easier to make Zappos a career and not just another job. Suggestions are always welcome, and many of these suggestions are acted upon, giving employees a sense of accomplishment. From the random parades, to the constant recognition of success, its easy to see why we've become one of Fortune's "100 Best Companies to Work For." I LOVE ZAPPOS!!!

HECTOR G.
employee since 2006

Zappos Culture is a way of living, a way to do things differently, breaking all pre-existing and traditional standards in the customer-service industry. After three years of having fun (what most people would call working), I had realized that if I ever leave Zappos, I would have to find something else to do beside customer service. Because I truly believe that I won't find any other company so oriented towards customers and employees as Zappos.

HELENA D.
employee since 2008

Zappos Culture is so WOW! That's the best thing about Zappos. Everyone here is out to WOW everyone else. Our customers can tell that we're happy. What a pleasure to work in a call center where people rave about our service and the rate of complaints is next to nil!

HELENE T.
employee since 2008

Zappos Culture is a unique way of life. That's what we are here at Zappos, UNIQUE! That's why we stand out to our customers, businesses and our community. We have adapted this way of life to try and connect (as Sean Stevenson puts it) with each other, customers and whoever comes to our office, but mostly to better ourselves in every aspect. That's what makes us the way we are!

HOLLY F.
employee since 2006

How many people can honestly say that they love their jobs? At Zappos, we all can. It is so much fun to come to work and talk to people on the phone about all the great things that Zappos offers. Customers always ask me how it is that I sound so cheery, but it's not hard to be cheery when your co-workers feel like family and you know that you work for a company that supports you, where you can be yourself. Our customers are a part of our family, too, and I hope that they feel like family when the call is ended.

HOLLY K.
employee since 2007

Z – Zealous
A – Alive
P – Precious
P – Playful
O – Original
S – Spectacular

C – Colorful
U – Unexpected
L – Laudable
T – Trendy
U – Unique
R – Remarkable
E – Energetic

IJEOMA I.
employee since 2006

I enjoy the culture that we have here because there is a strong emphasis on building relationships. I have made some connections with people here that will endure even if we must part ways. That is the most special element of our culture to me.

IRENE V.
employee since 2007

The Zappos Culture is incomparable. I've never even heard of any other company like it. At Zappos we are all a family, not just co-workers. It's great to see the smiling faces when you are walking in the door. Someone you may not know yet will still take the time to say hello. These are things that aren't commonly seen in other companies.

I have noticed that since working at Zappos, my whole perspective about work has changed. For once in my life, I don't dread coming to work! I feel very honored to work for a company as unique and amazing as Zappos.

ISABELLA P.
employee since 2010

I have been working here for only a month and the Zappos Culture is something I've never experienced before. When I applied to Zappos, I read about the culture and, to be honest, the Zappos culture goes above and beyond what I've read about in books and online. Actually experiencing the culture every day is a pretty amazing feeling. I am excited to come to work every day, because every day is always fun and new. It is great that I am able to deliver happiness to our customers and it has to do with how unique the Zappos culture is. I have great co-workers who enjoy coming to work, and I've never had a job like that before. I consider myself lucky and I love working for Zappos. This month has been an awesome ride with the company and I look forward to an exciting future.

JAIME S.
employee since 2007

The Zappos Culture helped me stop smoking! The work environment is so laid back, relaxed and informal that I didn't feel the need to take a break. At some workplaces, all you can think about is when your break is and when you're off. Just getting out the front door and lighting that cigarette is an act of relaxation. It's especially nice when you have a stressful job because that's all you can think about is, "When's my damn break?!"

Since day one at Zappos, I haven't felt like that. I told myself, "If this place turns out to be as badass as everyone says it is, then I should be able to stop!" So I tried ... and succeeded! No stupid gum, no books about quitting, no telling myself this is the last one and flaking out, and no setting myself up to fail! I don't feel the same stress that most others feel in their workplace. I don't feel like I have to run away or take that smoke break. Just being here made it possible for me to quit.

Like Dr. Vik always said, "If you set a goal for yourself and the goal is too tough, you set yourself up to fail! Then eventually, with all goals you set for yourself, you subconsciously have a deep-rooted negative feeling that you can't succeed, you can't complete your goals!" Well, his quote was something along those lines, but nevertheless, it was true! Zappos has certainly made my goal easy to reach! That just goes to show, being positive and keeping your thoughts and actions in check really does make the difference. And this is certainly a hard task, as many people have predefined thoughts that work sucks. You have to actively put in some very hard work to keep your thoughts and actions in check; that's the trick to creating culture in the workplace. Once you have everyone on board, then you find the workplace culture starts to become more natural and then the boring stuff like personal/professional goals and objectives become easier to reach!

I think we can chalk up our $8 million in sales to that!

Now I can walk up a flight of stairs without gasping for air! I can take my dog for a run and not want to fall over dead from blackened, unhealthy lungs! Satisfaction guaranteed! HA HA, I sound like a cereal box. Thanks for reading.

45

JAMES C.
employee since 2006

Zappos is LOVE!

Thank you for being you!

JAMES H.
employee since 2009

I love the Zappos Culture because it allows me to be myself and to pursue growth in the areas that interest me.

JANE J.
employee since 2005

The Zappos Culture reminds me of the thought of dropping an Alka-Seltzer tablet into a glass of water — you don't see it, but somehow it does something magical.

The personal connection we all have to one another is very unique and special. I am very lucky and proud to be a part of the Zappos family.

JANET P.
employee since 2009

Being part of the Zappos family and culture has been life changing. I am surrounded by people who really want to know what I am passionate about. They are interested in my goals and helping me achieve them. Our Ten Core Values are what makes us who we are as a team and individuals. We absolutely love our customers and are encouraged to go above and beyond for them, every day! We really are a SERVICE company that just happens to sell shoes!

JASMINE K.
employee since 2006

Zappos Culture allows me to be me. I'm not stuck in a mold that you'd expect from a booming business. I come to work enthused and feel as if I make a difference. I intentionally promote Zappos outside of work without even noticing it. I've grown both professionally and personally. I am inspired everyday by the interactions I have with both my co-workers and our customers. The people I work with are not only my co-workers, but also my family. But most importantly, I know that I am part of something special and am blessed because of the impact being here has made on my life.

Mahalo Nui Loa to everyone at Zappos who has made this journey one that I hope will never end!

JEANINE L.
employee since 2007

I don't know what else to say that I haven't already said in the past about Zappos, but I'll try to add something new this time. I'm so blessed and honored to be working for, well not just for, but with a company like Zappos. Forget the random parades, the free food, free benefits, holiday parties and happy hours, which are all wonderful, of course... this company is all about positivity and a unique bond shared by all. We truly are pumped for the future of Zappos and we all work towards it together.

Family is a word that is often used when describing co-workers here and you know what? It's true. I have met some awesome people here and have great friendships that will follow me for life now. I hear people talk about their "crummy" jobs and how they wish they could quit or get laid off. I then think how lucky I am to be able to say the exact opposite about my job. I hope always to be able to say it, too — cuz I ain't ever leaving!!!

JEFFREY L.
employee since 2006

This will be my fourth entry for the Zappos Culture book, so it's time to change things up a bit. It's time for... Haiku!

Zappos makes me proud;
we're like a family here.
One team, one vision!

JENN R.
employee since 2009

What does the Zappos Culture mean to me? Well, I believe the Zappos Culture is truly a way of life. I have been blessed to become a part of such a wonderful company for almost three months now. Ever since day one, everyone has been so welcoming, kind, and eager to teach me the ropes. It's like having a second family at work, and I truly enjoy leaving my house to come be with them every day! Frowns rarely exist, and all of our hard work is constantly praised! Of course, life gets rough for all of us, but the minute I park my car, and prepare to walk into these doors, I leave all my troubles behind. I feel as if the 40 hours a week I spend here are like 40 hours of therapy. This has truly been reflected in my family life on a daily basis as well. Zappos believes in the success and well being of its employees. They also EMPOWER US to provide all the tools to constantly WOW each and every single customer that we come in contact with. You very rarely have to transfer a customer to satisfy his or her needs. How cool is that? It feels so wonderful when customers tell you "I LOVE ZAPPOS," and on the other end we say, "WE LOVE YOU TOO!" Building this bond is such an amazing feeling! I have never experienced such a culture fit before at any of my other jobs. I say jobs, because all those building blocks have brought me right where I sit today, as I EMBRACE my future CAREER with Zappos. :-)

JENNA T.
employee since 2008

2009 was both the best and the worst year of my life. The best, because I welcomed my beautiful daughter into this world. The worst, because I lost the most important person in my life... my mom (who also worked here). How does this relate to Zappos and its culture? They were there for me, every step of the way. Whether it was throwing me countless baby showers or just giving me time for my family, I knew I could count on them. They say you don't realize who your real friends are until something life changing happens. Well, here at Zappos, I didn't realize I even had that many real friends until that happened! I was absolutely overwhelmed with how much support everyone gave me and how sincere everyone was. To this day, I know I can still count on many of them for anything, whether it's a shoulder to cry on or a babysitter. I have worked here for two years now and am still in awe of how life changing our Zappos Culture is. I thank God every day that I'm a part of it!!

JENNIFER D.
employee since 2009

The Zappos Culture has become very important to me in a very short time. This is the first job I've ever had where I am encouraged to be myself. I'm also able to share ideas and even complaints... without feeling like I'm going to "get in trouble" with someone. This has been, by far, the best place I've ever worked and I hope it will be the last!

JENNIFER F.
employee since 2009

When I think of Zappos and our culture, I can't help but think about a circus. I mean this in the nicest way possible. A circus consists of various types of individuals with a range of talents that they're able to bring to the group without being forced to conform to someone else's idea of how they should act, what they should wear, or who they should be. However, when you put all of these unique people together, you end up with a wonderful outcome. Our company reminds me of a circus for these reasons, not to mention that like a circus, we also have people in strange outfits, parties with fire breathers and carnival games, and the occasional visit from a llama. I love this place!

JENNIFER McG.
employee since 2007

I feel that our culture is an essential balance between "party all night" and "work all day". We learn, we teach, we party, we care. Zappos means a great place to work, with friends and family.

JENNIFER P.
employee since 2008

Finally, I've found a place that allows employees to really live the golden rule. I've never been happier in my life. I hope Zappos will always be this way.

JENNIFER W.
employee since 2007

When I leave work, I go to my apartment — where I live...

When it's time to come back to work — I come home to Zappos ...

JESSE C.
employee since 2005

As a member of the newly formed Learning Center located in Customer Loyalty, I've been thinking a lot about culture and the connections that we share with each other. I like to compare it to something we here at Zappos all hold near and dear to our hearts: Our success has not happened because of low prices, mass marketing, or gimmick-type sales. We turn first-time customers into loyal ones. They share their experience with friends and family, they blog about it on the internet, and they come back again and again. I think of our culture the same way. Zappos is full of the highest-performing people in the world. We perform at a higher level because we care about each other. Through the connections we share with one another, we strive to be better because we are inspired to do so. Sure, benefits are great, and free food is absolutely incredible, but when it comes down to it, I am who I am because of the relationships I've built. I want to be a better person for the people that I work with; I am proud to be a member of this family.

JESSICA B.
employee since 2006

The Zappos family has helped me to grow in sooo many ways. We work together, laugh together, and love one another. I really do think that we are the closest that any group of 500-plus people could possibly be. Because of that, and our common love for shoes/clothing/house wares/and more (okay, maybe that's just me) Zappos employees share a common goal. Working as a team speeds up our momentum and makes success that much sweeter. Success by definition may be to achieve something, but for me it's simply being a part of that something.

Thank you Zappos, my family, my friends.

JESSICA D.
employee since 2007

It is very hard for me to explain what the Zappos Culture means to me. Each time I am asked this question, the same combination of words runs through my mind, "happiness, friendship/family, motivation, kindness, fun, and different." The Zappos Culture makes me happy to be a part of this company; it has helped me make a ton of friends who are now more like family, it has motivated me to become a better person, it has shown me that there are amazing and truly kind people in this world. The culture fosters fun and craziness, and it is genuinely different from any culture I have experienced in my previous jobs. All in all, the Zappos Culture means the world to me and I will do everything I can to keep it alive and well.

Wow, so maybe it wasn't as hard for me to explain as I thought! Thank you!

JESSICA K.
employee since 2009

Ahh… the Zappos Culture and what it means to me, It means I get to come to work and be me! I am allowed to be creative and crazy. We are encouraged to connect with our customers and do whatever we need to make them happy, without asking permission. Our culture is more of a family then anything. We care for each other on a business and personal level.

I can honestly say Zappos is like no other company I've ever worked for. I would try to compare Zappos culture with that of my previous employers, but honestly, they did not have culture! Where else can you get paid to sit on the phone and shop with customers all day!

JESSICA O.
employee since 2005

Every time I think of the Zappos Culture, I think of "The Freedom to Change things". Zappos is an ever-changing environment that keeps its atmosphere open to accept these changes. As a matter of fact, evolving is a better description because we become better with each change that's made. I think both change and freedom are constants that propel us further and further in this world.

JESSICA P.
employee since 2009

I LOVE the Zappos Culture! I love that I can be my weird self at work every day and people don't even think twice about what I am doing or wearing! The Ten Core Values are at the heart of our unique culture. They set us up for a fun and open learning environment that promotes success. The core values are amazing and even translate into our personal lives flawlessly. They make me a better person every day and I am so thankful that I found Zappos!

JESSICA R.
employee since 2009

Zappos Culture: social, fun, candid, zany, unpredictable, exceptional, diverse, positive, current, original, accepting, odd, open, ridiculous, sublime and vivacious.

Zappos Culture makes me feel: proud, stimulated, normal, abnormal, empowered, privileged, beloved, linked, innovative, spoiled, inspired, challenged, bizarre and happy.

JIM G.
employee since 2005

The Zappos Culture is really hard to explain. We continue to grow, and yet we are still holding on to that small company vibe. I personally think it's awesome.

They say that when you get to be a larger company, one of the hardest things to do is maintain a good culture. Well, I'm happy to know that every day, we all strive to ensure that we still continue to have that vibe we had years ago. We still make it a mission to know everyone personally and you feel bad when you see someone in the hallways that you don't actually know! I think it's awesome! WOO!

JO L.
employee since 2007

Zappos Culture involves taking ownership of one's level of happiness. Once one realizes that they are the key driver to how good their lives are, they are able to enjoy the good vibes of Zappos Culture wherever they go. What a wonderful place to learn this lesson and accomplish great things at the same time!

JOEY M.
employee since 2009

The energy here at Zappos is amazing, from the first day of training. When I think of our culture, I think of the fun we have every day wgnhen we come to work. People are happy and the buzz of activity is always constant.

Our Zappos culture is such a tough thing to nail down, and it's always evolving and changing too. That's the most exciting part; it's like a game to see what part of us we can bring to work every day to make everyone else's day a little better and WAY more fun. Every day I come to work thinking I know what to expect, only to find out I have no idea what every day at Zappos holds.

JOHN B.
employee since 2010

Although I have only been here since January 2010, I can sum up my thoughts about Zappos with these simple words — I would be lost without you, Zappos.

JOHN D.
employee since 2005

"When I was a boy, there was one permanent ambition among my comrades in our village on the west bank of the Mississippi River. That was to be a steamboatman. We had transient ambitions of other sorts, but they were only transient. When a circus came and left, it left us all burning to become clowns. The first minstrel show that came to our section left us all suffering to try that kind of life. Now and then we had a hope that if we lived and were good, God would permit us to be pirates. These ambitions faded out, each in its turn, but the ambition to be a steamboatman always remained."

That's from Life on the Mississippi by Mark Twain, one of my favorite books as a kid. What does that have to do with Zappos.com and it's culture you might ask?? Dreams. Not being afraid to think about what you'd like to be, and what you can someday become. A mind of a child has no limits, but as we get older that way of thinking goes away. Zappos.com has a way of bringing it back.

49

JOHN K.
employee since 2009

Zappos has an incredible environment to work in. Never have I felt so comfortable with being myself in a large group. The culture here embraces our differences and our quirks and values them. An environment like that cultivates creativity and personal growth. I never feel like an idea of mine will be disregarded, or that my enthusiasm will be stifled. I've only worked here for three months, but I can already say with confidence that this is the best place I have ever worked.

JONATHAN B.
employee since 2008

I know that Zappos is the place I want to be! It is a career, as opposed to a job, and is truly an oasis in the desert of corporate mediocrity. Awesome people, great benefits and plenty of free T-shirts!

JOHNATHAN L.
employee since 2007

When I wake up in the morning, there are plenty of times when I think to myself, "Ugh... time to go to work again." I drag myself to the office, and then something amazing happens. I don't mind being here. In fact, I actually like being here. It really is my second home, and I'm happy to be able to say that. So many good people and special things go on. In high school, I had no spirit. At Zappos, though... well, I'm definitely behind Zappos. Tony's vision of Delivering Happiness is something that I can be proud to contribute to.

JORDAN R.
employee since 2007

Working at Zappos has been a fantastic experience. This is by far the best job I have ever had.

JORGE P.
employee since 2006

Being a part of the Zappos Cculture means becoming a part of growth and learning. You are constantly given the opportunity to improve yourself, be it personally or professionally. What's great about this is that, at the same time, you are given the guidance and tools you will need to succeed. Ask and you will receive. There is peer pressure, but it is positive peer pressure. Everyone around you wants you to succeed. We are geared toward the exceptional, rather than the average. The more people use the Zappos Culture, the better place the world becomes!

JOSEF K.
employee since 2008

Zappos. For me, this is the one job I simply love to wake up and go to every day. I've had a rough job history because I got so easily bored with my past jobs. Zappos makes every day new, fun and exciting.

I never imagined that one day I would like to go to work and assist other people. Zappos has made that possible. Looking back on how things started here for me, I see that Zappos helps you grow as a person. I've seen noticeable changes in my attitude and in the way I deal with others on a day-to-day basis. This is all for the better! I used to like who I was, but now I LOVE who I am. The Ten Core Values that we live by at Zappos are like guidelines to being a better you. That's the best way I can seem to put it. Not that there is anything wrong with anyone of us; this just "enhances" the user experience. That experience is your life. I appreciate all Zappos does for me as an individual, and as a whole, as a company, for what it does to make people as happy as Zappos can.

Thanks, Zappos for all you do for everyone.

JOSEPH A.
employee since 2008

The Zappos Culture means the world to me. It means waking up early to be here by 6am and being greeted by many "Hellos" and "Good mornings." People actually happy to be here so early. It also means sharing a conversation about absolutely nothing with someone you barely know, yet you walk away smiling and interested. A big part of our culture is the abundance of caring on a daily basis. People want to know how you are doing, they want to hear about your day. When everyone cares about each other, its easy to care about our customers. We generally want to help them because it's in our culture and we do care. When I leave here at 3 p.m. every day, I feel like I'm taking the culture of caring with me. I use it with my family, friends, and even in the general public. We embrace our culture here at Zappos, and use it to make the world a better place.

JOSEPHINE R.
employee since 2004

I have worked at Zappos since November 4, 2004! Every day I am WOWed by the sheer talent, energy, camaraderie and family spirit that surrounds me. I have been in the work force for 36 years! My family at Zappos gives me the opportunity to continue to grow and improve myself each and every day, as well as to contribute to our common goal, the pursuit of HAPPINESS!!!

JOSH P.
employee since 2008

You would think it would be so easy to just type how I feel about the Zappos Culture, but it's really not easy. I have waited till the last minute to think of something to say about our culture, but words cannot express how AMAZING it really is. Zappos is, hands down, the BEST company I have ever worked for and I enjoy learning and growing every day while being here at Zappos.

JOSHUA L.
employee since 2007

Zappos Culture is…

JOYCE E.
employee since 2006

Well, I have been employed now for three wonderful years. In June 2009, I began working on my very first specialty team. I joined the Order Verification team. One thing that I've learned while working on this team is this: No more curbside service. I've stopped giving my credit card to strangers, and I am very passionate about not having my credit card numbers stolen and very determined to keep it from happening (Core Value #9).

Anyway, moving forward, I will definitely not wait another three years before pursuing growth and learning (Core Value #5) and working on my next specialty team. Even though I've been with Zappos for three years, I met a couple of people for the very first time when I joined the team. At the same time, I do realize why it's so hard to leave a team once you've built a positive team and family spirit (Core Value #7). This, too is a FINE group of people.

I have a lot yet to learn, and I thank Zappos for giving me many opportunities to branch out. Shout out to the FAT team!!!!

JULIANNE R.
employee since 2007

Z (clap, clap... clap), A (clap, clap... clap), P (clap, clap... clap), P (clap, clap... clap), O (clap, clap... clap), S (clap, clap... clap), ZAPPOS!!! Just like everyone else in this company, I am a fan of the Zappos Culture and what is represented. I've been here for three years now, and I still feel blessed to be a part of such a great company. The support is always there. We all look out for each other, as well as for our customers. We continue to grow and change, and this helps us evolve. I love that we can all be ourselves. We have truly built an awesome family! Every day, I am thankful for everything Zappos has done for me. :-D :-* ;-P

JUSTIN "JAY" A.
employee since 2009

Zappos Culture means everything to me. I don't just apply the culture to my work time but also during my daily life outside of work. Here at Zappos, you're more than just an employee, you're part of a family. I've never had a job that would pay you to do some of the most unusual things, like parades around the building, literally yelling and screaming for a small purpose like graduating to the main floor. Another thing that Zappos Culture is about is our dress policy. You would think that the people high up in the company would be wearing suits and what not, but none of us do. We wear whatever we want that day and occasionally we'll have an ugly sweater day, or something along those lines, just for kicks. We have so much fun here we don't even consider this a job any more. Zappos culture is something that no other company can bring about.

JUSTIN F.
employee since 2009

Zappos Culture is one of a kind. I've had some jobs over the years that were just jobs — but this is far different. I find myself wanting to get up in the mornings and wanting to come to work. I have seen some things here that you simply won't see at any other company, which separates us and makes us different. What has Zappos done for me since I've started? Well it has made me a better and happier person. I'm almost always in such a good mood and seeing my team (family) every day makes coming to work even better. I've taken one of our Core Values very seriously and tried to apply "Being Humble" to any situation, and what a difference so far! You see everyone at Zappos using the Ten Core Values on a daily basis and you even hear our culture being spread to our customers. It's so pleasant to talk to our loyal customers on a daily basis because they are a reflection of us. Customer service is something that everyone does on a daily basis. I've been catching myself watching how other companies and individuals handle customer service and I'm sometimes shocked at what happens, so I'm very excited to be part of a company that leads the industry in putting the customer first. During training, we were told that we wouldn't just be working at some other job but we would be working for our "last" job. After being here a while, I can see how this is true. With all the training, skill sets and specialty jobs, there are endless opportunities to advance and improve. I, for one, believe this will be my last job.

JUSTIN H.
employee since 2009

The Zappos Culture is especially important to me because I have worked at other companies that tried to establish the same thing. Those other places failed pretty dramatically at trying to create the same kind of atmosphere, primarily because their main focus was on making their company look good. They didn't actually do anything to try and back up the culture — to live it.

Comparing my past experiences to my current place at Zappos is like comparing night and day. The culture here at Zappos is 100% genuine. You won't find anyone trying to "force" it, or merely "putting up with it" while they do their own thing. Every person here seems to truly feel like he or she is a part of it, and it's an amazing feeling. Not to hyperbolize, but it can really be a life-changing mindset if you allow it to be. The thing that really makes our Core Values shine is the fact that they aren't strictly work-specific guidelines; they are really general ideals that you can apply to your life outside of work and see very positive results. I've only been with the company for about three months now, but I can already tell that (hopefully) I'll be here for a long, long time!

KARA H.
employee since 2008

The culture at Zappos isn't just the Ten Core Values we operate by, it is something we live by. I have noticed that the Zappos Culture has changed not only how I provide customer service at work every day, but also how I view life outside of work. I started to take what I have learned from the Zappos Culture and integrated that into my daily life without even realizing it. I love it when I can end a call and I know that on the other end, that customer has a smile on their face. Being able to provide that type of service or an act of kindness in person is just as good a feeling that makes you just want to spread it to everyone else.

KARI Z.
employee since 2007

Zappos is freakin' fantastic! I've been working here for two years and it keeps getting better! I probably said the same thing last year... but it is still true to this day! The Zappos Culture here is extraordinary! It is so awesome coming into work, knowing that your co-workers are happy to be there and happy to see you! These people are not only your friends… but they become part of your family. I have met so many sweet, kind and funny people. Every time a new training class starts, I meet more! Thank you to everyone who has made and continues to make Zappos the amazing place it is… I won't be leaving anytime soon.

KATHERINE F.
employee since 2009

The Zappos Culture, to me, means we live and work by our Ten Core Values. My favorite Core Value is #1, Delivering WOW through Service. We have the unique opportunity of being able to handle each call by doing what is right for the customer. I know of no other company that offers courtesy exchanges, which is the ability to exchange items for the customer, move the money over, get the item out to the customer ASAP... all before having the original merchandise back to us. We handle each and every call on an individual basis with the freedom to go above and beyond to do what is right or help make it right… or in some instances, even referring the customer to another site for an item we don't have in stock! Wow! I am so proud to work for a company that truly offers exceptional customer service!

KATHERYN G.
employee since 2007

It is a joy to work for such a wonderful company. The culture is fabulous and keeps getting better and better.

KATHY H.
employee since 2005

Zappos is a great company to work for! I've been here for over four years now. It's so different from any other company I have ever worked for. Zappos encourages us to personally grow and to offer suggestions and solutions; at Zappos, unlike most other companies, our suggestions are actually read and considered. We are encouraged to be ourselves and to create a little weirdness. It makes it a fun place to work! Zappos continues to rapidly grow and it's been great to be a part of it all! Thanks for making it all possible, Tony!

KEIR E.
employee since 2008

I like that Zappos is ever changing. If you have attention deficit disorder, and I do, you will never get a chance to exercise it because we just keep on trucking!

KEVIN T.
employee since 2008

The culture here is amazing. I enjoy the fact that we are all like a family and act as a support system for one another. No matter what department or job title someone may have, he or she will take the time to sit and actually listen to you.

KIANA L.
employee since 2007

It's amazing that year after year, my excitement for being a part of the Zappos family continues to grow! I have experienced a lot of growth over the past year and it's all because of how Zappos encourages its employees to progress. Not only do you encourage it, you provide the resources and tools to help people reach their goals. I have never in my life looked forward to going to work, but I can honestly say that I really look forward to coming into the office every morning because I am passionate about the work I am doing and equally passionate about the people I work with. I've never been interested in creating outside relationships with my co-workers in the past, but Zappos has changed my perspective ... now, some of my closest friends are also employed by Zappos. Many companies talk about customer service but Zappos is different in that respect... we don't just talk about it, we live it, breathe it. and believe in it. I feel as though the opportunities are endless here. I couldn't be happier with things right now and look

KIM M.
employee since 2007

I have been at Zappos for almost two years now and it still amazes me every day that I found such an amazing job. I really don't feel like it's a job, I feel we have more of a family atmosphere and regardless of the titles (managers, supervisors, leads) everyone is treated equally and with respect. I love talking to the customers and hearing how much they love Zappos. Its been such a great opportunity for me to work for a company that cares so much about its employees and customers. The Zappos Culture allows everyone to be themselves and feel comfortable about who they are. It allows for open-mindedness and growth within the company.

Thank you for the opportunity to work for such a wonderful company.

KIM N.
employee since 2008

It has been almost two years now since I have been with Zappos, and it has been a great experience so far. Being in this culture has changed me as a person and in how I look at life. I hope to be with this company for a very long time so that I can continue to grow into a better person. I love my Zappos family, and I know that they will always be there for me.

KRISTY M.
employee since 2007

Happiness! WOW, what a concept. To allow your employees to be in charge of their own happiness. I started this job as just that, a job. Zappos has now become my passion... a passion that is present in my encounters with strangers, my interactions with family and friends and in my personal well being. I can, without a doubt, say that I am happy because of the passion I have for my life at Zappos

LAILONNIE H.
employee since 2008

What is the Zappos Culture? One of the definitions of culture is the product or growth resulting from such cultivation. I don't consider our culture a "product," but if you replace that with "family," it would read, "the family growth resulting from cultivation." That's what our culture means to me.

Zappos has been the perfect gift, job and experience for me. I'm very grateful for this wonderful place that I come to daily. Just when you think you can't grow any more, or play and be challenged, a new class is introduced, or a new sporting event... and then, of course, there's happy hour!!!! It's a stress-free, loving and "homelike" environment.

What's different about the Zappos Culture compared to other company cultures? I'm used to working for companies that do not appreciate you or what you contribute to the company. Other companies do not keep you in the loop or ask for your feedback. They also want you to get as much done as possible. (Quantity versus quality.)

It's nice to know that we can give honest feedback, suggestions and talk to management if needed without having our jobs be in jeopardy. Also, it's nice to say what we like or dislike when it comes to our health insurance. That's unheard of at other companies.

Zappos Culture is very diverse and very accepting. You can be your authentic self and that's okay,, which is also unheard of at other companies. At other companies they really don't care to get to know you on a personal level. I've met some great people while working at Zappos and I have "jewels" as friends here. I mean the type of friends that don't come a "dime by the dozen." One is even my BFF!

LAKESH M.
employee since 2007

Zappos was right when they said the culture here is different than anywhere else. I've been with Zappos for almost three years now, and I can truly confirm this. I've worked for a variety of companies in a variety of fields, none as creative as the culture here. I would have to say Zappos definitely is the best and most fun. We are encouraged to be ourselves whether we're a little weird or not!

LAURA C.
employee since 2007

Working at Zappos has totally made my life better in so many ways. We have some of the most amazing staff and I consider them my second family. We all support and encourage one another to excel in both our professional and personal lives, and we all understand what our main goals are. Our vision is priceless, and spreading happiness is just one of the reasons why my days are so joyful. I love Zappos and Zappos loves me, plain and simple!

LAURA R.
employee since 2006

When they asked me to put down what I think about Zappos Culture I had to think about it. It is not something that people run into everyday. I think that it empowers someone to do better, or do more for people in general. It takes getting used to and it is frustrating when you know it is possible but you don't see more people utilizing it. Zappos offers so many training opportunities for its employee that I would love to see other companies adopt ideas from Zappos' training in History and Communication to great speakers.

LAUREN C.
employee since 2006

The Zappos culture continues to grow and develop each year, just like the people and the company. I feel so fortunate to be a part of such a great experience not only for our customers but for everyone that works for the company as well. I have been with Zappos for a little over 3 ½ years and I'm still amazed and always wowed by the wonderful benefits and little things Zappos incorporates to make its employees happy.

Zappos continually evaluates everything it does and analyzes ways we can continue to better ourselves and give back. This mentality really pushes me to go above and beyond my own efforts and give Zappos the best of myself. I love working for such and innovative and creative company that is so humble and willing to listen and even implement ideas from all over the company. I am excited and proud to continue to help drive Zappos to even greater success in the many years to come! :)

LAUREN P.
employee since 2006

Zappos Culture is everything surrounding us, from the minute we walk into the building, to the minute we leave. You can see it in an employee you do not know holding the door open for you, your lead thanking you for all your hard work that day, or even in something as simple as your team decorating your desk on your birthday. These are just a few examples, but our culture is displayed every day. What makes our culture so amazing is that the people you work with are not just co-workers, they are family. We are one huge family at Zappos and that shines through on a daily basis. I just had my fourth anniversary at Zappos and honestly, it feels as if I have always been here. Our culture is what makes Zappos. I couldn't imagine being anywhere else or having any other job.

LAUREN S.
employee since 2008

The Zappos Culture isn't an adjective that we use to describe how something is done. Rather, it is a representation of the mindset and lifestyle we choose to embody. I've often compared Zappos to my previous employers and found that the use of the word "culture" with regard to them was a hollow word — a word that held neither real place nor clear definition.

Here at Zappos, the culture is the people who work, live and breathe Zappos. It is not something we strive to possess, but rather something we've already achieved. What I like most about Zappos is the freedom, the freedom to express myself, to live the life I choose to live... the encouragement that I get when I have an idea and want to implement it in the workplace and the "welcome-ness" that I feel when I come to work. We are one big family; when you speak of Zappos, you speak of each and every one of us. And I am a proud member of this family.

LEANN W.
employee since 2009

Zappos has made a big difference in my life. I have never been so happy at a job the way I am here. I truly feel like this is my second home and everyone here is my family. When my grandpa passed last year, many people let me know that they understood how I felt and that they are here for me if I needed them. It made me feel better about taking the time off that I needed so that I could come to work and be able to concentrate on working. Amazing — that is the best word I can think of to describe Zappos.

LETHA M.
employee since 2007

My third installment in the Culture Book and I still feel as passionate — if not more passionate — about this family. To see all of the major changes we have gone through over the years in the name of making our customers happy makes me feel so blessed to be a part of it. I can't say how much this company means to me. This is truly my family!

LINDA H.
employee since 2006

From an anthropological perspective, culture is the distinct way that people living in different parts of the world classified and represented their experiences, and acted creatively. If acting creatively is what we do at Zappos, I would say we are the winners and top rankers of all culture makers! Yeah, man!

My name is Linda and I'm coming upon on my fourth anniversary here at Zappos. I, now, am privileged to say I've seen many changes in my time with the company. A thought just came to mind: It would be grand to see our government function like Zappos and see all the changes day-to-day. We see what works with both our customer service and our employee service. That's right, you are reading correctly. Our management team provides a service to our employees as well. The people are certainly heard around these parts. I wish I can elaborate, but you would have to see it to believe it. I've never been so proud of a place I worked for in my life! When I'm asked what it's like to work for Zappos nowadays, I have so much to say that I don't know where to start and I can't seem to stop. Before I know it, the groceries are melting in my car. That particular instance was when I was at the grocery store just last night. True story.

Zappos is another set of parents or family that is always so encouraging, loving and supportive. Thank you, Zappos family, for how much you care about me and believe in me. I love my life and never want to work at another place again. I mean it. Can't wait to write in next year's book! :-)

LINDA R.
employee since 2007

There are so many things going on in our Zappos Culture that are truly amazing for us employees. I'd like to talk about just one. I am so impressed by the rewards we receive for just coming to work. For just showing up at the appointed time and day: I receive gifts, time off, recognition and get taken out to dinner. WOW — and I would have showed up to work anyway. Oh yeah, by the way, I also get a salary.

LISA N.
employee since 2009

Zappos Culture had everything to do with my decision to apply here. Once I was exposed to it, I knew I had to be a part of it, to show the power of WOW! I've never been a huge fan of change, often seeing it as a constant threat of instability in my life, but Zappos has shown me that when embraced, it can be the exact opposite. Being part of a company that encourages their employees to grow, to continue learning and to be proud of their individuality is a rare find. To actually care about and develop relationships with those you work around five days a week is a blessing. Selling shoes is what we may do, but being a company who care is who we are. Thank you Zappos!

LORNE S.
employee since 2006

The Zappos Culture is so much more than just a job. Our culture is what separates us from other companies. For example, we never stay more than three months in the same desk. We are always changing. I embrace this change. It's fun meeting new people, because our culture is people coming together and striving for one goal, our Zappos Culture.

At my last desk, we had set up a singing group. We were going to name it "The Zappetts." We were going to be three guys who would sing for everybody around us and have great fun. One of us made a statement, "This is what our culture is all about, having fun and enjoying each other."

We were going to ask Tony to sponsor us, but we have to learn to sing first.

LUCUS H.
employee since 2007

The Zappos Culture is a group of people with one goal in mind, to WOW, and they cannot deny IT!

LYVIER B.
employee since 2009

To me, Zappos Culture is inspiring, contagious and breath taking. It has consumed me in so many ways, I hope one day soon it becomes a virus and infects everyone on the planet. Zappos Culture is one of a kind. It is so unique, it is its own category. It should have its own meaning in Webster's Dictionary. What I like the most about our culture is that it is empowering. It's made me a better person and has allowed me to pay it forward. I have changed in person, mind and soul since I started working here. I love my Zappos!!

MARA K.
employee since 2005

To begin, I believe Zappos is like a fine aged wine. It gets better with age. I have been working for Zappos.com since January 31, 2005, and so many new and exciting changes have been made since then. When I first started, we did not have our Ten Core Values as they are now. We have great changes all the time. What company, I ask, will allow their employees to give input on changing policies that do not work well? If we have any questions or suggestions, our managers take them to heart and sometimes implement them. We have other companies that want to follow our example in terms of values — our call center, our customer service — because we are all about customers, external and internal. We are one large happy family, weird and wacky. I believe when I came to Zappos, I went to a family that I was missing for most of my adult life. It is so great my daughter is coming to join us at Zappos. Hopefully.

I want to thank Tony, Alfred, and Fred for making this such an amazing company. I was on vacation for three weeks and could not wait to come back. That is how wonderful Zappos is.

MARCIE W.
employee since 2009

The Zappos Culture, to me, means the following: Treating our customers the way Tony treats us — just like family. This is the way a company should run!

The culture is SO different here because people actually like their jobs, and people get along here. It's so different from other companies. When I first started, I was skeptical because this type of culture is so rare, and I had a hard time believing it existed. After being here a few months, I expect to be treated this way everywhere! We get spoiled without even realizing it.

The best thing about the Zappos Culture is that it rubs off on you and makes you a better person.

MARGRET C.
employee since 2008

Create Fun and a Little Weirdness.

Here at Zappos we are able to express ourselves freely. This allows us to be real people while doing our jobs. Sometimes it means being just a little weird or maybe just a little crazy. More importantly, we get our jobs done efficiently and we have happy employees all having a good time while at work. Who would have thought going to work could be the place to go and have a good time and lots of fun!?

MARIA E.
employee since 2006

Zappos Culture: The best way to define OUR culture is with pure passion. The ability to make others happy and genuinely care about NOT only our customers, but ourselves as friends and family. I have many great memories shared with my Zappos family and absolutely love working here. It's been an awesome FOUR years... thank you, Tony. And a special thanks to my fellow workers — it's been AmaZinG...Let's rock 2010!

<---o---> Hugs for everyone. I <3

MARINA M.
employee since 2007

The Zappos Culture is lived all the time. I love working somewhere that feels like my home away from home. Everyone is family here and I enjoy every minute of my day at Zappos. Zappos is one of the main reasons I stay in Las Vegas! Zappos Rocks!

MARISSA G.
employee since 2007

I have been with Zappos for almost three years now, and I must say that this is the BEST company I have ever worked for in all my working life. The culture is one of the many things that keeps me excited to come back to work each day. Zappos culture is different than other companies in that we are a huge family, we can be ourselves and everyone works like a family. There are so many growth opportunities within our company. I love the open door policy. I love how our managers and supervisors always show interest in our goals outside and inside of Zappos so they can help us progress and get to where it is we are trying to go.

I would not choose anywhere else to work.

MARISSA J.
employee since 2009

I think the biggest component of the Zappos Culture is our family spirit. It is truly unbelievable to see how someone progresses once they change that "work" attitude to one they would use with their own families. I firmly believe that I have two families now — my blood relatives and Zappos. I cannot even begin to explain what my Zappos family has come to mean to me. I know that others genuinely feel that way too. I know, because I have seen the bond in action. Without the family spirit, I don't know if the Zappos Culture would same.

MAJORIE L.
employee since 2007

Working at Zappos has had a very beneficial effect on my life. I like coming to work and knowing that there will be lots of smiles and good will. It is a far cry from some of the jobs I have had, where grumpiness and frowns dominated the day. If problems come up at Zappos, solutions are arrived at with determination and positive attitudes. Our customers always seem to be amazed with and appreciative of our culture. They can feel the good vibes through the phone! I am planning on Zappos being my last employer. I doubt very much that I would be able to find a more congenial or satisfying place to work.

MARK C.
employee since 2008

The Zappos Cculture is being yourself and enjoying life! How many people can come to work in pajamas 5 days a week!!! Haha, yeah, it's pretty crazy but that's what keeps us here! Good place to work, good people to work with...who could ask for more!?!? I'm happy and I'm thankful that I'm a part of the Zappos Culture!!! ^_^

MARLENE K.
employee since 2005

Our Zappos Culture nourishes you with down home goodness. It's like comfort food for your soul.

Thanks!

MARQURITA L.
employee since 2008

Zappos Culture is awesome! I feel like I work with family, not just co-workers. We actually know things in detail about one another. Not like "Don't put those reports there, she'll tear your head" off kind of detail, but the real one. Like, knowing when my birthday is, without having to check my "file." Or that I'm a nut about gifts — just ask some of my teammates around the holidays. I'm rambling, but if you're reading this and you know me, you're probably smiling because you know exactly what I mean.

MARY T.
employee since 2007

What is Zappos Culture to me? That is simple. It is my way of life. The culture at Zappos is truly life-impacting. I see and take things a lot differently now. I also handle situations from a whole new perspective. The people I work with here are so much like my second family. To call this place my job is truly a blessing. F.A.T (Fred - Alfred - Tony) has really built something that could be life/economy changing. I know this first hand because I can hear it in the customers' voices. They are so happy that they get to speak to a live person and not even that, it's someone that actually wants to talk and assist them. The Zappos Ten Core Values are something that I think we all need to incorporate into our daily lives.

MAURA S.
employee since 2003

The other day one of my co-workers and I made up a song about a new project we're working on. We sang the song to our entire team to introduce the project at an offsite meeting. I then finished up the meeting by doing a cartwheel.

That's the Zappos Culture. :)

MEGAN P.
employee since 2006

Working at Zappos is like falling in love. You can't explain how you feel, you just know it in in your heart.

MELANIE M.
employee since 2009

I felt as if I found love at first sight with Zappos! From the first day I went on tour here, I knew this was the place for me! The culture here was a perfect fit!! It took me five months to get hired here, but it was well worth the much-anticipated wait!! Persistence has more than paid off for me! They have WOWED me even more now that I am a part of this awesome company! I found that part of the culture here — delivering WOW through service — was exactly how I thought things should be and how I was raised. It is amazing to me that we are empowered to actually treat customers the way we feel they should be treated, instead of following all the usual corporate red tape. Another part of the Zappos Culture that I love and embrace is having a family and team spirit. I was blown away when I got to my area to work and realized how genuinely friendly and helpful everyone is. I found that as a company, we are always striving to come up with innovative ideas, letting our creativity flow to keep our team unified. Everyone has a great time contributing their ideas! I feel it is the glue that keeps us all together. Our management team actually cares about our feedback and takes our input into consideration. They request our ideas as we work as a team to drive positive change, improving operations in-house as well as for our customers. (Something that was not always so readily embraced in some of the other corporate cultures that I have been a part of.) I am so very grateful to be a part of something so that is willing to give so much back to its employees and customers. I love that I am encouraged to grow both personally and professionally! What an awesome life to live — I love my job!!

MELISSA C.
employee since 2006

The culture at Zappos goes beyond these walls. We carry it in our hearts as we spread Joy, Happiness, and Laughter to the world.

MELODY M.
employee since 2007

Another year has just flown by and the amazement I felt when I first started has only grown over time. There is no better place to be than where we are. I can't remember what my life was like before I worked here. The idea that we are helping people every day, working with a smile on our faces and making friends with our co-workers — who eventually become as close to us as our own families — are beyond believable.I tip my hat to this wonderful place and thank everyone who has been supportive of Zappos Culture. I also thank those who embrace our core values and apply them to their everyday lives. It's a great feeling to be a part of what was once a dream but is now a reality. I cannot wait to see what our future has in store for us. To another amazing year! Cheers!

MERENAITE S.
employee since 2008

I am blessed to be part of such a great company. The culture here encourages me to be positive and open minded.

MICHAEL M.
employee since 2008

The Zappos Culture is all about creating a fun and, ultimately, a positive place to work. This is apparent in every aspect of what we do. From parties to the off-the-wall decor in the office, it's all there. I have never worked in an environment where the employees lived and breathed the company in which they are employed, but you see it here. People are happy and we exude that both internally and externally. This is what I love about the Zappos Culture.

MICHAEL S.
employee since 2009

Zappos Culture is about being a blessing to others. I'm here to be a blessing in someone else's life. We are not selling products here, but touching the lives of people all around the world. I love the fact that I work with people who see and want that on each and every call or email they take in our call center. No other company in sales has the goal of making a customer say WOW! because of great service. I love the fact that I am who I am when I come into work. For once in my life, I am who I was supposed to be 24 hours a day, seven days a week.

MICHELE N.
employee since 2009

When I think of the Zappos Culture, all I know is how I feel, how I'm excited to be here each day and how much fun I've been having. I come from stuffy corporate jobs where everyone frowned on having fun and laughing, and each day I felt like the life in me was being snuffed out until I was literally DEAD sitting at my desk each day. People who know me know I love to laugh, have fun and am always smiling. So, NOW that I'm here, I feel so alive again!!!! Mahalo for creating such an awesome company culture!!!

MICHELLE M.
employee since 2006

What I like (okay, LOVE) about our culture here is the family environment! We are encouraged to build relationships and this has resulted in some really WoWish friendships! I met my husband here and several best friends. Having such close ties helps us all be on the same page in delivering WoW to our customers and of course, to each other. I also love how we are all important and everyone matters. It's true, we all have an important role in making Zappos into what it is — a different and awesome place to work!

MICHELLE S.
employee since 2008

The Zappos Culture is something truly special. I write this on my 40th birthday, which I had been dreading. I was feeling a bit down until I got to work and saw my desk decorated with balloons, flowers, and pictures of my favorite bands. And my fellow team members came in carrying potluck dishes and dressed in 80s fashions! That is just one snapshot of what the Zappos Culture is all about: people who genuinely care about one another, going above and beyond for each other

MICHELLE T.
employee since 2009

I have only been at Zappos for a very short time (six months), but ever since the first day, I've felt like I was part of a family. It is not every day that you can walk into a place, especially your workplace, and feel like you are part of a family. Zappos has shown me that not just at work, but everywhere that you go in life, you should feel like you are part of something bigger than yourself. I surely hope that I will be able to grow, and succeed, with my new Zappos family.

MIKE S.
employee since 2005

Zappos Culture is the overall environment — space, attitude, freedom, encouragement, mentality, philosophy, management style, and actual physical surroundings — which all work together to create a total milieu which attempts to make each individual better and happier on a whole, so that each one of us will then spread this to each other, our customers and everyone we encounter.

NAMIT B.
employee since 2009

I cannot say enough things about the Zappos Culture. I have only been here four months and I've never connected with so many people in my whole life. This place truly has a family atmosphere; people are so kind and helpful. I'm having so much fun going to happy hours and participating in group activities. There are so many things I'm looking forward to in the coming months. I have no doubt that this is going to be a fun first year. Thanks Zappos!

NANCY H.
employee since 2007

I have been here at Zappos for over two years now and I am still saying to anyone who will listen that Zappos is the most amazing company I have ever worked for! I have to say thank you to Tony, our CEO, for having the vision he had — and still has — for this company. The fact that a CEO could care so much about his employees and the culture of this company is just phenomenal. When the focus of a company is on their employees first, it is only natural that those employees would want to go above and beyond to give the same focus and concern for their customers. It is just amazing how much excellent customer service can impact not only the customer, but also the growth of a company. Thank you, Zappos, for giving me the opportunity to help you grow while also helping me to grow!

NATASHA G.
employee since 2005

The Zappos Culture is AMAZING! As soon as you walk into the doors you are instantly greeted by smiling faces! No matter what your mood was prior to arriving at work, it instantly changes in a matter of seconds! I can honestly say that I am extremely blessed to be surrounded by such an outstanding group of people. Working for Zappos has truly changed my life. I look forward to what the future may hold for my Awesome Zappos Family and me!!

NATISHA D.
employee since 2006

This is by far the best company that I have every worked for. I can't even say the word "work" when it comes to Zappos. This is by far the best company that I have been apart of!!! That's how I feel about being here, that I am actually a part of something great! I am truly amazed that we have collectively managed to maintain our culture and our emphasis on family spirit, year after year after year! It's a wonderful feeling to know I've contributed to what we are today and what we will be tomorrow. I'm inspired, I'm dedicated, I'm passionate, I'm loyal, and I'm truly blessed to be a part of such a wonderful company!

Thank you! :-)

NIEVES S.
employee since 2009

According to Janet Lane "Of all the things you wear, your expression is the most important" and I think that the employees' expressions exhibit the great culture at Zappos. I've worked in other jobs where people didn't enjoy their tasks and that inevitably shows. I love that everyone is in a great mood when working.

NIKISHA P.
employee since 2006

The Zappos Culture is amazing. What sets Zappos apart from other company cultures is that everyone lives by it. We are what other companies strive to be. I wouldn't trade it for anything.

NIKKI S.
employee since 2007

To me, Zappos culture means I really can be my-self. I really can voice my opinion. At my previous job I wasn't allowed to have an opinion, or when I was, it was given to me. I had ideas to improve our business but it didn't matter, no one wanted to hear them. At Zappos, if I have an idea, or if I think something needs to change, I can talk about it, and what's better, I can be hon

NOEL B.
employee since 2007

Zappos is a place where I can feel comfortable about being myself. It is a judgment-free zone. I am pretty comfortable with who I am, but at other work places, I have felt like I had to be someone else; like I was acting. Here, I feel welcomed, supported and loved. Thank you Zappos!

OSWALDO S.
employee since 2005

The Zappos Culture is the very thing that keeps our company going. Without it we probably would have had a dull environment that may have hindered the growth of this humble little company. And who would want that?!

There are not many places that can compare to Zappos. Of course, there are other places that make much more money, but their focus is their bank account, not the hearts of their employees and most importantly, their customers. Because our culture keeps us from losing sight of our customers, we can never give it up to become just another company!

PAMELA A.
employee since 2009

When I first moved to Las Vegas this past year, I had no idea what I had gotten myself into work-ing for Zappos. I can say that my overall experi-ence has been life changing. From the beginning, I felt a more unique atmosphere than at any other job I have ever had. Having a bad day at Zappos is kind of impossible because everyone around you wants to make you feel better. Everyone smiles, and if you're not having a good day, someone will make you smile!

My Zangstas, which means everyone from my training class, have been really wonderful to me in this difficult transition... moving away from everything I know to not knowing anybody in the city I live in! I have built relationships with people at Zappos that I will absolutely have for the rest of my life. I know that anyone who becomes a part of our Zappos Culture can testify to the fact that it makes you a better person. You start to realize that you are being extra thoughtful to people that you don't even know, no matter where you go! The greatest thing about our culture is that you truly feel that your co-workers genuinely care for you and want to see you do well. Whenever I hear people talk about how great Zappos is, whether it is a customer or someone on the street, it makes me proud to say I work here! I am happy and lucky to be a part of an epic company that is only going to grow into a leading company in this industry because of our amazing culture!

PATRICE C.
employee since 2007

Zappos is a life experience for both employees and customers. As employees, we are inspired and encouraged to pursue growth and learn-ing in a positive family manner. We embrace our customers as part of the Zappos family and really believe in a "Personal Emotional Connec-tion" with each and everyone we come in contact with, at Zappos and in our personal life as well. We choose our attitudes every day, and I choose the positive, life-changing attitude of the Zappos Culture.

PATRICIA B.
employee since 2009

When I think of Zappos, the one word that comes to mind is individuality. Here at Zappos, it doesn't matter what your background is, or where you came from — you are welcome here. You are welcome to express yourself; in fact, you are encouraged to do so without negativity, without judgment... We just ask that you have some fun and create a little weirdness to help embrace and drive change.

Here at Zappos:

You are empowered
You are celebrated
You are an individual

PATRCIA N.
employee since 2006

I have worked at Zappos.com for over three years and every year it gets better and better. I cannot wait to get to work and talk with our customers and see my co-workers. Our culture has made this company the place people want to come to for a tour as well as come to work. I have talked with people who wished we had locations in their state and even thought about moving. This just makes me proud and lets me know how lucky I am. I always encourage people I meet or talk to who embrace our culture to know that they can also have it. They can take it upon themselves to talk with the people in their company. I suggest they take a tour, so they can give their insight for what they experienced.

For me I have grown so much and see my personal life in a totally different way. I don't stress over things that change. Instead I look for the positive in that change. Our culture influences us in such a way that you really don't notice it. It just seems natural.

Embracing our culture.

PERRI G.
employee since 2006

Coming to work every day with a smile on my face.

Understanding that we are not just a workplace, but a company with a vision that we are passionate about.

Learning and believing in everything Zappos stands for.

Taking the time to get to know fellow employees on a personal level.

Unbelievable company spirit.

Random acts of kindness/happiness/weirdness.

Ending my work day with a smile on my face.

That's what the Zappos Culture means to me!

QUINTAYE P.
employee since 2006

The Zappos Culture is very unique. The minute you step into our lobby, you will see the difference. Zappos sets itself apart from all the rest and is one of a kind in all aspects of the company's operations. We aren't afraid to be different and are actually encouraged to be different. In my opinion, no other company will be able to duplicate what Zappos has done or can even come close to it. I look forward to coming to work every day because I know I can be myself.

I am encouraged to grow personally and professionally here, I have awesome co-workers around me and the list goes on and on and on ... I feel privileged to work for such a great company!!!!!!

RANCHEZCA V.
employee since 2009

I am still in awe of the Zappos Culture. I cannot believe I work for a company like this! First and most importantly, Zappos is a family, and like all families, it takes care of you. Another thing I love about this company is the energy that you get from just being here. We are encouraged to be ourselves, to be creative and have fun. Zappos is an empowering and inspirational place to work. Every day I am here is a good day!

RANDALL H.
employee since 2008

I have been fortunate enough to be a part of Zappos for the last two years, and I can definitely say that they have been some of the very best years of my life.

Over the last two years, my quality of life has improved quite drastically. I have spent some time thinking about what is different now that things have turned around, and there is one common denominator. Zappos.

Zappos encompasses the qualities of a great company, and it is easy to see why. Zappos is run by GREAT people! From the moment you walk in the door, you can feel the energy and the excitement radiating throughout the halls. I have never been somewhere that has been so accepting of people from all walks of life, and I have never felt more at home while at work.

When I first started working at Zappos, there was energy and a high that came from just walking through the doors. This is not uncommon to feel when you begin a new chapter in your life. What is uncommon is for this feeling to radiate for two years straight! I can honestly say that I could not be more proud of the job that I have, and I feel privileged when I get the opportunity to tell others where I work.

Zappos Culture is very simple: be passionate about what you are doing, work happy, work hard, and have fun! Zappos proves that the old cliché, "A happy employee is a productive employee" is no cliché at all. I come to work every day, knowing that I have a higher purpose and knowing that my actions have a direct impact on the success of our company. I am blown away on a daily basis by the impact that this company has had on my work career and, what's most evident to me, on my perspective on life in general. The thought of a company — my job — having an impact on the way that I function on a daily basis is a truly overwhelming feeling. Working at Zappos, and the experiences that I have encountered as a result of working at Zappos will have a lasting impact on the rest of my life!

RANIELLE R.
employee since 2009

Being able to work at Zappos is like winning the lottery when it comes to finding jobs. It's like stepping into a fairy-tale world where everybody is happy, nice, and encouraging in all that you do. Every time that I enter the Zappos building I feel both humbled and blessed to be able to be a part of something most people can only dream of.

REBEKAH N.
employee since 2006

The Zappos Culture means that when I come to work it won't be like any other place I have worked at. It means that I will have fun and be able to talk and laugh with the great friends that I have made while being here. Zappos isn't just a job, it's a home away from home and we are like a big family.

RENA D.
employee since 2004

Zappos is my home away from home! I enjoy every day that I am able to spend here. I have now worked at a company that truly embraces the true meaning of family. The amazing people that I work with are my family in and outside of work. We all share a special tie that brings us together... the fabulous company that we work for. We all work together to provide outstanding service to customers, whether they are customers on the phone or vendors who stop by the office. I love Zappos for its unique culture and am very proud to be a part of it! I'm always inspired by our culture to be the best that I can be. I look forward to years ahead.

RENEA W.
employee since 2007

The saying, "Often imitated, but never duplicated" comes to mind when I think of our Zappos Culture.

To describe our culture in a few sentences is just about impossible. Where else can you throw team parades for no reason at all, have a company party with employees dressed as Bridezilla and Elvis running around, or be able to recognize a co-worker's willingness to go above and beyond by giving them a $50 bonus?

The atmosphere is so unique in that our culture is like no other. I can't imagine what can be done to top what's already BEEN done. I'm truly looking forward to another epic year at Zappos!

RIAN C.
employee since 2009

Family. If I had to describe Zappos in one word it would be family. I have never been in a working environment that felt so warm. I went through training and we learned a lot because we create a indestructible bond. This is a bond that grows everyday as we get to know the amazing people in this company. I moved to Las Vegas alone but Zappos has provided me with a family here. Us newbies will carry the torch of our great culture and may it live forever. Thank you so much, Zappos, you have made me a better person.

RICKI M.
employee since 2004

Every year, for the past five years, I've written a few words about the Zappos Culture and how it improves the lives of all of us here at Zappos. After all, being around upbeat, positive, happy people is certainly contagious. During this past year, I've notice a ripple effect that goes beyond these walls and this company. I know it started among our direct competitors as a marketing (or survival) tool. Now there are other types of retailers that have begun to offer free shipping and English-speaking telephone representatives. I'm impressed. Soon, perhaps, it will become the norm and any company that doesn't offer free shipping will vanish from sight. It's not just retailers who are picking up the ball. I was having problems with my old cell phone and put off calling the carrier for weeks. When I finally called, I spoke with a truly helpful representative. I was numb. On the one occasion recently I had to speak with a government employee who went above and beyond, I was blown completely away! Maybe you've noticed, the sour-faced, bored, disagreeable people at the DMV have all been replaced! Could our culture be spreading?

RITA S.
employee since 2006

Every year I am more amazed by Zappos than I was the year before. Our culture, our growth, our goals, our family. Just when I think it's as good as it could possibly be, it gets better. I believe that the reason for this is our positive energy. Just as the bell cannot be un-rung, our positive energy resounds universally. There is no limit to our potential. I feel so incredibly fortunate to be a part of this ever-growing and changing energy.

ROB S.
employee since 2004

Each day the Zappos Culture shows me something new. It's like a never-ending story that's always building towards a climax that I'm now convinced will never come. The excitement of this pursuit makes me feel like an extreme sport junky. I can never get enough, and each turn of the page only inspires a greater thirst for the next. The characters in this story are full of creativity, passion, and wisdom. I'm WoW'd by the interplay of emotions and relationships. The impact of each interaction adds a new layer to the experience. What a place?! What a story?! Dang, this is cool!

ROBIN G.
employee since 2006

Unbelieveable! Here I am three and one half years at a job that is still Unbelieveable! Words are not enough to describe the intensity of my job. My job is an event. It is a happening. It is ever-changing. The culture, the family, our mission are always ever present and embraced. This is no 9 to 5. This is truly 24/7. How I do go on...?

ROCKNE H.
employee since 2009

From an outside point of view, you hear a lot about the Zappos Culture and think, "I don't think it's as good as they say it is," or "You gotta be kidding?! They have a nap room?? No Way!" A lot of doubt arises. Until you have the amazing opportunity to work here. Then you discover that everything you hear is absolutely true. And more...

Throughout my very short ten year workforce career, I have had the opportunity to work for many companies. I have experienced some great workplace settings, some places I've considered a regular 9-5 and some places I couldn't wait to deliver my two week notice to. No other company I've worked for can compare to this company.

Moving to Las Vegas in October 2008 is when I first heard about Zappos. My first impression was, "what the heck is that name?" The website was great, containing a lot of great items. The customer service was amazing.

The orders were delivered in a very timely manner. I thought to myself, "Maybe I should give this place a try as my next 'job'."

It wasn't until I stepped into training class on day one, when I knew I belonged to this company. Every day brings something new and exciting. The motivation that managers, leads, supervisors and even your own coworkers give you, is out of this world. To top it off, the amazing team and family spirit within this company is what made me determine that Zappos is not a NEXT job, but my LAST job, my "career".

No one can ever foretell the future, but one can create a pathway through determination for future goals. My goal is to be a part of this company for a very long time. And as I write this message, my eyes fill with tears for the extreme love I have for Zappos. This is where I belong.

RON M.
employee since 2009

I remember the first time I walked into the Zappos doors for my first day. I was nervous and excited. I soon found that even though I had never met any of my peers, they would still become my family in just a short amount of time. I'm truly lucky to work at such an awesome company that encourages its employees to be so close with their coworkers even if they are of different levels in the company. I can hang out with my leads and senior reps and that's just plain awesome.

ROSARIO S.
employee since 2006

The Zappos Culture is so unique. What makes it so unique? Nowhere in this day and age will you find a company that values its employees and customers to the highest level. Employees are committed to work together to provide world-class customer service. I am blessed and fortunate to work for a company that CARES.

RUBEN R.
employee since 2009

Free lunches. Free T-Shirts. Free KINDLES!! Oh my!! And that was just in my first six weeks with Zappos. That's just some of the many wonderful perks that we get as employees. I have never worked for a company that genuinely seems to care for their employees and their wellbeing the way that Zappos cares for us. That is part of the CULTURE here at Zappos. I worked eight years for a certain home improvement retailer that had the reputation of being a great place to work. It was a good job, but they didn't "walk the walk" the way Zappos does. I look forward to coming to work everyday, and the Zappos Culture is a BIG reason for that.

RUBY A.
employee since 2008

I have been with Zappos almost two years, and this is the only company I have ever worked for that has a culture within the work place. The Zappos Culture, to me, means allowing me to be myself, while enjoying and having fun serving our customers.

Zappos was open and honest with us when the company was purchased by Amazon, it was like nothing really changed. They kept the communication flowing through this process. They even offered us a retention bonus! I have worked for companies in the past that just closed the doors without any thoughts about their employees. I love working for Zappos, because it is not about how young you are! It's not about how old you are! It's about how weird you are!

I heart Zappos. Do you heart Zappos, too?

RYAN I.
employee since 2007

To me, the Zappos Culture is freedom... the freedom to be who I am and not be scared about being judged. It's the freedom not having to wear a suit and tie unless I feel like sporting it. There's no pressure whatsoever. I like the feeling that I can go into work with pajama pants and a tuxedo top. Sure, it'll be weird, but that's the point!

The Zappos Culture has also been an inspiration in my personal life, inspiring me to pursue things that I would have never dreamed about approaching. Because of the culture, I've changed from a couch potato to a hiker! It has opened my eyes and given me comfort to know I can do anything as long as I stay dedicated. None of my previous jobs have come close to presenting something this unique or encouraged such self-motivation. It's given me a desire to go all out and try anything. The sky is the limit and I can only thank the culture at Zappos!

SAMANTHA Q.
employee since 2009

Working at Zappos means that everyone is encouraged to be himself or herself. In fact, it's encouraged within the Ten Core Values. I appreciate the request to "create fun and a little weirdness." I've worked at a few places where "weird" was a horrible brand for one to receive. Here, it's celebrated.

I can't think of anywhere else where you can turn your head in both directions from your desk and see a gigantic Burt Reynolds picture; a lead's picture decorating her area as a clown, queen, pirate, Shrek, streamers all around in different colors, a Christmas tree with baby shoes all around, snowflakes dangling from the ceiling, circus signs, a homage to Canada, and another to Freddy Krueger... to mention just a few things. There are different facets of culture throughout Zappos. CLT is much different in its culture than Dev or Merch or H.R. But that's part of the magic here.

I feel fortunate to be able to add a little bit of myself into culture. Everyone who has ever been here has added a little bit to what everyone sees as our awesome culture.

SANDRA J.
employee since 2009

The Zappos Culture seems almost fictitious when you hear about it. You just don't want to believe people when they tell you about the culture. It's so great to be able to be a part of it! I believe it's what makes people say, "I want to go to work!" At least that's how it is for me. It's fun to be around people who are entertaining. It doesn't make you dread walking through the doors. You have so many different personalities walking around here dancing, acting goofy and just having a good time while being able to do their jobs. It's great to see parades go by and birthdays and decorations all the time. It just puts you in a great mood.

SCOTT K.
employee since 2004

Zappos Culture, to me, is about the people. We have an awesome group of folks at Zappos, all driving together in the same direction.

My co-workers are everything to me. I enjoy laughing with them, growing beards with them, sending Star Wars emails to them, eating Potluck food with them, giving cool nicknames to them, doing parades with them, coaching them, sharing ideas with them, telling fart jokes to them, forwarding funny pictures to them, doing projects with them, calibratingwith them, going to the IZ Ultra Lounge with them, troubleshooting with them, and growing Zappos to the next level with them!

SEAN H.
employee since 2009

I can truly say that the culture here at Zappos has changed my life. In the short time I've been working here, my perspective on so many issues has changed and I have grown a lot as a person. I'm pretty sure anyone in my position would have the same feelings. Working with so many different people, from various backgrounds and with cultures of their own, has helped me to mature and truly accept people for who they are. Thinking of the Ten Core Values here at Zappos in every aspect of life has improved both my morale and my productivity. This is the first job I've had where I look forward to coming to work every Monday morning; that in itself is a great reflection of our Zappos Culture.

SEAN M.
employee since 2006

The things that I like about the Zappos Culture is how it inspires all of us to raise the bar in our professional and personal lives as well as promoting connection and communication.

SEAN E.
employee since 2006

I look at the Zappos Culture as a professional and personal guide. I feel that I have matured in a positive aspect with its guidance and I wake up everyday feeling grateful. I also feel that the culture is one-of-a- kind and unforgettable.

SHANNON C.
employee since 2008

Before I started work at Zappos, you could say I was what is called a "job hopper." I was great at getting jobs, but after several months I would find a reason not to stay at that job. Perhaps it was the way the management handled their staff, or maybe just the work environment.

Now that I'm nearing my second year at this utopia called Zappos, I am proud to say that was in the past. It is an absolute joy to work at this most wonderful job. I look forward to coming to work every single day. Our team is like a family, and that nurturing atmosphere reflects on the way we want our customers to feel as well. I hope to stay here indefinitely and am excited about growing with this amazing company.

SHANNON M.
employee since 2007

I have been with this awesome company since August of 2007. I always wanted to work at a company with a vision that included seeing employees as people, not just workers. That is truly what it is like here at Zappos... there have been some tough times and the way that the company handled the situation gave me a bigger level of respect for my job as well as the people above me. I can honestly say upper management takes care of the little people too. :-)

Most companies don't know how to adjust to growth. Not Zappos! We have mastered keeping the culture alive in the midst of the awesome growth that we continue to have... I understand that everything isn't going to be perfect, but to me this is extremely close to perfect. Since I have become a part of Zappos family, I have embraced the Ten Core Values that we have in place here and applied them to my entire lifestyle. I talk about Zappos all the time, and I find myself feeling bad for others who work for a company that doesn't have the culture that we have. I love coming to work and feeling like I'm just going to visit with my extended family. With the economy the way it is, Zappos has continued to move forward to the next level. There's an awesome plan for this company and I'm so blessed to be apart of the Zappos adventure. Thank you, F.A.T., for having the vision to know that we love you all and will continue to do all the steps needed to take Zappos to infinity with everything that we do!

SHANNON R.
employee since 2007

Our Zappos Culture is fun and zany, support-ive and growth-producing, full of on-the-spot change. It provides us with chances to try new and adventurous opportunities, and is always amazing. My life has become so very enriched by serving at Zappos and by connecting with the truly wonderful people that are members of this fine family. Would I ever want to pursue a career elsewhere? Not on your life!

SHARON R.
employee since 2007

Zappos is a most amazing addition to my life. Instead of dreading going to work like so many folks do, I actually look forward to my "adven-tures" at Zappos each day! What a difference Zappos has made in my life… the beliefs, values, and inspirations that I treasure in my personal life are also part of my daily work with the Zappos Culture and Core Values! It's a most wonderful extension of my life — the Zappos family. This atmosphere can only exist and grow to such a great degree because of the one at the top who practices it, cultivates it, and teaches others — Tony Hsieh.

Thank you, Tony, for making this possible.

SHAVONE T.
employee since 2006

Culture refers to the cumulative deposit of knowl-edge, experience, beliefs, values and attitudes acquired by a group of people. Anyone who is familiar with our Zappos Culture can attest to this. Our culture is unlike any other and nothing will ever change that. Three years and counting… GO ZAPPOS!

SHAYLEEN H.
employee since 2009

Zappos is my vacation away from the real world. I can come in and always have a smile or two (or 20) waiting for me. I have had the best work experience ever being here, met some of the most amazing people, and have come to recognize strengths in myself that I didn't realize I had. I hope to continue to grow as a person and keep on smiling! Thanks, Zappos!

SHEENA G.
employee since 2008

I think that the Zappos Culture is a force to be reckoned with. The Core Values that we live by have a direct effect on my work, but also carry over to my personal life, the way that I deal with stressful situations, school, family life and more. I love my Zappos family and I am so grateful that no matter what, if I have a problem, I know that I have someone to go to who will empathize with me and help me find the best solution possible, or set me straight if that is what I need. That's not something that can be said about the environ-ment at other companies, and it's not something that I have ever experienced prior to my time here at Zappos.

On any given day, it's guaranteed that we will laugh together, have a little fun (and weirdness!), and take care of customers any way that we can. I understand why my friends think that I am a Zappos fanatic… I can't stop talking about all the wonderful things that this company, my family away from home, has done for me. The last year has been a huge journey for the company as a whole (Amazon and Zappos, sitting in a tree …) and for me personally (shout out to the Senior Reps), and I can't wait to see what I will have to rave about next year.

I heart Zappos!

SOFIA K.
employee since 2009

I have only been with Zappos three months, but that's long enough for me to know that I never want to work anywhere else again. Zappos is truly a great place to be. I love that everyone seems friendly, accepting, and happy to be at work. It definitely makes it easy to get out of bed in the morning. Unlike other places I have been employed, I don't find myself counting down to the weekend. Also, it's nice to actually be given the ability to do my job, and do it well, and feel as if my contribution to the company is valued. A lot of companies say that they are about service and the customer, but they send mixed messages when the emphasis is placed on getting to the next caller as soon as possible. Here, I can take my time and resolve all issues, and I am em-powered to take care of 99% of the customer's needs. Never mind about companies that say they care about their employees. I have never worked for a company that does so much for their people. I truly feel lucky to be here.

STACY H.
employee since 2006

Coming to work at Zappos is like going to visit Grandma's house as a kid. You are spoiled, have fun and get fed. At Zappos we get fed so much that I am convinced I will not lose any serious weight until the day I leave. It makes me think about the letters people write when they have to leave. Usually it is due to moving out of state because, well, really, why else would you leave Zappos? The emails are sent out to the entire floor to say goodbye to their work-family. We typically throw a mini-happy hour for the person who is leaving and demand to see them back for visits.

Our Zappos Culture is more than just ten ideas to live by, or a fun environment, or even happy customers. It's looking at those around you, those you will never see but hear their voice on the phone, or read their words in e-mail, as family. When you can see the world in this caring light, you become a better person and the joy spreads. The Zappos Culture is paying it forward to everyone who comes in contact with us. Our vendors, our employees, our customers, and even our tours get joy out of the experience that is Zappos. Thank God for Grandmas and Zappos!

STEPHANIE B.
employee since 2007

Our amazing Zappos Culture is so unique, everyone here is proud to be a part of it. Our culture allows us to be ourselves and have fun. We're actually encouraged to act silly and be weird. We even get to shave the CEO's head if we want to! ;) Have you ever heard of a company where the CEO lets his employees shave his head?!

The main difference between Zappos and other companies is our Ten Core Values. We live them every day while most other companies don't. Everyone here genuinely cares about each other. Zappos Culture really and truly is the best, and working here is an honor and a blessing. I hope that people who come in contact with our company will understand how we operate and why we act the way we do. Work is important and it gets done, but having fun is also a part of life and we're definitely living the life at Zappos!!

STEPHANIE C.
employee since 2007

As I come up on my three-year anniversary, I can't think of anything to say about the Zappos Culture, other than it is still a wonderful, beautiful thing, that I come to work with a smile on my face and leave with a smile on my face. I am still in awe of the amazing people that I work with and I am grateful that I have a team that has pushed me out of my comfort zone to be better. I can't wait to see what the rest of the year has in store for us!

STEPHANIE W.
employee since 2004

I've been at Zappos for five and a half years now. I can't imagine working anywhere else ever again. The Zappos Culture is like no other. It's being yourself and being valued for your individuality. It feels so great to be given the liberty to use our own judgment, to be trusted, to be heard. We are encouraged to pursue growth and learning, given skills that will help us both at work and in our personal lives. I feel spoiled by how well we are taken care of here. I enjoy the fun activities, parades, potlucks, dress-up days. Never in my life have I been happy to get up and go to work, it is a true blessing to be here.

SUNSHINE J.
employee since 2010

Zappos is the best social experiment I've ever been a part of. What a novel idea! Be nice and helpful to others. And be yourself! This is the most interesting job I've ever had. I feel as if I make an actual impact at work every day. I wish the same job satisfaction for everyone. (I just started.)

SUSANA P.
employee since 2007

Zappos Culture, to me, is not just a "what," but a "how." It is obvious anytime you walk through this office … you see parades, potlucks, fun and weirdness all over the place. It's plain to see from the outside looking in. The "how" is the best part. How can we accomplish having so many smiling faces, so many parties, so many different activities and still function for business purposes? The answer is simple, really. When you take a group of people and provide them with a single vision that the entire company lives by, Delivering Wow through Service, you get hard workers who love their jobs and enjoy life in general. Other companies also have visions, however, those can differ depending on who you ask. One vision is the way to go. Viva Zappos!

TABITHA J.
employee since 2009

I was hired at Zappos about four months ago and that was the beginning of true happiness in the workplace for me. I had been in the corporate world for about 16 years and have never been as comfortable to be myself as I have been here. The culture is like none other that I have ever been involved in, and you can feel how important it is to the company as well as the employees. I honestly feel like I am a part of a team and family all wrapped into one. Zappos Rocks!!!!

TAISHA T.
employee since 2006

Zappos Culture means a lot! Our Ten Core Values are just like Wu Wei in Taoism. When you embrace these core values, they become a way of life. Every day I find myself in situations where the actions of our core values have to go into full effect! I mean, it really says a lot when other companies take an interest in what we believe in as Zapponians and pay to learn what now comes naturally to us. What makes us different is that we have such a diverse environment — everyone is allowed to be themselves without judgment! At other companies, it's all black or white, and some employees never even see their CEO. What I love about our culture is that it's so accepting! The family spirit and environment makes coming to work a huge reunion every day. If you love what you do, you'll never have to work a day in your life!!

TAMA C.
employee since 2007

While most companies want to stamp out individuality, our Zappos Culture invites and embraces uniqueness. Rather than rewarding drone-like behavior, each of us is rewarded with the ability to be our own person. We are allowed to flourish, grow, and in turn nurture others to do the same, instead of withering on the vine of "corporate syndrome." I believe that holding dear to our Ten Core Values frees us to soar into a future of unlimited possibilities.

TAMI L.
employee since 2007

The Zappos Culture is unmatchable, incomparable and unsurpassable. Each day, when I walk into the building, I know there will be something fun, inspirational, and educational... and that I will personally learn something new or experience something for the first time. I am thankful we are able to express our individuality and creativity throughout the entire Zappos family.

TAMIKA T.
employee since 2006

Moving from the East Coast to Nevada was a big step but becoming a Zappos employee was the best move I've made. I can't think of a better place to work! Our culture and team spirit makes us unique and constantly inspire us to give 110% inside and outside of work. This will be my fourth year at Zappos, and each year it gets better. I can't wait to see what the future holds for us!

TAMMIE C.
employee since 2006

Zappos culture, to me, means that Zappos all about improving the mind, values and unity. I think Zappos embraces everyone that walks through the door and finds a unique way to incorporate each one's knowledge, diversity and experiences to build the culture that is here today.

TAMMY R.
employee since 2009

What does the culture of Zappos mean to me? Well, culture can be defined as "the quality in a person or society that arises from a concern for what is regarded as excellent in arts, letters, manners, scholarly pursuits, etc." This is definitely what Zappos is and does. It's a powerful force you feel from the first moment you walk into the building. It's as simple as someone who smiles at you, holds the door for you and asks how you are. You can tell it is genuine, not forced or phony. This is something that continues to be reaffirmed as you go through training and start to form an unexpected and amazing bond with your fellow trainees and your co-workers.

Everything that is done here exudes quality … the manners of the employees, the facilities, the opportunities to pursue growth, both profession-ally and personally, and most importantly, the people! I've worked in a small-town elementary school where the staff was like a family, but never have I been in an environment where people truly treat each other like family. I have enjoyed working with some of my past co-workers, but not until working here have I ever been able to say that I LOVE the people I work with. I know that I have formed a bond with people here for whom I would do anything in or outside of work and they, in turn, would do the same for me. There is no price you can ever put on knowing that you have such a positive place to come to work 40 hours a week and a support system that is always there for you!!!!!!

TAMRA J.
employee since 2008

Zappos Culture has changed my life. I have become a better person because of Zappos. The friendships you make here will last forever! It just makes you want to be a better person and go above and beyond in everything that you do.

I find myself holding the door for people, when others let it slam in my face. When I see someone that needs to pull out of a driveway or merge with traffic, I go out of my way to let them in. I know that when someone is courteous to me on the road, it makes me want to go out of my way for others. I have found that I am a more patient and understanding person at home and on the job.

I think the Golden Rule holds true: "Do unto others as you would have them do unto you!" If everyone were to follow that rule, or essentially, to live the Zappos Culture, can you imagine the kind of world we would have?

TANAI M.
employee since 2008

The Zappos Culture is different from the culture of any other job. At other companies you must fit the mold or conform to their beliefs. Here at Zappos, we are encouraged to be different and think outside the box. Employees are encouraged to be the best that they can be and to grow, not only professionally, but personally as well. Since my time here at Zappos, I can truly say that I look at the world differently and have changed for the better in so many ways. I look forward to the future to see how much more I can better myself here and what Zappos has in store for me. :)

THOMAS S.
employee since 2008

The foundation of the Zappos Culture is our belief in and the guidance we get from our Core Values. We are a mixture of many different backrounds and environments. It's a beautiful thing to work with such a diverse group of people whose commonality is that we are all guided by the same Core Values.

THOMAS T.
employee since 2007

Zappos is the BIZNASS!!!! I have worked here for three years and some change and I am happy to report that this company is still a fantastic organization to work for. The people are great! The environment is positive! The culture is one of a kind! I believe in Zappos and Zappos believes in me. Although the people are not perfect, Zappos has systems and policies that we as employees and customers can rely on and trust. I still love this place!

TIFFANY L.
employee since 2005

Zappos' culture is like no other. It is a culture of family, of friends, of making others happy. It is about being a part of something bigger than just the bottom line. It is a place where you can be who you want to be, express yourself in your own unique way and feel comfortable and accepted for doing so. Zappos is a place you enjoy coming to every day and where you never know what to expect. The one thing that is a constant is that we are a little fun and weird; one day we could be having a parade, and the next we are celebrating Cinco de Mayo! The opportunities at Zappos are endless, and I am thankful every day I come to work. FAT is something most people think of in a less than positive manner; here at Zappos, it is something I aspire to be more like (F = Fred, A = Alfred, T = Tony).

I wouldn't want to work anywhere else EVER!!!

TOM S.
employee since 2007

Zappos Culture is about being part of a family. I consider all of my co-workers surrogate brothers and sisters. Everyone truly cares about you and always asks how you are. Too, if you need anything there is no hesitation with asking a co-worker and usually they're willing to help.

What sets Zappos apart from other companies revolves around the culture. I know of no other company that does so much for their employees from the awesome free benefits, no co-pays, free food, building a kitchen that serves delicious food, happy hours, awesome parties and employee surveys. Zappos truly cares about their employees' happiness, which results in making the customers happy.

I love the Zappos Culture because never before have I worked at a place where you look forward to being at work. The management team definitely has a passion for what they're doing and want to make Zappos the best and most successful company for years to come.

TYSON W.
employee since 2009

Georg Simmel states that culture refers to "the cultivation of individuals through the agency of external forms which have been objectified in the course of history." Nowhere have I seen this statement put to more positive use than here at Zappos. After 17 years of bouncing around the country, working in various restaurants, I have found a wonderfully fulfilling experience that embodies an inherent goodness within itself as a participating body and, in turn, projects that goodness upon those with whom it comes into contact.

To express the old Latin axiom, "Dulce et decorum est."

VERONICA J.
employee since 2005

Zappos: a culture of ideals. At the heart of it, our Ten Core Values probably aren't all that different from those of many other companies (although, to be fair, there are probably very few others who would promote the creation of both fun AND weirdness). We might not always be as open and honest as we'd like to be or as we'd like to think we are; we may sometimes fall short of the goal of doing more with less; we might not always be excited to embrace every change as much as we had hoped; but so what? We're human. And for a bunch of humans doing their best to deliver the very best service around, I think we're doing a hell of a job — not because we always reach every goal we set, but because we always *strive* to be the best we possibly can be. Our culture means never giving up, and for that, I give us an "A" for effort.

VINCENT V.
employee since 2008

Zappos is awesome! The Culture here is a breath of fresh air. You can tell Zappos is a "little different" as soon as you walk in the door. I love working for a company (which is more like a family) that cares about its customers and employees. The Culture here is a very BIG part of Zappos and we don't want it to go anywhere. With the "work hard, play hard" attitude, it allows us to take care of business and enjoy ourselves at the same time. Having our Culture, which keeps us close, makes Zappos more than just a job. I enjoy being with Zappos and plan on enjoying many years here!

VIOLA H.
employee since 2007

The Zappos Culture allows each one of us to come to work and be ourselves. We have been given the freedom to "let our hair down" and enjoy doing our jobs. This is the only company I have worked for where I can say I look forward to coming to work.

We have many different age groups and ethnicities working here, which gives us an opportunity to learn about other cultures. You can say that we are the "Zappos Melting Pot."

Zappos is the new Empire State of Mind!

WANDA H.
employee since 2005

The Zappos Culture is so unique. I love that I am free to be me, and I believe that our core value, "Create Fun and a Little Weirdness," was included just for my benefit. My fellow employees are all so wonderful. You can strike up a conversation with anyone here. I feel that my co-workers honestly care about me, as I care about them. Zappos definitely has a family atmosphere. You care about and trust your family, and that is what we share here. This is such an amazing culture when there are so many employees or, to be more accurate, friends. Every day when I come to work, I feel welcome, cared about and that I am an important part of something very special.

WAYNE A.
employee since 2008

I am still happy to be working for Zappos after 18 months. The culture remains different and more personal than any other place where I've worked, even after many years in the work force. At this point, I'm happy to be employed, given the current work force climate in the country. I hope to be able to take part in new functions at Zappos this year and after a new shift bid to take place in March. I hope that will come to pass.

WILLIAM B.
employee since 2007

There is a bigger picture here ... I think I can see it, I can almost see it. It's kind of like this vague mirage on the horizon. My mind wants to think it is an illusion because this vision I see has never been seen before. An altruistic business...? Is that an oxymoron? How does Amazon fit in? Do we still have an airline in this mirage?

My only hope is that I make it to this vision, grow with this company, evolve with my second family, and follow a richer path for my life as a result of my job... yes, I said it, because of my job... is this real? Any day now I expect Rod Serling to step through a hole in space/time and tell me that all of this has been a dream, the mirage on the horizon is nothing more, an imperceptible wisp of a non-reality. Pinch me, slap me, throw cold water on my face... no WAIT! Don't! I want to stay right here, and if it's not real, then call me crazy and throw me in a cell. I am staying right where I'm at.

YAHAIRA Y.
employee since 2008

It feels great to work for a company whose name has such a positive connotation throughout our community. Whether I'm curing my hot chai craving at a coffee shop, grabbing a goody at a small bakery, or trying shoes on at a well-known retailer, the reaction is always the same! "You work for Zappos? I've seen your company on TV! It looks like a really fun place to work!" or "Zappos folks are always stopping through here. You all seem so nice!" I've yet to hear any negative reviews and not only does that make me feel proud to be a part of the family; it makes me want to live up to the standard we've set... inside and outside of work.

DETE
DELIVER
A

TEAM

SPIRIT

HONEST

HUMBLE

OPEN

POSITIVE

CHANGE

OPEN-MINDED

INED

SERVICE

EMBRACE

CREATE

COMMUNICATION

FUN

DRIVE

LEARNING

WEIRDNESS

WOW

NTUROUS

GROWTH

PASSIONATE

RELATIONSHIP

FAMILY

PICNICS

Jester's Lounge

drink

MERR

EAT

IMEN

ZAPPOS IS GOING **GOING** MED

IEVAL ON

YOUR A

O

POSITIVE

DRIVE

ADVENTUROUS

FAMILY

DETERMINED

SERVICE

EME

WEIRDNESS
CREATE
HONEST
EN-MINDED
COMMUNICATION
GROWTH
FUN
TEAM
DELIVER
WOW
SPIRIT
RELATIONSHIP
EARNING
HUMBLE
ACE   CHANGE
PASSIONATE

AARON T.
employee since 2005

The Zappos Culture is unique and ever-changing. I think as each year passes, my outlook on the culture of this company is always a little bit different, but the foundation of it remains the same: Every day when you walk through the door, you're allowed to be yourself, express your own ideas, and share your very own, unique personality with the people you spend a third of your day with (sometimes more).

It's not often that you can come into a corporate setting and feel as though the people aren't judging you, but, in fact, feel like your extended family. The "Positive Team and Family Spirit" that drives this Culture Machine is made up of a bunch of moving parts... the people. So, each and every day, we're cultivating and carrying forth this culture into new years and new decades, one person, one day at a time... I'm so grateful that I get to be a part of that.

The Zappos Culture has inspired me and many others to make it part of our lives outside of work. I take the positivity, nuances, and values that I learn at work and apply them to my family, my friends and my own personal endeavors. So, in short, the Zappos Culture is, quite simply put, a Lifestyle!

AILA M.
employee since 2009

I have been with Zappos for five months; so far, so excellent! The impression I have to date is that this is the best of all worlds:

• Values that stand the test of time, i.e., customer service, caring for people, work ethic, honesty.

• Of-the-moment company with relevant ideas for the future.

• Entrepreneurial spirit, in the truest sense of the word.

People are people wherever you go, but this company truly respects and values everyone, customers and employees alike. Isn't that where you would want to work?

ALANA P.
employee since 2006

There is a saying; life is a succession of moments, seconds and minutes. To live each one is to succeed. Every part of who I am in my career today, I attribute to Zappos. No matter what the accomplishment or failure, I embrace every moment. The foundation that has been provided to me by Zappos is priceless. This company's vision is one that I am extremely proud to say I'm a part of.

ALESHA G.
employee since 2004

Zappos is such a special part of my life and I appreciate every day that I get to wake up and come to work. I get to see my friends and family laugh and cry sometimes. I don't think I would have had the opportunity to become so close to so many people had it not been for Zappos. The Zappos Culture is the glue that holds family together. Because of our culture, we have grown and nurtured each other over the years. We have some of the best relationships in the industry and our vendors feel like they are a part of our family too. I said it before and I will say it again. I couldn't see myself any other place. Thank you, Zappos, for all that you do for us each and every day.

ALEX D.
employee since 2005

In the past four years or so, as the company has grown, I've seen the Zappos Culture evolve in many ways.. However, our culture has always remained true to its original spirit. With these changes in our company, I too have changed in many ways. I've realized that this is genuinely more than just a job to me. My co-workers are truly like my family in many, many ways. More than once over the years, I've noticed myself finding faith in my job, and the people I work with, when times became trying in other aspects of my life. I've always trusted that the company will recognize me for the hard work I've committed myself to and, in my opinion, it always has, in one way or another. At every other job I've ever worked, it has honestly been just a place where I toiled for 8 hours a day in order to subsist. On the other hand, I can veritably say that I love what I do here at Zappos, for the company, myself, and the people I'm lucky enough to work with nearly every single day.

ALISON C.
employee since 2008

Zappos is an amazing place to work. Having worked for many other retail organizations, it is refreshing for me to be at a company that truly values its employees along with the talents and ideas they bring to the table. Everyone here has the ability to make a difference in the company. Regardless of position, or length of time with the company, anyone with an idea has the power to make it happen. Thinking "outside the box" is encouraged. I feel fortunate to work in a creative, dynamic environment like this. The Zappos Culture inspires me on a daily basis. Thanks!

AMBER R.
employee since 2005

Why I love Zappos so much... it's because I can truly be myself at work. It is very important to be who you are and be accepted for it. ZAPPOS ROCKS! Enough said!

ANDREA L.
employee since 2007

I often remind myself how lucky I am to work for such a great company. Zappos allows us to grow, be creative and most of all, to have fun. It's so important to enjoy where you work and the people you work with. Since the first day I started (almost three years ago now) I couldn't imagine working anywhere else. I couldn't ask for anything more! Thank you, F.A.T.

ANONYMOUS

I've been here for over four years now, and the company never ceases to amaze me. We strive to be the best in every aspect of the business, and Zappos has continued to remain focused on the culture for each and everyone's lives here. Challenging barriers constantly appear, but we adapt and overcome. While others around us may be surviving or just showing some signs of success, we continue to move forward and improve. The Zappos Culture is truly defined by the employees. Whether we are working or playing, we are always giving 110%. We know how to have fun. We know how to be serious. We know how to embrace and drive change. Other company cultures may stay the same; we update ours and make it better. Why is that? The Zappos Culture is in constant motion, and we, as its employees, are always striving to be the best.

ANONYMOUS

Working at Zappos has been so much more than just a job. It has been a life-changing experience and the past year has been no exception. I have been lucky enough to be a part of a team that truly functions as a cohesive group. We have always been friendly, but the friendships you form grow every year, and more and more, they are your friends first and your co-workers second. They carry you through bad days and tough times; you never dread a day of work when it means coming in to see your friends.

Prior to working at Zappos, I had not been able to find my niche in the Las Vegas area. Now I am thankful every day to have become a part of something so great, and to have something that is more than just a job.

ANONYMOUS

This past year has been beyond amazing. I've come to realize the incredible family I have away from home. We laughed, cried, fought and hugged it out over and over again. We are all stronger for it. We've become leaders in our own right. These girls are not just my co-workers, but my sisters too.

ANTHONY S.
employee since 2008

Never in my life have I been so fortunate to work with such great people! I have worked with so many different companies that promise their employees a lot. Zappos has the respect of its employees because it goes beyond promises — Zappos just does. I feel such an intense sense of gratitude to work here because I know that Zappos cares about its employees as much as their customers. Working at Zappos has been an honor.

ASHLYN B.
employee since 2009

I've been working here for a little over three months and I can say that I'm truly amazed and blessed to be working at the best company ever!! When I was getting ready for my interview I read a ton of articles and watched a ton of videos about Zappos and, although they were amazing, they couldn't possibly translate the amazing aura within these walls — there's such a sense of family and pride and true happiness. When I first started everyone on my team and in the company was so accepting of me and really went out of their way to make me feel at home. I am soooo lucky and I LOVE it here!!!!

AVA Z.
age 10

Zappos makes me think of fun and excitement. I think the people who work there are more like brothers and sisters, and fathers and mothers than co-workers. I love visiting Zappos. My favorite thing to do when I'm there is go to the cafeteria and get free ice cream bars! The rules are different at Zappos; everyone is encouraged to be who they really are. Zappos has inspired me to create my own business and I will, someday soon. I will try to create a culture like the Zappos Culture, but even better — stay tuned.

AVNEET S.
employee since 2009

Culture is a big thing for me. It tells a lot about how a person was brought up; it's a way of life; it makes you who you are; I guess we can say that it builds character. I am fairly new to this company but in a way it feels like I have known every single person here my whole life. Countless numbers of times, I have been at a restaurant or a grocery store and run into someone who works at Zappos, who I may or may not have met before, and it seems like I ran into a cousin or some other family member.

Two stories I want to share with you all:

After only being here for three months in an entry-level position, I took a bold step and asked Tony, Alfred and Fred to dinner, for no particular reason — I just wanted to get to know them better and say thank you for everything that they do. I didn't know what to expect but I knew it was worth it. Within 30 minutes I got an email asking about what time and date I was free. I literally had nothing to discuss with them — I even thought I would be wasting their time but we went to dinner and it was fantastic, something I would remember forever.

Secondly, I came up with an idea that we should have a Facebook application to better market our products to the younger demographics. Whether it was a good idea or not, I was able to speak my mind, share ideas, be creative and make mistakes. Within a week, I was able to get in touch with our development team and have this thing tested out.

Besides selling merchandise and looking at profitability, we really focus on inspiring others, giving customers what they want and having better relationships with our vendors.

If I was to narrow down all the Core Values and our way of thinking, it would be: Creativity. Passion. Trust.

I am going to let you all in an insider secret — the happier your employees are, the harder they will work. The happier your customers, the more they will shop with you. The happier your vendors, the better relationships you have with them (and we all want a better relationship with people in sales right?)

I am so happy to get up in the morning and come to work, because it isn't your typical workday. I am allowed to share ideas, do something different every day, and help this company grow! I have the opportunity to move to any department that I am qualified for, learn about new things and grow. What more do I want in life?

BILL J.
employee since 2004

Being a part of the Zappos Culture has made me realize that coming to work doesn't have to suck. Zappos employees are like family to me and working on the Outdoor buying team is like hanging out with good friends. It's hard to believe I spent 14 years working for companies that never really understood what it takes to make the workplace feel more like where I am today. I feel fortunate to be able to work with great partners like Matt Dyson from Sperry Top-Sider, Katie Davis from Columbia Sportswear, Jenny Fredricks from Ahnu Footwear, Dan Hill from Lowa Boots, and Bob Nagy form Montrail footwear. I've learned so much about the industry by working so closely with these amazing people. I'm surrounded by great people in the office and I work with the best people in the industry.

This is the best job I've ever had!

BRADEN M.
employee since 2006

If success could be measured, the Zappos Culture would be worth its weight in gold. Philosophically and economically, placing emphasis on company culture is the best investment for your business. Yet, in the worst economic downturn since the Great Depression, the idea seems foreign in the marketplace. The constant focus on growth and profit have blinded the vast majority of domestic commerce from one of its most valuable assets: the employees. Zappos' progressive business model has created an environment unparalleled by other businesses. Happy employees make happy vendors and customers. It's simple. At least, Zappos make it seem simple. Our culture is as unique as the individuals who create and perpetuate it. Our culture creates a personal, emotional connection with our customers and our vendors. It is a fresh reminder that business isn't just about dollars and cents. I have been employed by Zappos for four years and remain inspired by my all co-workers and proud of our efforts.

BRIAN W.
employee since 2007

My thoughts in a Haiku:

Many days spent here
Happiness in each of them
Many more to come

BRIDGET D.
employee since 2009

Zappos Culture is a very unique thing. Everyone who works here loves what they do and it makes work more enjoyable. I think this company stands out from the rest because of the employees' enthusiasm and love for this company. We all work very hard and play even harder. It is a wonderful combination that keeps our culture at its finest. I am proud to be a part of this company.

BROOKE P.
employee since 2005

Our Zappos Culture is the glue that keeps our company together. Our passion is exemplified in our culture. We all have boundless passion for this company and our daily work here is a labor of love. I take so much pride in my work, as do others who work here. This magical culture is the breeding ground for productive, creative, and happy workers. We are constantly challenged to think outside of the box and to take big risks. This type of freethinking is not encouraged in most companies. I'm lucky to have been a part of the exponential growth here over the last five years.

CAMERON G.
employee since 2005

What is the Zappos Culture to me? It's an attitude. A genuine happiness. A deeper connection. A meaningful purpose. A constant evolution. Zappos is built on relationships; they are the foundation for all our achievements, both personally and professionally. I have made so many lifelong friends in the last five years, and because of it there are so many things to be thankful for. So please value your relationships, for they will certainly define your destiny. :)

CARLA L.
employee since 2006

We are so lucky to have the Zappos Culture, which creates a working atmosphere everyone loves. It's looking forward to going to work, seeing the friendly/smiling faces in the hallway, people who hold doors for you, looking at the clock and realizing the day flew by, and celebrating with co-workers when we reach a goal. It's so great to be with a company that says they will grow managers from the ground up and really means it. Everyone works so hard and works well together. People stop what they're doing to answer a question and take the time to make sure that the answer was understood. It's unlike most companies out there. I think that's why Zappos has been as successful as it has been. Everyone here is passionate about the culture and I see it growing and changing (for the better) as the years go on. Go Zappos!

CASSANDRA L.
employee since 2008

When asked what Zappos Culture is to me, I must say it is the reason I wake up happy to go to work every day. I love not knowing what to expect, knowing that my ideas are listened to and my motivational team is there for support. Zappos Culture is why we succeed and still strive to be even better. :)

CAT S.
employee since 2008

This is my third culture book entry, and it's crazy for me to think about how quickly the past two years have gone by, and also how much I have changed over those two years and three culture book entries I've submitted.

When I first started at Zappos two years ago, I wrote my first culture book entry about three days into my new job and life here. I remember how much everything stood out to me because it was so different than any previous job I have had. People held doors for you and smiled, people said hi to you even if they didn't know you, there were crazy parades, happy hours, costumes, parties... but this was normal every day life at Zappos, I quickly came to realize. This wasn't special treatment for specific people because it was their first day or birthday, this was special treatment for everyone, every day.

My initial shock and surprise has definitely worn off, as I've learned to expect the unexpected here, but I am even more grateful and appreciative of the everyday life here at Zappos because of this culture. Whether it's ping pong balls falling from the ceiling, basketball hoop tournaments down my team's row, or someone simply saying hi and holding the door for you, the culture at Zappos has really grown to be more a part of my entire life than I had expected. I am stoked to bring visitors in and introduce them to people and show them around because I want people to be able to experience our culture and understand why this company is so amazing.

The Zappos' culture is definitely one of a kind, but I think there are many things we all learn and take away from working here that helps develop our culture even more as we share it with our friends, family, guests, vendors, etc. Our culture and environment has encouraged me to really reach out and push myself to greater limits, both personally and professionally. I know that I have never felt as enabled and supported as I do here at Zappos because of the environment we have created. Our culture is important and I try to absorb it from as many aspects as I can — personally, professionally, mentally, and educationally (not sure if that's a word, but it fits the flow).

I know that our culture here will only grow and strengthen as our company continues to grow, and I am stoked to be a part of such an amazing and inspiring company where I am able to learn and grow with along the way. This culture is definitely something awesome and something we can all be proud of. I know that I am not the same person I was two years ago, or would be today, if it wasn't for the influence of Zappos and the culture here that has become such an important part of my life. Thanks!

CATHLEEN T.
employee since 2007

What does the Zappos Culture mean to me... For my first year, I wrote about how great it finally was to be able to work with people who were just like me... for my second year, I wrote how I felt as if this were a theme park — the happiest place on earth. Going into my third year, I still feel all these things. However, I now feel as if I work with family. I was recently promoted and my entire team helped me with getting over the anxiety I was feeling about taking my assistant buyer test. When it was done, everyone came up to me and hugged me — I felt so much love, I cried!! I am so blessed to be here, living my passion on a daily basis and working with people who are my family.

Thanks!

CATIE S.
employee since 2008

I was trying to convince a previous work buddy to come to Zappos and this individual asked me "What would it take for you to leave Zappos?"

I sat staring and squinting at my computer wondering what it would take. The lottery wouldn't do it; I would get really bored. Being Anthony Bordain's sidekick wouldn't do it; I don't think being famous would be awesome at all. Getting to try all the ski resorts in the world wouldn't do it; I couldn't deal with the weird tan line from the goggles. Being a shoe tester for Acne or Gucci wouldn't do it; I don't love Sweden or Italy.

I wrote "That's a good question." and I'm not a fan of that response. So I erased it and simply explained all the reasons why I applied to Zappos and how lucky I am that I got in this place. Since my buddy asked me that question, I have thought more about it, and it is a good question — but my most honest response is, "I can't see myself leaving, ever."

And that's why I came to Zappos in the first place.

CHRIS P.
employee since 2004

The doorbell rings every so often at my house, and without hesitation, my two daughters run thru the house screaming, "Zappos! Zappos!" They do this whether it's a package from Zappos or not. It's so funny that every time that bell rings, it reminds them of UPS delivering Zappos packages. These experiences with my girls also remind me of one of the things that I love most about being at Zappos: our focus on the customer experience. What's cool is that it's not only a company initiative, but also a people initiative. Every person cares about the future of our company and every person knows that it's the customer experience that is going to keep Zappos a premium and ever-lasting company. The Zappos Culture plays a big part in this, of course, as it is the single biggest thing that attracts these wonderful people to our company. I consider myself to be very fortunate to be part of such a great company that really challenges us to better ourselves and be part of something bigger than life itself.

CLAIRE S.
employee since 2007

Z oetic
A dventurous
P layful
P owered by service
O pen-minded
S ervice

C reates a lot of fun and weirdness
U nique (??)
L aughter
T eam and family spirit keeps our culture strong
U ndeniably humble
R eally passionate
E mbraces change

CORRIE H.
employee since 2009

The Zappos Culture is fun, creative, spontaneous, motivating, purposeful, weird, inspiring, developing, challenging, giving, empowering, cheerful, and happy.

Zappos accepts people for who they are and encourages them to be who they want to be.

DANA Z.
employee since 2009

I just celebrated my first six months at Zappos … and the honeymoon continues! I have truly found my paradise. I have always enjoyed life to the fullest and to be able to work with such amazing people who share my same passion and values in life is just the icing on the cake. There is no question in my mind that it was fate. Zappos is truly "Powered by the People." Thanks for creating something so special that will be talked about for many years to come. I am thankful to be part of the Zappos Family.

DAVID C.
employee since 2006

The Zappos Culture is a something that cultivates creativity and next level thinking. It gives you the freedom to express ideas and explore different ways of doing things. By giving everyone at Zappos the freedom that our culture gives them, we insure that we will be on the forefront of everything we pursue.

DAVID H.
employee since 2009

If I had to sum up our culture I'd say it is about having fun, taking pride in what you do, and striving to be the kind of person that truly makes you happy! And we at Zappos want EVERYONE to be able to experience that right along with us!!

DEBORAH W.
employee since 2009

Being an avid shopper and in the footwear industry for over 20 years, I shopped and knew about Zappos. Who would have thought that I would watch the Nightline spot on TV about Zappos, then find myself working here. I remember thinking how lucky the employees were to work for a company like Zappos. To be able to express yourself in your own way and to have everyone embrace it. I have been here for five months and everything that was on the show is true!! Quite remarkable!!

I went from being one of the few people to create wackiness at my previous employers to being one of approximately 800 employees that do the same.

In the summer of 2009 both of my parents passed away right before I started working at Zappos. I also moved across the country in order to work here. What was probably the hardest year of my life turned out to be one of the best. I am fortunate to be here and to have found a new family.

DYANSA C.
employee since 2007

I love my job! I love my job! I love my job! It has now been over two years for me here at Zappos and I still drive to work every morning singing the same tune. I love my job! I have been very fortunate so far in life and have worked at some really great places. Each was unique in its own right and the people I have come to know have really made each one even better. I must say that Zappos has its own unique culture that has hit me right in the heart. I will do whatever it takes for Zappos to be successful because my team does everything to make me successful. What more could you ask for in an employer? It does make me sad that many people will never get to experience a place like this and never understand why we are the way we are. I am just so thankful to have a job where I love what I do and love the people I work with. That includes all my great reps. Thank you for the knowledge and training you have given me and thank you, Zappos, for choosing me to represent you!!!

EILEEN T.
employee since 2002

The Zappos Culture is work hard, play hard and remember what you learned as a child... treat others as you would like to be treated! Zappos is all about the customer experience, and a customer is everyone we come into contact with, whether it be an employee, vendor, etc. We are family and there is no distinction between work life and personal life because we're always working towards a common goal. And it's not work if you love what you're doing!

ERICA W.
employee since 2004

A small example of the culture at Zappos: the feeling I get when I walk through the doors in the morning and Roz greets me is irreplaceable. It's like going home for Christmas! Amazing how I can feel this more than once a year.

I am honored to be a part of our family. I know this is a rare feeling, so my promise is to make others feel something similar. I am excited for our future.

ERIKA C.
employee since 2004

After five and a half years it amazes me that the culture here remains the same. The only thing that changes is the strength in our relationships and the bond we share with one another. Through our Zappos Culture, I continue to gain some of the best relationships that I will cherish forever. I even found my husband here, and in three months I will have two wonderful baby boys that I might not have if it weren't for the love I found at Zappos. For that I am truly grateful.

FRED M.
employee since 1999

2009 was a big year for Zappos. See if you can find a few of the things that happened!

```
P  T  R  U  D  A  M  A  Z  O  N  M  A  R  R  I  A  G  E  G  X  Q  T
V  B  T  H  Y  O  O  E  C  E  V  B  J  S  R  M  R  R  D  M  F  M  E
E  E  P  I  P  E  L  I  N  E  S  D  E  E  S  B  U  D  D  R  F  G  N
D  B  E  L  B  M  U  H  R  H  R  X  Z  O  O  M  N  F  J  G  T  G  Y
T  U  T  J  T  N  S  E  S  E  V  E  P  I  H  S  R  E  D  A  E  L  E
D  K  F  O  R  T  U  N  E  S  B  E  S  T  C  O  M  P  A  N  Y  D  A
S  I  U  M  R  D  B  R  R  D  J  V  R  G  N  J  H  E  S  E  V  B  R
X  S  B  W  O  W  X  E  Y  E  B  R  M  R  X  Z  E  T  A  L  W  E  A
Y  S  D  D  R  U  C  O  L  T  H  I  N  G  E  H  E  S  V  L  N  D  N
L  I  B  V  H  D  K  D  R  R  G  R  D  X  M  R  D  H  R  U  D  R  N
I  N  G  S  W  E  S  A  P  P  R  E  N  T  I  C  E  D  V  M  T  O  I
M  G  A  D  L  R  E  S  U  L  T  S  E  E  V  A  G  E  Z  M  E  Y  V
A  H  B  H  S  X  V  B  R  E  R  D  Y  R  H  S  E  H  J  Y  W  K  E
F  R  Y  D  E  L  I  V  E  R  I  N  G  H  A  P  P  I  N  E  S  S  R
C  V  S  W  G  E  T  B  L  U  E  N  X  J  Y  K  P  T  S  G  J  T  S
W  C  S  Z  X  N  R  H  D  T  E  G  L  E  L  D  N  I  K  M  R  S  A
Z  X  N  R  J  K  Y  K  G  E  W  H  M  V  I  D  E  O  P  N  T  D  R
A  L  I  G  N  M  E  N  T  U  Y  J  E  S  E  W  A  G  H  N  J  Y  Y
M  D  G  G  V  E  Y  W  E  C  I  V  R  E  S  R  E  M  O  T  S  U  C
```

GALEN H.
employee since 2004

It has been six years now that I have been privileged enough to be part of our wonderful Zappos Culture. To me, the Zappos Culture is a feeling of pride, ownership, loyalty, spontaneity, fun and family. It is wanting to make the world a better place through the little things. It's about wanting to make people genuinely happy. In essence, it's about creating something wonderful, not only for our children's children, but for the nation and eventually. the whole world. I personally feel very proud to be part of our wonderful culture!

GRAHAM M.
employee since 2006

Say what you will about Nick's "Desert Boot Drama," Fred's "Leap of Faith," or Tony and Alfred's "Pizza Pyramid Scheme" — all vital pieces of the Zappos lore — but the Zappos Culture gets its true strength from the bottom up.

Now, I mean no disrespect to F.A.T. or the like. Our founding fathers paved the way, and without them we might all be working at Amazon.com or some other crazy place (wink, wink). But the point I'm trying to make is that we've got ourselves one crazy supply of "tour stop" deserving lore at every level in this place. The way Roz at the front desk makes everyone who walks though the door feel better than their mom ever has. The way Kathleen on the 6pm Team volunteers to go home at night and sew costumes for half the company, while single-handedly taking care of her 10-year-old son. The way Dave in IT plays the guitar, and dons a poncho and sombrero while fixing computers every afternoon. The way Bill in Performance greets those touring the office by devising complex pranks that would make both Wile E. Coyote and Ralph Waldo Emerson proud, all while beating every goaled sales metric of the year.

Executives, watch out! You've got awfully big shoes being filled, literally, in the case of Fred's shoes.

HEATHER C.
employee since 2007

I remember when I was 14 or 15, I had a palm reader tell me that one day I was going to be a speaker for a great company. That always stuck with me. Then one day, while I was on the phone with a customer, it came back to me and I instantly put two and two together. To me, Zappos Culture means that we are all speakers for this great company. We are representatives of our company and our culture... ALWAYS. Whether we are at the grocery store or in a vendor meeting, we stay true to ourselves — and everybody we come into contact with appreciates it. Our culture is infectious and I would never want to work anywhere else.

Now, if I could only remember the rest of what that palm reader told me...

HEAVEN T
employee since 2006

"You have brains in your head. You have feet in your shoes. You can steer yourself, any direction you choose." — Dr. Seuss.

Zappos solely sold shoes online when I started, and now it has grown to include everything from shoes to house wares. The number of great people I have the privilege to call co-workers have grown so much the past four years. I've not only grown in the company as an employee but as a person as well. I have come to appreciate Zappos for being my encourager, friend, and teacher. We party hard and we work harder. How many people can say that about the place they work for? Thank you, Zappos for the great memories, hard laughs, and for helping me steer myself in a positive direction.

JACQUELINE M.
employee since 2007

Efforts have been made to try and replicate it, even to duplicate it... but the Zappos Culture is a truly genuine, one-of-a-kind, extraordinary phenomenon that can only be experienced through working at Zappos. After the first encounter, some may still doubt its true existence, some have hesitations believing that it is not a facade, while others struggle to comprehend how it is possible that something like this can not only exist 24/7, but continue to grow daily!

Not long thereafter, the realization starts to sink in... there is no doubt; there is no hesitation in believing... you have become a piece of this phenomenon! And you thought that working here was going to be "just another job!"

JARED F.
employee since 2009

A year ago I was having fun teaching people how to ski and I realized I am only happy when I enjoy what I do. Now I'm doing something I enjoy and I'm working with people that are equally as passionate about their categories as I am. This difference can only be attributed to the culture that Zappos has created. It's more than a daily arcade basketball tournament, but those are fun too. It's the accepting people that make Zappos truly great by allowing people to be who they are. The culture has created at Zappos a fun environment that doesn't make me look back. Plus it doesn't require shoveling snow.

JARETT A.
employee since 2008

Zappos is a melting pot of overflowing energy and personalities. There are very few places in this industry where you can continuously feel inspired, fulfilled, and welcomed with open arms. I feel like I spend more time at "work" and with "colleagues" than anywhere and with anyone else in my life. I am so very thankful that I can come to a "workplace" that is truly more of a community and have colleagues that are much more like extended family members. Zappos is "fantasmigastical," a word that, like this place, is indefinable."

JAY A.
employee since 2009

This is my first year at Zappos. In fact, I have only been here a few months. I have spent my life and career — over 20 years — working at various large, small and private companies. I spent the majority of my corporate time trying to fit into the corporate culture of the company where I was working at the time. I never thought about being myself. Instead, I thought about what the company expected and what would advance my career. The really frustrating aspect of this type of "adapting culture" is that it is constantly changing when your manager, director or VP changes. In essence, you were so busy trying to adjust to what you thought your immediate supervisor or the company wanted you to be, you totally lost yourself.

When I started at Zappos, I wasn't even sure who I was anymore and was tired of trying to reinvent myself for the sake of fitting into the current edition of the corporate culture. But now, after a few months at Zappos, I have to say the most refreshing aspect of Zappos versus any other company that I have worked for is that I don't have to figure the corporate culture out. They really want me to be me! Nothing to hide, nothing to fit into — I just get to be me. And the more that I am me — genuinely me — the more people have responded to me and, more importantly, the more it has made me happy. It is a form of Bliss!

JEANNE M.
employee since 2006

"You'll never sell shoes on-line" —
Was prevailing wisdom in '99.
Tony didn't listen when this was said,
Proved them all wrong instead,
Now selling clothing, handbags, and glasses for wine!

Our culture's what's gotten us here today,
Through Core Values we live every day.
Wowing customers by the millions,
Now selling product in the billions,
There's nowhere that I'd rather stay!

I never dread coming to work,
Virtually nobody here is a jerk,
Surrounded by my best friends,
Our dynamic atmosphere never ends,
Though outsiders may think we're berserk!

Our management never fails to inspire,
And as we carefully choose who to hire,
Instead of a job it's a calling,
Other places now seem appalling,
There's no other workplace I desire!

In my four years I've been able to deduce,
We learn, we take risks, yet we produce,
Every day we Deliver Happiness,
And don't confuse this with sappiness,
And we always have plenty of Goose!

JEFF B.
employee since 2006

Culture is what keeps me here at Zappos. It keeps me sane even while work can be insane at times. I love the fact that we can be ourselves at work. Hard work is what our culture is all about... and of course the laughs, cheers, shots and beers mixed in. We are one of the few companies that can pride ourselves on being unique. I don't just like our culture, I love it. I will be here as long as the culture stays strong, and by my prediction, I will be here for a very, very long time.

JEFF G.
employee since 2006

What does Zappos Culture mean to me? This will be my fourth entry in our Culture Book. After being here for over three years, this is by far the best place to work. It's not about the glitz and glamour; sure, the drinking and partying are awesome, but it goes deeper. Zappos Culture is about being yourself, whether you're fun and a little weird or quiet and a little shy. It's about accepting and respecting each other, building relationships to get the job done. That's the secret to delivering WOW!

JENNIFER M.
employee since 2006

Zappos is an explosive combination of friendship, laughter, growth and opportunity. I've been so lucky to be able to experience this environment for over three years now!

JENNIFER S.
employee since 2007

Zappos Culture is an amazing feeling like no other.
The way I can truly be myself is like no other.
The support I get from my peers is like no other.
The smile it puts on my face on a stressful day is like no other.
The connection I feel with the company is like no other.
I am so lucky to be working at Zappos and enjoy a company culture that's like no other in the world!

JENNIFER T.
employee since 2009

What Zappos Culture means to me? It's a tough thing to put into words. But, to pretty much sum it up — it's refreshing and motivating.

JESSICA M.
employee since 2009

The Zappos Culture, to me, means freedom. Freedom to express myself, create friendships and be creative in everyday situations. Freedom from the typical, the mundane, being stuck in simply living and not enjoying each day. Freedom to develop and grow personally and professionally. It's the ability for each of us to push ourselves to truly find ourselves and what's important.

JOSH S.
employee since 2006

Every year it becomes increasingly difficult to write these. The best stories/experiences/jokes have all been told in my previous entries. So this year, I'm going to talk about something that happened to me very recently. As time passes, it is slowly starting to blow my mind.

Here at Zappos, during tours and pump-up talks to vendors, we claim to have an amazingly close culture. Close enough that some people … nay, most people … even say that we are like a family around here. I find this statement to be nothing short of the truth.

My story: About a week ago, I received a phone call from my mother, saying that my grandmother had just had a pretty intense heart attack, had been taken into surgery, and was "not looking good." I jumped out of my chair, packed up my stuff, and bolted out of the office to race to the hospital. Since it was the middle of the day, I mentioned to my boss that I had a family emergency as I was passing out the door. When I came back the following day, the co-workers that sit near me expressed extreme concern about the seriousness of my situation the prior day. Everything ended up well with my grandmother, but it meant so much to me to see that my team had so much concern when they knew things weren't right in my life. I always knew that my team and I were a close-knit group, but this unfortunate event showed me how deep our caring for one another really goes. Without question, I know that my team is here for me, as I intend to be for them.

KAILEY N.
employee since 2009

To me, the Zappos Culture is something I aspire to grow within myself on a day-to-day basis. As a semi-new employee (I've been here for eight months now) I have been so impressed with what I see every day. I am so blessed to have such an amazing job, a great environment to work in, and great people to work with. I continue to feel like more of a part of the culture each day and I can't wait to see what exciting opportunities Zappos has to offer!

KARA T.
employee since 2010

If the Zappos Culture were a drink, it would be red wine; it tastes sooo good and can get you silly, but has nutritional and health benefits too!

KARRIE M.
employee since 2006

It's amazing how each individual contributes to and owns the Zappos Culture. Whether it is through someone simply smiling at you in the hall or holding the door for you, to Zappos Idol and random dance contests, the culture exists all around us at Zappos. Through the diversity of people, we are able to evolve in the way that we promote the culture and, through this, we continue to set ourselves apart as a unique company culture.

KATHY K.
employee since 2006

Zappos Culture to me can be quantified in each and every moment that a vendor has said to me that in their decades of working in the shoe industry they have never felt such a feeling of togetherness as they do when they work with Zappos. It is remarkable to me how I found myself in a company that stands by its Core Values. It doesn't matter how many hours a day you put in because you truly love what you do and you wouldn't want it any other way. The passion, challenge, growth and opportunities are endless and I feel fortunate to be a part of something so special.

KELLY R.
employee since 2006

Somebody pinch me! Is this real? I have been working at Zappos for four years now and it still seems like a dream. Zappos is unlike any other place I have ever set foot in. I still remember the day when I interviewed for Zappos. I went through a half day of interviews with many people. I remember interviewing with Fred. He never cracked a smile! He asked me "If you won the lottery, what would you do next?" If I had known that an honest answer was encouraged then I probably wouldn't have give your typical "let me please get this job" kind of answer. He asked me if I had any suggestions that I would change to the website. I gave him my suggestion and I got an email two days later showing me that they had implemented my suggestion on the home page!!! How cool is that! That was over four years ago and it is amazing that Zappos is still about taking anybody's idea and making it happen if it makes sense. Zappos is also about going to work every day and truly being yourself. I think that makes people happy! I think that is probably what I value about my life at Zappos the most. That I am truly happy every time I walk through the doors.

KEVIN W.
employee since 2004

If you mention Zappos to one of our customers you'll probably hear about the amazing product selection and service we offer. If you mention Zappos to one of our business partners you'll probably hear about the amazing growth and success we've had. However, if you ask our employees what they're most proud of you'll probably hear about our Zappos Culture. Above all else, our culture is what drives our success and keeps us coming back each day inspired to continue it.

KIM B.
employee since 2007

I have worked at Zappos for about three years now, and it has been the best three years of my life! I have made some really great friends who I truly consider family!

I wake up every day and look forward to going into the office, every day is a different day, you never know what's going to happen! I love the energy that flows around the office; it definitely feeds from one person to the next!

One thing that is special and unique about Zappos is our culture and core values! This is something that I have never experienced at a company, and it is now something I cannot ever imagine being without. Zappos has really made a great impact on my life!

KRISTIN C.
employee since 2009

During my senior year at Purdue University, I took an e-retailing class and we often had guest speakers. One night, we had a speaker from Zappos and before the class started, every single person was handed a Zappos "Culture Book." I spent the entire class reading through all of the excerpts and looking at photos. A year later I found myself digging up that very same book to see if I would fit in with those strangers that are now a family to me. I never imagined myself sitting at this desk writing a page of this book, but I am so happy to be doing it. Zappos is my first job out of college and I can't imagine a better one. I guess it's a good sign that it was my boss's first job too (seven years ago!). I don't know what I expected when I moved to Las Vegas, but it was not a petting zoo at work, head-shaving day, Zoktoberfest, filming a skit in the middle of desert or an LMFAO music video, team outings at Mt. Charleston and the M Resort pool, or the multitude of activities to come. Ohh — and I've learned a lot about buying too;) This place is crazy! I'm so glad I made the decision to become a part of it.

KRISTIN H.
employee since 2006

To me, Zappos Culture can be best described as that warm feeling you get when you walk into your parents' house. You're not fearing what the day is going bring you, but instead anticipating your workday. Across all of our many departments, those who have truly embraced our culture understand that they are a part of something unique and special. Knowing what we have accomplished in the past ten years will help us to blow past all of our future goals. Here's to an exciting 2010!

LAUREN G.
employee since 2006

The Zappos culture is very special and hard to put into words. I think each person in our company contributes a little piece of themselves to create the happiness that is within the walls of this place. Working here for a few years, I have seen a lot of growth and change, but certain things always remain... the feeling that I get each day when I walk in the front doors and see familiar, smiling faces... the delicious smell of popcorn in the lobby... the gloooorious sound of karaoke in the lunchroom... the sound of cow bells and dinner bells ringing when a tour walks by... the sight and sound of laughter in the hallways... and the feeling that I get knowing that I am surrounded by people who are happy and very lucky to be a part or this incredible company.

LEEMARIE S.
employee since 2006

I love coming to work every day and being able to express my opinion and truly be heard. I love that I laugh at least twice a day. I love that I am constantly challenged to better myself both professionally and personally. I love the Zappos Culture!

LINDSAY R.
employee since 2007

I am so fortunate to be part of the Zappos family. Never before have I been part of a family that motivates and challenges me on a daily basis. From winning bets that allow me to shave my boss's head to motivational speakers that inspire me to push myself to the next level and get off my butt... this place is awesome!!!

MATTHEW T.
employee since 2007

I first heard about Zappos through the Culture Book. I was at another job, and they wanted each of us to read a section of the book. My boss explained that, "It's a company that sells shoes, handbags and other stuff. We want to make our company just like Zappos." I thought, "What does this have to do with our job?" I took the book home and started reading. From the first entry, I knew Zappos had something special that our company didn't. I was racking my brain and thinking, "How can our company be like Zappos? Everyone at Zappos wants to be there — they actually enjoy going to work. There's no way our company could ever achieve what they have." After much thought, I finally found a solution: I'd just go work at Zappos. I wanted to work somewhere where I didn't have to go to work, but where I get to go to work. I've been at Zappos for three years and hope to be here for many, many more. And it's all because of the Culture Book.

MEGAN R.
employee since 2007

I have had the privilege of working for Zappos for almost three years now and I can't think of any place else I'd rather be for the next ten years! The Zappos Culture is what makes us unique! It's what makes me excited to go to work every day. The promise of change, the opportunity to grow and learn daily, the element of fun that's incorporated into our daily work lives and the chance to work with some of the most amazing people I've ever met! When I look at the people around me, I don't think of them as just co-workers, I think of them as family. We have a family culture here that focuses on encouraging one another to grow and be successful. I feel so lucky to have the opportunity to work for such an incredible company that through the years has preserved and sustained the culture that sets us apart in the industry! I'm sold :)

MEGAN T.
employee since 2008

I absolutely love being a part of such an amazing company. The people, the core values... I love it all! I'm very excited to see what the future hold for us.

MEGHAN B.
employee since 2005

The Zappos Culture is constantly evolving, but to me, one thing it has always represented is freedom. The freedom to be creative and think outside of the box, to be unconventional, to follow personal passions, to try new things, and ultimately the freedom to be yourself.

MICAELA M.
employee since 2007

I'm still in awe with this Zappos Culture. I know I'm a lucky girl when I can call my co-workers FRIENDS (and mean it)!! These are the people who inspire me to "work hard, play hard" and to set big goals as a professional and person. This culture inspires me to be a better ME!

MICHAEL F.
employee since 2008

I'm sitting at my desk in my sweat pants eating a cheeseburger and drinking a ginger ale, a meal I got in our very own lunchroom. What an office job!

MICHAEL F.
employee since 2007

Because more and more people are becoming familiar with Zappos, when people ask me where I work and I tell them, I notice a subtle swell of excitement beaming my way just before they tell me, "How cool that must be!" Coming to a place like Zappos every day is cool... I know that is simply put, but after many years in the workplace, it is not often that I have been able to say that. What has stemmed from our amazing culture is opportunity and growth that continues to excite me. Our culture is just so unique and has such a positive effect on everyone connected to it.

MICHAEL N.
employee since 2003

This April will be my seventh year at Zappos! It's funny, every year I sit down at my desk and think about this and it always comes back to this: Living the Golden Rule. When you treat people the way you want to be treated, the world is a better place. It's much more fulfilling to be nice to someone and "WOW" them, putting a smile on their face. And it should not stop at the doors of the Zappos office — do it all the time! You will be a much happier person yourself, too. To me that's what our culture brings out, spreading happiness.

NATASHA P.
employee since 2005

The Zappos Culture is about believing.
Believing we can accomplish anything.
Believing we can get through the day and tomorrow will be better.
Believing that you are supported even during the strangest of times.
Believing that we can do the impossible!

NICOLE S.
employee since 2006

Zappos is a place where I know that I will be understood professionally and personally. I am a little weird and that is ok!!! I also know that just like a family, if there is something that I am struggling with, I know that I have the support from my team and friends here at Zappos to help me through anything I need. I love Zappos and the way it allows people to be themselves… just caring human beings that happen to sell shoes, apparel, beauty, and home, etc!

NOEL C.
employee since 2006

Everyone says that they love our culture … and at 6pm it's no different.

It's Friday night at 9 p.m., I am sitting with my entire team having dinner. And a co-worker shouts out, "Crap!! I forgot to do my culture entry. It was due today!!"

So, here I am at dinner. With my co-workers that I chose to spend Friday nights with. And I am typing my culture entry to "get it in in time" on my Blackberry. Who wouldn't want to work with a group of individuals so amazing that after you've spent over 40 hours a week working with (and sitting four feet apart), and you STILL get exited to go out with them after work? On a Friday! That's our culture. And that's how 6pm rolls!

Holla!!

PAUL P.
employee since 2006

The Zappos Culture is contagious regardless of how you're feeling on a given day. You can walk through the parking lot in the worst mood, and once you walk in the doors, all that easily melts away. People genuinely care about each other here and let it show. This is reflected in peoples' work. If you allow people to be themselves and give them the necessary tools, they will genuinely try their best for the company and for the people around them. You are not expected to fit a corporate stereotype here and it is much appreciated by all. Thanks for another great year.

RAVEN M.
employee since 2008

Excitement, opportunity and the ability to take risks is what the Zappos Culture means to me. To be able to inspire, motivate and spark people, to want to change and grow to be more like our company and our culture is almost surreal. It's hard to define what this feeling is because it's almost inherent in everyone who works here, but to me it's the ability to wake up every morning and be motivated, happy and excited to come be a part of this phenomenon we call Zappos. Unlike many other companies out there, Zappos allows you to push the envelope, think outside the box, and try to find new ways to shape and define the market. I feel lucky and privileged to be part of the Zappos family; to me this isn't just a job, it's an opportunity to change the way people think of retail, customer service and how to do business.

REBECCA K.
employee since 2004

To me, the Zappos Culture encompasses so much more than what I can write in a small paragraph...which is why one would have to read the entire Culture Book and every entry to understand how it defines this amazing company. As the years go by (this is my sixth year at Zappos!) the culture makes me realize how spoiled I am to work here. The excitement when you walk through the doors in the morning is catchy. The energy of the people around me is magnetic. The way we are encouraged to be imaginative is inspiring. The stories of customer service are uplifting. The silly daily happenings are fun. All these things make me want to come to work every day. I have people tell me on a regular basis how lucky I am to be working for such a great company. I always tell them I'm more than lucky. I realize I have the opportunity of a lifetime and I'm not gonna take it for granted!

RICHARD Z.
employee since 2010

My oldest daughter, Olivia, attends Loyola Marymount University in LA, where Tony once won the LMU Entrepreneur of the Year award. One day last year, she was walking to class with two boys from the LMU business school. The guys started to talking about Zappos, what an amazing company it is and how they think Tony is a "super cool guy and the most amazing business person ever." My daughter was very proud and blurted out "I know Tony!" Needless to say, the business schools boys didn't believe a freshman girl would know anything about their idol, Tony. Before she could tell them her Dad also worked for the Zappos, the boys darted off to class. Weeks later, I told Tony the story and we both laughed. Tony then took out his Blackberry and texted my daughter the following message: "Hey Olivia, any time you or your business school friends want to come to Vegas for a tour of our offices, just let me know ... see you soon! Tony". The next day while walking to class with the same two boys, Olivia opened Tony's message and giggled. One of the boys said "What's so funny?" Olivia replied "Want to go to Vegas?" The boys read her text and couldn't believe their hero Tony had sent her a text. They both yelled "We're going to Vegas, baby!!"

ROBERT P.
employee since 2007

Having worked in many retail establishments, I never knew of a company having a Culture. I have worked for small companies and major department stores and the culture there is basically making sales and keeping the boss happy. Coming to Zappos and hearing about this culture thing, I was a little confused. Culture, what's that? Is it like what your home country is about?

Well, Zappos Culture at first is a little shocking because everyone is happy, friendly and having fun while working. The culture is addicting and soon you start to feel it and understand it. It's about being you and not having to stress that the CEO or VP is coming for a visit and you have to spend 48 hours straight making sure everything is perfect. The Zappos Culture gives you freedom to have an opinion or make suggestions. It's about working hard and partying harder. It's about growth for yourself and your carrier. It's about loving what you are passionate about and feeling enjoyment when something is accomplished. Creating such a culture takes involvement from everyone here and no one is afraid to express what their culture involvement is. Zappos is a unique and amazing place. Thank you, Zappos.

RUDY R.
employee since 2005

I believe that Zappos Culture is what keeps our company the best place I have ever worked for. When I started at 6pm last year, I was concerned that the culture would change. I had heard that we were going to be completely separate from Zappos. I am glad that the Zappos culture from is still the same for 6pm. I know some changes will take place, but the culture should stay the same. In my mind, the unique culture we have the privilege to live in keeps us being the best. I feel that we all participate in activities, decisions, parties. I feel part of something bigger than me. Is not about just being the best, but trying your best. About a company that gives us another side of the business world that is life. What we can do to be happier and more fulfilled in our lives. I feel part of a community that reaches out to the world. It is like nowhere else I ever worked. The closest would be Whole Foods, but at Zappos I never felt more whole in my entire life.

SCOTT J.
employee since 2002

This will be my eighth year at Zappos.com, or to put it another way, one-quarter of my years on Earth have been spent with an ever-increasing amount of Zapponians whom I consider part of my family. I have been truly fortunate to be part of this company and its incredible growth. I feel that our recent marriage with Amazon.com has only strengthened our service commitment to our customers and I can't wait to see what 2010 brings!

SHANNON R.
employee since 2009

I love this company! I came from one of Fortune's «best companies to work for.» They are truly a great company but they were missing something... culture and core values!

Zappos is a breath of fresh air and I am so blessed to have been invited to join such a great team of real people.

SHYLOH C.
employee since 2007

This is my third year writing in the Culture Book! I can't believe how time has flown! I remember the days when reaching $2,000 in apparel sales was cause for celebration as it was a record day!

I am thrilled to be part of a company that makes people happy as well as making their lives easier — all through personal connections with our customers! The internal atmosphere at Zappos is no different. This amazing company encourages me to make lifelong personal and professional friendships. I am consistently challenged by a category that experiences record growth on a daily basis! I make a difference at Zappos. Zappos makes a difference in the world. It is a wonderful partnership!

STEVE G.
employee since 2008

To me, Zappos Culture means the freedom to achieve professional goals in a friendly, fun environment. Thanks for providing this.

STEVE H.
employee since 2004

The Zappos Culture has continued to evolve over the years. The most amazing thing, and one thing that really illustrates the strength of our Culture, is the way it's stronger now than it's ever been after all the changes of the last year and a half. Zappos has been through tough economic times, difficult decisions and a merger with Amazon and at the end of the day our Culture continues to grow. The continued strength of our Culture is a true testament to all employees and friends of Zappos.

The Culture is what brings us all together and defines the Zappos family and brand. It's difficult to remember a time when the Core Values weren't a daily part of my life both professionally and personally. All the friends I travel and hang out with are the same people I work with every day; I don't know of any other company or organization in the world where that happens. I look forward to Zappos' continued growth and know that our Culture will help keep any changes that happen in the future both positive and successful.

STEVEN P.
employee since 2008

Zappos truly has a fantastic culture. It encourages thinking outside of the box, recognizes the importance of team/family, and promotes personal and professional growth!!!

SUNDAY P.
employee since 2010

I just started here but I already feel at home. Everyone is genuinely friendly and enjoys what they do. I love that Zappos is a large company with a small company feel. I already feel that my opinion counts and I am not just another employee.

TERRA E.
employee since 2007

It truly is an awesome feeling to be excited about coming to work each morning. It's even more awesome to be able to still say that after three years of working at Zappos. We continue to grow and grow but so does our Zappos culture and that's what makes this the best job I'll ever have. Our culture is one of a kind!!

TERRY I.
employee since 2007

Zappos Culture allows us to stand as individuals and continue to grow as a team.

VALENCIA F.
employee since 2007

Being a part of Zappos has truly been an unexpected experience. I came into Zappos with no knowledge of shoes, brands, lifestyles, and definitely no experience with buying them except for my own personal use. My background is working as an Executive Assistant, Accounting, Payroll ... office work. I was just excited to get a job as an office assistant for this company. I had heard so much about, but didn't quite get it.

Over time, I have been given the opportunity to become a Merchandising Assistant. I am buying shoes! The people I work for believed in me, encouraged me, taught me and continue to teach me and I am grateful to be able to challenge myself in a world I knew nothing of. I don't know of many companies who would give their employees the opportunity to grow into a position that they have no experience in. Zappos is amazing in that way. It encourages the growth of all employees and gives us the tools to do so. All the while, this company continues to WOW us with all the happiness they spread with the parties, parades, All Hands meetings, etc.

I finally get it now. Thanks, Zappos!

YEVAN C.
employee since 2008

Zappos is a healthy heart. A healthy heart circulates nourishing blood throughout all the body to keep it strong, healthy and nourished. Zappos circulates hope, joy, love, goodness, kindness and happiness to all we meet. Thanks to our great culture, our pursuit of growth and learning, and our amazing leaders, peers and peeps, we will continue to infect the world with a healthy blood supply. Goodness and happiness in equals Goodness and happiness out! I am so blessed, and grateful to be a part of our vision and purpose to make the world a better, safer and happier place. Let us always see our vision through clear eyes and a pure heart.

ZACHARY B.
employee since 2010

This is my first year here at Zappos, and I can't say enough about this company and its culture. I have studied the Zappos Culture in college, and it has been everything I have studied and then some. I am extremely excited to start my Zappos career because so far it has been everything I have wanted to be a part of my career, which is: work hard and play hard, working with a bunch of happy people who are helpful and like a family, and dealing with products I know and love and wear myself. I cannot wait to see what Zappos has in store for me in the future.

HEALTH AND WE

Laugh[...]
favorite[...]
Hilarity brings clarity.
Live well, Laugh a[...]
Let the FUN sh[...]
La[...]
www.laugha[...]

WEICOME
ZAPPO[...]

just because Fred, Alfred and Tony (aka FAT)

like to dress like Interplanetary Rock Stars of the Future (aka IRSF)

at our annual Health and Wellness Fair (aka HWF)

doesn't mean we take these things any less serious

(KWIM?)

LLNESS

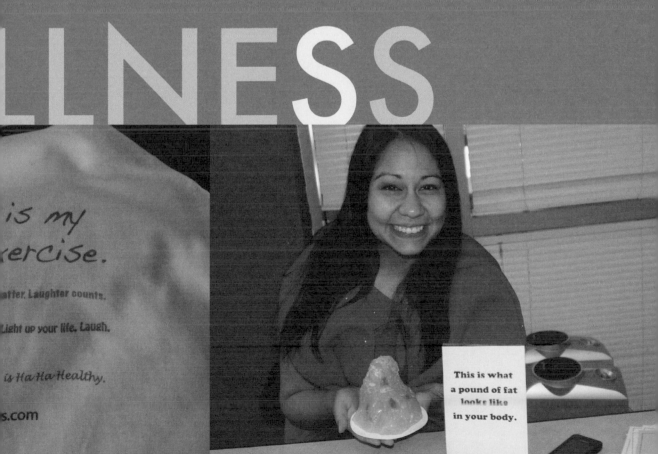

is my

rercise.

atter. Laughter counts.

Light up your life. Laugh.

is Ha Ha Healthy.

s.com

This is what
a pound of fat
looks like
in your body.

All Hands
Meeting

Death of Cla

before we launched our redesigned site this year
it was only right to bid a respectful farewell
to the passing of the original site (aka "classic")
that helped start it all in 1999

there wasn't a dry eye (or nose) in sight

ssic

HULA

HULA

AT ZAPPOS **LIFE**

IS

A BEACH

COMMUNICATION CHANGE OPEN DE
DELIVER
FAMILY ADVENTURO
FUN
PAS:

HUMBLE DRIVE SPIRIT

PEN-MINDED RELATIONSHIP

OSITIVE **WOW**

RMINED CREATE

EMBRACE HONEST

SERVICE LEARNING

NATE GROWTH TEAM WEIRDNESS

ALANE C.
employee since 2006

Zappos is the first place I have worked where I even heard about "Company Culture". I have found that this sets Zappos apart from other employers; Zappos really cares about our happiness and maintaining a "Team and Family Spirit." I have a great family at home (lots of kids, step-kids, grandkids and many in my extended family). However, I don't get to spend much time with them as we all have our lives and our jobs. So coming to work at a place that feels like an extension of my family makes work a happier experience. It keeps me connected to belong to a "family" at work. All the people I associate with here at Zappos are warm, caring and friendly. I truly feel that most of my friends here would do anything for me if I really needed them to. Thanks for providing a safe, friendly atmosphere where I get to spend my days, instead of somewhere that I "have" to go.

ALFRED L.
employee since 2004

On October 13, 2008 at 2:52 AM Pacific Time, after seeing our daily sales report email, I replied to all with "Are we staring into the abyss?" Obviously, that was not meant to be sent to all. Here was the email exchange I had with Fred after:

Fred: Oops.

Alfred: Yeah. Meant to send to a smaller group. Have Kris trying to recall it. Couldn't sleep but obvious still sleepy.

Fred: I can't sleep either. Haven't been able to the past several days. Either something is technically wrong with the site that we aren't seeing or the past weeks economic crisis has cut our sales by a third. I'm not sleeping because I'm very concerned it's the latter. We are potentially facing one of the greatest challenges we ever faced.
Alfred: I agree. It is darkest before it becomes pitch black. ;)

This is not very inspiring nor one of our finest moments. The uninspiring opener was originally from philosopher Friedrich Nietzsche who said, "When you stare into the abyss, the abyss stares back at you." What he meant has been left to a lot of interpretation.

For example, how can the abyss really stare back? Some have interpreted the line as nothing stares back – an even darker interpretation – but the movie "Wall Street" has a more positive spin with: "Man stares into the abyss, and there's nothing staring back at him. That's when man finds his character. And that's what keeps him out of the abyss."

There was no doubt that the second half of 2008 and beginning of 2009 were some of our dark times with a financial crisis and a deep global recession. What is inspiring is that we looked deep into ourselves, got aligned, came together, and got ourselves onto better pastures. That is the power of our culture. Our future is very bright, but there will also be more dark days along the way. We know we can get through it because we know from experience that we have the strength of culture to look deep into ourselves and the courage to just keep moving forward.

AMANDA K.
employee since 2008

I came to Zappos thinking that I had worked for some pretty great companies in the past. I had co-workers that became my friends, and I had a pretty fun time at work. That perception changed once I started at Zappos. Almost immediately, I realized how distorted my definition of a great place to work really was! My co-workers at Zappos have become like family to me — they have embraced me for who I am and I never feel like I have to apologize for it! I can honestly say that they have made me laugh, made me cry and everything in between.

Whether we are learning to make pizza (and finding out that one of us thinks that Madrid is a city in Italy), watching the new "Twilight" movie together, creating unique ceramic art pieces for one another (some more successfully than others), watching one of our co-workers win big on a TV game show, or showing off our amazing ice-skating abilities, it is always an adventure and brings us closer together. This is the thing that truly makes the Zappos Culture so special — the friendships and relationships that are built both at work and away from the office. Knowing that I am surrounded by such great people every day makes coming to work exciting and fun and I look forward to walking through the doors each morning.

AMBER W.
employee since 2008

The Zappos Culture seems to be unlike that of any other company. I consider myself fortunate to have only experienced the Zappos Culture with reference to the corporate business world. This has been an unbelievably great place to work while attending college. The flexibility of my schedule has been perfect while attending school, but also the ladies of the legal department have been so completely friendly to me from the beginning and accommodating to me throughout the time that I have been here, which I had never experienced in a job before and may never again. I enjoy everything that I have learned from all of the "projects" I am assigned, as well as all of the silly fun associated with being a part of Zappos and its culture.

AMY B.
employee since 2007

Thanks to the Zappos Culture, I spend each day working with people I respect and have fun with, in an atmosphere that encourages me to grow both professionally and personally.

ANDREA W.
employee since 2007

The Zappos Culture encompasses a unique, rewarding and very fun environment. I embrace the culture at Zappos and consider it an added benefit.

In the few years that I've been at the best company ever, we have achieved so much together. I can't wait to see what the future holds for us all!

ANDREW K.
employee since 2007

Your manager is a true friend, which actually proves to be an asset, not a liability. Your new hires and hiring managers express appreciation thoughtfully and unexpectedly. Your CEO, COO, and "No Title" negotiate a switch-out, rather than a sell-out. Your peers care to ask about family trials, and devote prayers to positive outcomes. Your abilities and limitations are mercilessly challenged, redefining views on both.

ANDREW P.
employee since 2008

I like the Zappos Culture because it makes a Zappos work day go by so much faster and better than a day at most other jobs and at Zappos, people like to have fun.

ANNE F.
employee since 2008

It's hard to narrow down so many fabulous aspects of a company into just a few sentences. But I think my favorite characteristic of our Zappos Culture is our sense of family. My colleagues are my brothers and sisters. Not only do we see each other all week, but we are always together on the weekends. I love that we can express our individuality in our rows and that we sit among our colleagues instead of in offices. I love that we are encouraged to experience several different departments in order to find our niche. I love that there is a grey area and not everything is black or white. These are just a few wonderful characteristics of our company, and I am so blessed to be a part of it.

ASHELEY L.
employee since 2009

Here is the best way I know how to describe my feelings about the Zappos Culture.

At Zappos, culture is in the small moments… like when you realize you just made a customer happy and that same moment many other Zapponians are getting that same pleasure. The combination of the happiness of the customers along with the happiness of the Zapponians creates a nostalgic vibe. It's not a job. It's meaning.

AUSTIN K.
employee since 2008

The Zappos Culture means that I do not have to hide the silly things that I do for fun from my coworkers because more than likely, there is someone who does the same silly stuff for fun also. In addition, it is also very likely that we will gather and do these silly things together outside of work as friends, more than just coworkers.

BARRY V.
employee since 2007

To me, the Zappos Culture is about freedom. It provides freedom to the individual by allowing each personality to be genuine. It provides freedom to the professional by offering an environment in which to learn and succeed. It provides freedom of happiness because every day at Zappos is what you make of it. It is a wonderful company, filled with wonderful people. We are free!

BERNADITA B.
employee since 2007

Zappos Culture is very extraordinary, and that is why a lot of people really love to work here. Management is really willing to help their subordinates grow.

ZAPPOS culture to me is:

Z – Zappididah, zappidiyea, wow oh wow, what happy place to work and have fun.

A – awesome company, awesome people

P – people oriented

P – party people, they know how to party - drink, dance and have fun

O – open minded, overexcited company, always willing to help

S – superstar in customer service, we know how to deliver WOW through Service.

That is why we are all Zuperstars… yeah

BEVERLY S.
employee since 2005

Zappos Culture Haiku

I LOVE potatoes
Potatoes versus Zappos
Zappos wins 1 – 0*

*Disclaimer: If you've studied the genealogy of a Haiku, there are supposed to be five syllables in the third line. When reading my Haiku, please keep the dash silent and pronounce "0" as "oh," not as "zero." That way, it qualifies as a true Haiku. all Zuperstars… yeah

BRANDIS P.
employee since 2005

What I love most about the Zappos Culture is that when I wake up in the morning and come into work, it's more about me coming in to hang out with friends and... oh yeah, I have a job to do as well!

BRUCE R.
employee since 2006

The culture here has been a blessing where I'm free to be me, pursue my passions and enjoy my environment. The phrase Powered by Service doesn't just apply to how we treat our customers, it applies to how we treat each other.

CARLOS V.
employee since 2008

The Zappos Culture is definitely unique. Working at Zappos has been a great experience for me. Working here makes me feel like I am a part of great team of people with great values. I am so happy to be part of such a wonderful family-oriented company!

CHARLES A.
employee since 2001

I like the Zappos Culture because it allows one to explore other educational and career options. Many other companies hire for positions they need filled and are only interested in helping employees attain higher levels in those positions. Here, if an employee wants to pursue a career in another department, it is encouraged.

CHERYL F.
employee since 2006

If you can wait and not be tired by waiting...

This is the place where you want to be. Some things are slow growing, but worth waiting for. Relationships develop slowly, but are grounded in a firm foundation of hours of shared experience.

If you can dream — and not make dreams your master,

If you can think — and not make thoughts your aim...

We've strayed on one side or the other, caught up in dreams that consume every roadblock of rationality, of calculation and measured risk. We've pulled back and held on to methods and modes of thinking long antiquated by our growing size and our persona in the public eye. Somewhere in the middle is the aura and the buzz around the average day.

If you can meet with triumph and disaster

And treat those two imposters just the same...

Something we pride ourselves upon, full on your face, just not too hard. Plan for a pillow to soften your fall. We'll pick up the damaged, but not the irrevocably broken.

If you can bear to hear the truth you've spoken

Twisted by knaves to make a trap for fools,

Or watch the things you gave your life to broken,

And stoop and build 'em up with wornout tools...

We all have our motivations, great and small, for getting up in the morning and making the most of each second of each day. Though these motivations are not always in harmonious agreement, their overall alignment keep the ship sailing in the right direction through the murkiness of skepticism and cynicism that tries to pervade from without and sometimes seeps from within.

Yours is the Earth and everything that's in it...

Including this little piece of it that makes up Zappos.com.

CHRISSIE Y.
employee since 2007

Friends, shoes and parties.

CHRISTA F.
employee since 2004

I had my five-year anniversary in December of 2009. The day I started seems like both yesterday and a very long time ago.

So far in my fifth year with Zappos, one of the most amazing moments for me was at an All Hands Meeting where Sean Stephenson spoke. Sitting in that huge ballroom, before Sean started speaking, watching 750-plus employees flow into the room, feeling their energy and connection and realizing that my team had a hand in hiring all of those amazing people, it was surreal — one of my best moments at Zappos, and in life.

They say happiness comes from having a higher purpose. I feel blessed for having had a small part in the higher purpose and vision that is Zappos.

CHRISTIAN J.
employee since 2008

I feel encouraged to work at Zappos, because it not only gives us the opportunity to have a job, the Ten Core Values here help us to forge better and productive relationships with people, and to do our job with enthusiasm and companionship. The essential foundation for achieving these goals is the Zappos Culture.

CRAIG A.
employee since 2005

What to say about culture at my home and family, Zappos? Well, I think it's been incredibly fun and interesting to watch the culture change and improve over the almost five years I've been here. I think what I'd like to add this year is that my perspective on the culture of Zappos is all about happiness (thanks for inspiring, Tony). I usually can't wait to get to work and start the day. I thoroughly enjoy the time I spend with my Zappos family members and can't imagine spending my time anywhere else. As a result, I'm going to do everything in my power to help inspire others to find their happiness.

CYNTHIA T.
employee since 2008

Zappos is a place where I feel like I can be me. It is the anti-high school. You don't have to worry about not fitting in. It is not about clubs or cliques. I can just be myself and not worry about anyone judging me.

DAISY L.
employee since 2005

Homage to Vagge

1. Peace and tranquility
2. An understanding of the problem of evil
3. A continued appreciation that opposites require each other
4. Find the chosen one
5. Freedom from desire
6. Make Emo Sean happy (a paradox)
7. Increase efficiency
8. Be more like Daisy's parents
9. Keep hope alive
10. Love

DAVID L.
employee since 2007

There are no words I can use to describe what the Zappos Culture is to me more succinctly than that 14-year old girl on Jerry Springer, who said, "I do wha waannnn!!!! I do wahhh waaaaaAannn!!!!"

The moral of this story? Culture at Zappos: We do wah we waaaaaah.

DAVID T.
employee since 2008

I can't believe how time flies when you are having fun. I have been here almost two years now and it's just getting better and better. I am lucky enough to be the manager of two great areas. Helpdesk and Facilities. My job is to make sure everyone smiles. I am able to do this by making sure we have great heart-healthy food coming out of the Zappos Bistro every day or finding some way to make someone's day a little better with that a helping hand from the Helpdesk. I love Zappos.

DEBRA J.
employee since 2007

To me, the Zappos Culture means that I can breathe. I can try to stretch myself and not be afraid of failure. The culture has allowed me to go outside the box of my cubicle and learn new things, experience new things and live the WOW factor. I love this freedom and sometimes I have to remind myself not to take it for granted. I know from personal experience you do not find this out in the working world very often, so it should be cherished.

Thank you.

DEREK F.
employee since 2007

I look back at my last three years with Zappos and realize how lucky I am to have a job at this wonderful company. I know I write this in probably every one of my Culture Book entries, but I love the fact that I am still excited every day to wake up and come to work. I have absolutely loved every minute of my job so far, and I look forward to every minute of it to come. Bending Core Value #10 a bit, I'd just like to say, "Zappos Rocks!"

DEVLYN T.
employee since 2005

I've recently realized how much the Zappos culture affects my life OUTSIDE of work. I find myself using the Ten Core Values to help make decisions that don't have anything to do with Zappos. It I ever feel like giving up on a personal goal, I remind myself to be passionate and determined. When I'm struggling to communicate with a family member, I remember the importance of building open and honest relationships. If things aren't going the way I'd planned, I will embrace the change. The Core Values are more than just a way to behave at work. I get to see the Core Values in action on a daily basis. Because of this, I am continually inspired by all of the amazing people at Zappos. And the inspiration doesn't just fade away when I walk out the door to go home. I try to live the Core Values every day, whether I'm at work or not. They stay with me, no matter where I am.

DIANA G.
employee since 2005

Zappos is the only place I have ever worked for that has a Culture and cares so much about their employees. Our Ten Core Values are something we all respect and live by. At some point, you can't help but COMPLETELY catch the Core Value bug. And all of the sudden, you find yourself taking that bug into your personal life. I often find myself mentioning the Core Values when my friends and family do something that relates to them. I also find myself smiling at random people at school and at the grocery store — they probably think I'm crazy. =) But we should all spread it around and deliver happiness to the whole world!

DORSEY T.
employee since 2007

Every day, it's a joy to come to work. My co-workers are like family to me. Yes, we do argue and fight amongst each other, like all families do, but if there is a problem or a need that one us may have, we all come to together to help each other, and to take care of Zappos and our customers. In the past three years I've been here I have seen the company grow so much. I'm proud to work for a company that actually values its employees.

ELIZABETH G.
employee since 2006

The Culture of Zappos
is friendly and bold,
With a mix of great people
both youngish and old.

We encourage each other
To work hard and succeed.
With a culture that smothers
A happiness seed.

Our lives are all filled
With a smidgen of silly.
But not too much craziness.
Promise ... no, really.

It is nice to wake up
And be happy to come here.
Verses having to schlup
To a job that is weary.

It is hard to describe
The culture that's here.
It is family, and friends
And I hold them all dear.

ELLEN W.
employee since 2009

The Zappos Culture is camaraderie, support and encouragement of an individual's ideas, and respect for individualism.

ERIC K.
employee since 2008

Situational comedy. And yellow bananas.

ERICA J.
employee since 2007

Zappos Culture to me can be summed up with a few select "Eric-isms" (the other Team Relations Specialist):

– "I'm clapping in my heart."

– "Off the cuff..."

– "Speak your truth!"

– "I love ding dongs"

– "Chaka Khan Bang-la-Gong!"

– "It's a treasure trove of things."

– "I've been to Barcelona, Italy"

– "Oh My Gazzzzz!!"

– "Ahhhh-mazing!"

– "How do you rejuvenate?"

– "Share with me..."

– "I've got change in my car."

ERIKA D.
employee since 2007

The Culture at Zappos is what makes Zappos so special. It's working hard during month-end close and drinking hard at the vendor party.

HOLLIE D.
employee since 2006

What does Zappos Culture mean to me? That is such a hard question because it means so much. It means hard work and dedication. It means fun and family. It means challenges and pushing the limits, while feeling safe and supported in your endeavors. It means being yourself and not having to apologize for it. It means change and that being different is a good thing. It means risk and fear, but success and joy all at the same time. It is unpredictable, exciting and like no place I have ever worked. It truly brings a new meaning to the term "work" and makes your job worth doing.

HOPE L.
employee since 2007

Zappos Culture is home. It is where I want to be. It is inspiring, thought-provoking and wonderful. I will tell you a little story of an experience that will stick with me for the rest of my life. Now, it's not anything big but you know the saying, "It's the little things."

So, I went on vacation. Most people have done this before. In a normal job you would come back to work and everyone would hardly look up and say, "Oh, hi, how was your trip?" However, at Zappos I came into work to a chorus of greetings and "We missed you!" I was truly shocked. It truly made me appreciate the team and family spirit we have here more than anything. This was just a drop in the bucket to what the culture has meant to me over the past two years. I heart Zappos with all my heart!

JACOB P.
employee since 2003

As a recruiter here at Zappos, I get asked what our Zappos Culture is like every time I do an interview. I do a lot of interviews, so you might think I get tired of being asked that question. And you know what? I don't!

I was first asked this question six years ago. Back then I talked about frozen flying turkeys from past jobs I had and how I never once put a thought into company culture. Zappos changed all that for me though, and today, as was the case six years ago, Zappos Culture means the same thing. It's the way we treat each other. It's the genuine smile people have on their faces when they walk in the hall. It's the friendships we formed in and out off the office. It's our Ten Core Values. It's the amazing atmosphere, people and bonds I have been a part of for the past six years. It's also about how for the past six years I have been able to work the frozen turkey reference into this book.

JAMIE N.
employee since 2004

After five years, I still love coming to work. Zappos is never boring and every day presents interesting and unique challenges that have given me the opportunity to learn and grow so much. I get to work with amazing people at one of the best companies in America. I feel very lucky!

JEANETTE T.
employee since 2007

Out of all the companies I've worked for, Zappos is by far the best. I look forward to coming to work every day, because each day is different from the next. There is always something exciting going on, like parades, carnivals and even a "Fifties Day" ice cream social. So, tell me have you ever seen the CFO of your company get his head shaved? Well, I can honestly say that I have, and not just once, but several times. Zappos is open and honest with all of its employees and keeps us abreast of what is going on with the future of the company (I really appreciate that). I am proud to say that I work for Zappos.

JENEEN M.
employee since 2006

Dear Zappos,

Thank you for living free, for bucking traditional corporate "values," and for kicking @$$ in the process. I don't ask what I want to be when I grow up anymore. You answered the question for me.

Love,
Jeneen M.

JENNIFER S.
employee since 2008

Never have I felt so accepted for my love of zombies!

JERRY T.
employee since 2005

I wake up every day thinking I'm the luckiest person on earth. Every day that I come to Zappos I can hardly wait to get thru the doors to help WOW our employees and vendors/visitors. We are at an exciting time, with the culture permeating from every nook and cranny. As the Mayor of Zappos, it is my privilege and honor to be able to live the dream and help others see The Vision.

JESSICA V.
employee since 2010

The Zappos Culture offers an environment where people can grow as individuals. We are not restricted to certain responsibilities; instead, we are handed opportunity. This is a rarity, and I feel fortunate to work in such an encouraging and liberating environment.

JIMMY A.
employee since 2005

There once was a guy from Kentucky,

Who had a great job. Oh how lucky!

The culture was sweet, and the people were neat.

For his birthday, he got a cool ducky.

JOSE N.
employee since 2009

Zappos Culture to me is so different from other jobs that I have had. At my other jobs, everything was all about the money. Here, you can share your ideas with everyone. This makes me very comfortable in what I am doing now. I am very happy to be here at Zappos!!

JOSIE D.
employee since 2006

I know it's been said a thousand times before, but the people I work with are more than friends, they are family. I have as much fun with them outside the office as I do inside and it makes coming to work every day a pleasure. Building a positive team and family spirit is easy with such a great group of people. I'm fortunate to have them in my life.

JOSIE D.
employee since 2006

I will start by saying that working at Zappos has been the most amazing experience I have ever had, and I feel grateful to be part of the Zappos family. If I had to tell you the best part of working at Zappos, I would have to say it is the employees. I enjoy coming in every day, our benefits are hands down the best. Zappos is first class about everything we do and it has brought me to a better place personally.

KAILA T.
employee since 2007

It used to be that anytime someone would bring up Zappos, I would automatically think of shoes. Now, when someone brings up Zappos I think of family. What a difference, huh? I've worked at Zappos since June 2009, right when I turned 18 and I can honestly say that as a first full-time job, this is such a blessing.

Since I've been here, I've met so many great people and have already created loads of memories. Coming into Zappos, I don't think I realized how much of an experience I would take from it. From the day my training began, Zappos started to teach me little life lessons. Our Ten Core Values are ten life lessons that I learned the very first day. There are a few that I value most, for example, Core Value #5, Pursue Growth and Learning. This is something that I'm constantly doing with my life. I always say that every day people should leave room for improvement. The second that someone thinks they know everything is the second they shut out all possible knowledge. Zappos gave me the chance to improve myself every day. From classes to QAs to switching departments, I was able to learn and do so many things within eight months. The WOW customer service we give our employees, visitors, and vendors is the WOW service Zappos provides for its employees every day. Everyone at Zappos is like family to me. And LUCKY ME, every time we hire more people my family gets BIGGER AND BIGGER! :]

KATRINA J.
employee since 2006

As we continue to grow here at Zappos.com and become a bigger and more successful company, I am very glad to see we still have the feeling of a tight-knit family unit. It gives me great pride to know that we all contribute in our own departments and with our own individual talents, to the combined success of Zappos.com. We are a force to be reckoned with!! Others may try, but I am sure they are not having as much fun as we are along the way.

KEITH G.
employee since 2005

I have been working with Zappos for ten years now. There have been many highs and lows. I guess the main thing is to have more highs than lows. Somehow, when things got difficult the company always managed to come out better then it was when it went in. This is due to the great leadership and company culture. When we had layoffs, it was a very difficult time and Zappos made sure the employees were always taken care of.

Zappos was recently acquired by Amazon. Again, the leadership made sure all of the employees were taken care of and Zappos was able to keep its culture.

This is something that all of us at Zappos need to ensure we never take for granted. I am sure there were long hours and a lot of negotiating with Amazon in order to keep what we have. Once the acquisition was complete, Tony and Alfred bought everyone a Kindle, which was unheard of. When there were some employees who said they would pass on the Kindle, they decided to give all employees the option of the Kindle or a $250.00 gift card. They did not have to do this. This type of dedication to employee happiness goes a long way. It shows up in Zappos customer service and great partnerships with vendors. I would like to thank everyone for the hard work and sacrifices that were made along the way to help build Zappos to what it is today.

KEITH H.
employee since 2009

I have been at Zappos just about a year and I definitely can say I have seen the Ten Core Values being used daily. I am impressed by the very thought of a company taking care of its team members. We are truly a family of Zapponians. I look forward to many years of being a Zapponian.

KELLY H.
employee since 2008

The Zappos Cculture is almost impossible to explain in mere words; it almost HAS to be experienced. I cannot imagine complete strangers stopping me to ask if I work for Zappos (because I am wearing a Zappos T-shirt) and if it is really like what they have heard. The best part is, I get to tell them that it's even better!

Even my 88-year-old grandmother thinks Zappos is cool — and that's saying something!

KRIS O.
employee since 2005

Can you believe it? Ten years went by real fast. Sometimes, I think back through all that we've been through, and I swear I didn't expect this.

There's so much more of *everything*. We're not a start-up anymore. It's still fun, though. And I'm happy about that!

KRISTY M.
employee since 2007

Zappos is a land where I can be myself. I don't have to be a cookie cutter image of ""professional"" in order to be taken seriously and trusted to be capable of doing my job. I love the open-mindedness of our company and our family.

I *heart* Zappos 4evAr!

LAKSHAN F.
employee since 2008

In a transient city, Zappos has a unique culture that is far from transient. As long as Zappos continues to empower the individual to live and breathe the values upon which our culture is based, it will prevail. These values help create an environment that instills "genuine" customer service, the essence of the Zappos brand itself. I feel privileged to be part of the Zappos family, where being happy is a byproduct of the culture we so dearly hold true.

LINDSEY K.
employee since 2005

What does the Zappos culture mean to me? Well, I have written what it means to me for the last couple of years and each time, I feel something different. What I appreciate the most about the culture at this point in time is how everyone has the opportunity to grow personally and professionally. We are given many opportunities to help us reach our goals. It is also an environment where you can be yourself and explore your interests. The environment is very encouraging, friendly, innovative, fun, open-minded, inspirational, and most importantly, shows that Zappos is a place that cares about its employees. It is great to feel valued as an employee and to know that the company truly cares about our happiness and our wellbeing. I am proud and honored to be part of the Zappos family.

LISA M.
employee since 2004

The Zappos Culture is about change. Many other companies are afraid of change or are too set in their ways to acknowledge that they need to change. I have always enjoyed contributing to the change at Zappos. I look forward to further contributing to the change and experiencing the company as it grows in new directions.

LOREN M.
employee since 2004

CHANGE

By the time this Culture Book is published, I will have been at Zappos for more than six years. These last six years have been some of the best I can remember. Granted, I can't remember much farther back than that anyway. I have been witness to an incredible amount of change over the years and through that change I have grown. I don't mean I have gotten taller or bigger, but the Zappos 15 has definitely visited me.

What I'm trying to say is that I have learned to not only accept change, but really embrace it. I now look forward to change and I get excited by the thought of mixing it up. I have seen the company grow year after year from 80 to 180 to 300 then 500 and 1000 team members. At the time I write this we have close to 2000 Zappos team members between Las Vegas and Kentucky. I have had the opportunity to see our product base grow from shoes to handbags to apparel, electronics, house wares, cosmetics and more. I have been witness to many record days, from the first million-dollar day to the most recent seven-million-dollar day. Over this time I have watched us react, adapt and overcome hard times as well as celebrate the good times. However, with all this change and growth, one thing remains the same — our steadfast adherence to our culture and Ten Core Values. Since early on, the Culture and Core Values have been the guide that allows all Zappos employees to flourish in our ever-changing environment.

It is this ability to focus and unite around a common culture that has allowed us to remain successful through all these years. We now enter one of the biggest periods of change I have been part of at Zappos, our marriage to Amazon. The funny thing is, at most companies this might be the worst thing that could happen. Even from outside the company I hear people making comments about this change being the end of Zappos as we know it. Well, I call shenanigans! If the past is any inclination of the future ... this is going to be the best year ever at Zappos!

LOUIE M.
employee since 2006

To me, Zappos Culture means having a better quality of life. I find that my most enjoyable experiences have been while at work or with people that I have met at work. I have not worked for every company in the world, so I would be lying if I said this is the absolute best place to work, although I like to think it is. What I truly feel sets Zappos apart is its ability to have such a large corporation and still feel like it did when I worked in a company of ten people … as if I am friends with everyone and they are my family away from family, even though there are 800+ in our corporate headquarters.

Zappos encourages everyone to be who they are. Oddly enough, who we are works so well amongst everyone. There is never a dull moment at work, whether it be stress, success, happiness, or sadness. We are a family and at any point in time we ALWAYS come together to make the best of any situation we are presented with. I truly believe that you get what you give. Our employees give off a positive energy that is reflected when you look at what our culture is all about.

MAJA L.
employee since 2008

What Zappos Culture means to me is that I am encouraged to be a nerd! And that makes me very, very happy :-)!

MALLORY J.
employee since 2007

The Zappos Culture to me means I can do and be who I am without being judged in a negative way. It gives everyone the opportunity to grow and achieve their goals without being pressured and told what they should become.

MIGUEL P.
employee since 2008

When I start thinking of the Zappos Culture, a sea of feelings comes flowing up. How do I put these feelings into words? It is extremely difficult to express all the awesome things Zappos has given me, as well as the professional and personal growth I have experienced here. I know that the Zappos Culture makes me a better person, which, in turn, helps me teach other people how to be better. If anything, this culture gives me the opportunity to be better every day and it allows me to keep growing. I know that I'm extremely happy to come to work every day because I'm passionate about what I do. To me, the Zappos Culture is all about belonging to a family full of great people who are always willing to help and be there for you.

MARCIE A.
employee since 2008

I heart Zappos & my Zappos family.

MARGARET M.
employee since 2007

Zappos is truly a land of opportunity. I feel so blessed to be a part of an organization that encourages individual growth in all the different forms it takes. The Zappos Culture provides the infrastructure for employees to feel empowered to pursue their passions and to push themselves to be better all-around human beings. The Zappos family provides reassurance and support for those who choose to pursue different interests within the company. Employees are embraced and welcomed with open arms to new teams while they are remembered and celebrated by their old teams. Co-workers not only support each other's professional development but they also become friends and support systems. The heart of Zappos is its employees. I am inspired by the depth and richness of the Zappos spirit. It motivates me to explore unchartered lands in an effort to enrich my life and strengthen my contributions to the company.

MARIA U.
employee since 2008

Zappos para mi es la compañía diferente a las demás por su cultura. La cultura encierra principios muy fuertes que no solo toca el corazón, diría yo que toca el alma. Ahora que conozco su cultura, pienso deferente, siento deferente y amo mi trabajo y para los que trabajo. Ahora veo Zappos como mi hogar y a la gente como mi familia. Creo yo que la cultura son los principios que vienen de una gran familia y Zappos es una gran familia. La humildad se me hizo muy importante, es algo que pienso no se debe perder. Gracias a Tony a todas esas personas que crearon los valores de Zappos. Pienso que para dar esas clases que ofrecen a la compañía, hay que tener mucho corazón. Gracias a toda mi familia y a Zappos.

MARITZA L.
employee since 2008

Zappos Culture means having the title of 'Cruise Ship Navigator' and never working on a boat. It means coming into work to plan events, handout Zappos schwag, and help judge eating contests. I am one lucky sailor to have the opportunity to be a part of this great company. Zappos, I salute you!

I'm on a boat! I'm on a boat! I'm on a boat!

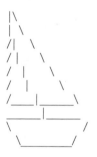

MARK G.
employee since 2009

Prior to coming aboard at Zappos, I read a lot about the Zappos Culture and spoke with former colleagues who worked here. They tried to give me a feel for what the culture was like. After working here for a few weeks I quickly realized that the only way to fully understand what everyone was describing was to be fully immersed in it. It's an amazing experience fueled by exceptional people.

MARY D.
employee since 2007

In all the years that I have worked, and with all the companies that I have worked for, I have never seen or felt what I feel here at Zappos. Our Zappos Culture is made up of people who live and believe in our Ten Core Values and make them happen everyday. It's the most positive feeling and up-lifting experience I have ever had in a workplace. I look forward to coming to work every day and I'm so happy to be a part of the Zappos team.

I could explain the core values and what they mean to me, I would rather say, they are a part of me. I believe the equation is, The People + Ten Core Values = The Culture, which turns into HAPPINESS every day.

Thanks for letting me share

MARY F.
employee since 2009

WOW… where do I begin… I have worked for more years than I want to admit and the Zappos Culture makes Zappos like no other company that I have ever worked.

I have worked in customer service at companies of various sizes. They all profess to encourage creativity and personal growth in a family environment. Experience has taught me that these are meaningless statements. However, at Zappos, they are absolutely true statements and so very much more.

I have never had a job for which I truly enjoyed getting up and going to the office. Every day at Zappos is like a day on "Fantasy Island." Zappos employees are a collection of dynamic people with different ethnic backgrounds working together, living and breathing the Zappos Ten Core Values, not only in our business environment but also in our personal lives. We are truly a family and daily, we realize that the Zappos Culture allows each one of us to be the absolute best we can be.

MEGAN A.
employee since 2007

I love the Zappos Culture. It's not something you see everywhere. It sets Zappos apart from the rest of the corporate world. I hope we always stay different and we don't forget how special what we have is.

MICHAEL A.
employee since 2006

The unique thing about Zappos, of course, is our extraordinary culture and the people who work here. The true test of a great culture is whether it can be sustained over time and through periods of change. As Zappos has continued to grow over the years, our commitment to culture remains strong. Even with our steady growth and our merger this past year with Amazon, our culture remains the most important aspect of Zappos and will ultimately determine our success in the years to come. It's up to all employees to drive the culture and to continue to make Zappos a great place to work.

MICHAEL H.
employee since 2008

Our culture is about enjoying the drive to work. It's about creating a safe, fun and productive work environment. This environment enables us to come together as a team to progress toward our personal, professional, and company goals. It is something to look forward to every day, enjoying the drive to work.

MIKAL G.
employee since 2007

The Zappos Culture means the world to me. It is what I fell in love with at this job, and it's what keeps a smile on my face every day. There are a lot of really great people here at Zappos, but it's more than just the people with whom we work. It's a way of measuring the value of our company, above just profits or our brand. Our culture spans farther than our advertising or word of mouth ever could. It shows in the way that Zappos cares for its employees, how our employees care for Zappos, and how Zappos treats its customers. It is built into everything we do as a company. I believe I am a better person because of the culture we have here. Zappos has taught me so much over the last 3 years, things I use daily in my professional and personal life! All I can say is I LOVE this place!!!

MIKE K.
employee since 2000

The year 2009 was a pivotal year for me, as I returned to Las Vegas to take charge of the Tech Support operation at the Zappos offices. Upon returning, I saw this opportunity as a challenge; an opportunity to gain a fresh, new perspective towards Zappos after two and a half years of being out at the warehouse. I also gained a new IT team and looked forward to meeting a whole new set of people.

With this renewed outlook on the company, I see that Zappos is resilient to the obstacles we incur, such as running out of space, competition from other retailers, and experiencing growing pains over a long period of time. I see that we can truly come together as a team. Zappos continues to succeed and thrive in an ever-changing global economy.

MIKI C.
employee since 2006

To me, Zappos Culture is something very unique and special. Our culture creates an environment that feels like family and you want to be a part of that family. I look forward to coming into work each day. At Zappos, we have the opportunity to grow both professionally and personally, challenging ourselves to excel. It's a really great place to work.

MISSY R.
employee since 2005

I love, love, love Zappos! Seriously, I love Zappos! If you didn't know, now you do!

I have been employed by Zappos since July 19th 2004, and each day, I still walk through the door amazed. What amazes me is seeing the company getting stronger and stronger than ever! I started with about 90 people in the 500 E Warm Springs office, but just like The Jeffersons' song, "Movin' on Up," we now have three buildings located on Corporate Circle. While Vegas was booming and growing, so was Kentucky with two warehouses filled with even more wonderful Zapponians! Life is great! During 2009, ZAPPOS and AMAZON GOT MARRIED... life is fantastic!

When I am asked about the Zappos Culture, my response remains the same. Zappos Culture is extraordinary and very unique itself.

To all the new Zappos employees, expect the unexpected.

Slainte!!!!

NICHOLAS B.
employee since 2005

Zappos Culture, to me, is being able to work at a great job, and be surrounded by great friends. Over the past year I have learned so much by doing so many different things within the company. I go home every evening with a new sense of accomplishment.

NICK V.
employee since 2003

A guy goes to work. On any given day, he may witness a parade, hang out with a llama, or get serenaded by a wannabe mariachi while getting his computer fixed.

With all the extracurriculars going on, this guy is still able to complete a lot of stuff. Even more impressive is that The Company generates impressive financial numbers. Not bad for a bunch of crazies.

PAM T.
employee since 2003

I'm a happier person than I was before joining Zappos. I've learned a lot, experienced a great deal, and made lots of friends. All this, while Zappos continues to invest in each of us.

Our Pipeline keeps our culture a priority through a rigorous hiring process, followed by providing continuous training, career paths, and leadership development. Our culture provides an environment in which people are free to be themselves and empowered to make decisions everyday.

Our Core Values are the framework for all of our decisions, serving as our guiding principles to simply do the right thing for our culture, business, employees, customers and community. The Zappos Culture is extraordinary and we have a responsibility to continue cultivating and protecting it. It's a privilege to be a part of our history!

PATRICK S.
employee since 2001

Zappos Culture to me is a very dynamic work environment that promotes thinking outside the box to continually evolve organizational efficiencies. The status quo is by far the weakest spoke in the Zappos wheel, with creativity and leadership being the strongest. The hub of the company is the team concept with all the departments working for the common goal, as well as willing to make sacrifices for the greater good.

This synergy among departments helps bring morale to the next level by strengthening the bond between all employees.

PATTI C.
employee since 2005

Zappos is an exciting place to work. No two days are ever alike. The energy that you feel when you walk in the building is amazing. The feeling of working with family is strong. And we are one big family. Our culture and core values are with us always. After all these years I can honestly say I still love coming to work every day.

RACHEL B.
employee since 2005

Once I got the email reminding us that it's time to write about our Zappos Culture again, I was racking my brain trying to figure out something to write about this year.. Then, after our team finished welcoming and greeting our new- hire class, I knew what I wanted to share.
For each new- hire class, our team gets up excited — well, after a few coffees, it is 7 a.m. nonetheless :) — to welcome them to Zappos. We each share our heart-felt stories about our experiences of first coming to Zappos and try to talk about what the Zappos Culture means to us. As each member of our team walked up to do their class intros last Monday, it hit me. We each have a great and touching story... which each one of us has heard and can re-tell many times over. :) But, every time one of us re-tells our story, the rest of our team laughs, tears up, cheers... and usually there is even a little craziness.

Vanessa, sorry to call you out, but I laughed so hard I was crying during your "chewing incident" in the midst of Loren's intro. :) Sorry, back to the point. What I noticed was that we were not only sharing our experiences in hopes of conveying into words what our culture is to the class, we were also showing the class, through our interactions, what it is like to live in it. We each not only support each other, but truly care what each of us has to say... enthusiastically. We hope the class is inspired by our stories and is excited to join us in our commitment to make our culture better each and every year. That's all until next year, folks. :) If you ever are hanging around 2300 at 7am on new-hire Monday, come and join us....

RACHEL P.
employee since 2008

To Me Zappos is much more than a job. I wake up in the morning, and instead of wishing that I could just go back to sleep, I am excited to get to work and see what the day has in store for me. There's always something exciting to look forward to. It is crazy how much Zappos has affected all aspects of my life. Zappos Culture has made me strive to be a better person. I have learned so much in the time that I have been here and I continue to grow every day. I am proud to be a part of this culture and I look forward to see where it takes me!

RACHEL M.
employee since 2007

One of my favorite things about the Zappos Culture is that it fosters a freedom of expression that empowers us to be endlessly creative, whether in thinking up new business ideas, finding more efficient ways to carry out tasks, or simply in expressing ourselves as unique individuals that together make up the collective Zappos family.

RAN G.
employee since 2009

I have been working here for almost a year now. It's the best year ever. I can't believe how much fun I have at work. I've never had this kind of feeling at my previous jobs. Thanks to Zappos Culture, I feel this isn't just a job, but a place where I can express passion for my work.

RANDALL B.
employee since 2009

What I love most about our Zappos Culture is how it truly turns into a way of life. If you truly believe in the Ten Core Values and what they stand for, you'll implement them in your everyday life as well. Even if you don't mean to, it happens. I look forward to seeing my co-workers each day at work, as well as growing together here as a company. I believe in the Zappos way, and with the pipeline classes, growth is a way of life, not an idea. We are a FAMILY, and that's the best part of it — all your co-workers, leads and supervisors want to see you do well. Thank you, Zappos.

RAYMOND A.
employee since 2004

Zappos Culture is the difference between waking up and thinking "I can't wait to get to work today" and thinking, "Man, is it morning again." I am going on my sixth year here at Zappos and have held many positions. It doesn't matter if someone says, "Hey, Ray, we need you to scrub the toilets today." I would smile, don my gloves and tackle the task as asked. I'm just happy being here every day!

REBECCA H.
employee since 2007

The Zappos Culture, to me, is the environment where I can be my best self. Our culture reminds me to be patient, generous, and kind. And, because I'm living that every day at work, it spills over into my personal life, and I find myself more patient, more generous, and more kind there also. In that way, the Zappos cCulture not only benefits me, but it also benefits my friends and family. I'm lucky to be a part of a place like this.

RENNA C.
employee since 2007

I am extremely thankful to be one battery that powers the Zappos way of life. :)

RICHARD E.
employee since 2008

The Zappos Culture is the most essential factor of our success. While skills and knowledge are the basic requirements to get work done, it's a company's culture that makes the difference between a job and a career; between a money-focused business and a customer-focused business; between a retailer and a partner. The Zappos Culture promotes growth, commitment and cooperation among all employees. I love coming to work here every day. The team environment has helped me to pursue my career goals, while at the same time working together towards our company goals.

I have grown here and I have seen my co-workers grow as well. I love reading the Zappos props and hearing customers express how pleased they are with Zappos. The way we work with vendors by making them feel like partners is another example of our culture. As we grow as a company, it's up to us to maintain the Zappos Culture.

RICHARD H.
employee since 2005

Writing this year's entry to the Culture Book on this eve of both Valentine's Day and Chinese New Year's Day means something very special to me. In one short year, the Zappos China operation expanded from one single employee to more than twenty of them. Tony sometimes talks about the blurring between work and family as a result of practicing the Zappos Culture. Well, in the Zappos China office, the blurring is not only 100%, but also 24/7, because all the employees actually work and live in the same building! This unique arrangement, coupled with a team of almost all new hires, presented a unique challenge to not only make it work, but also to work quickly. Fortunately, we learned from Tony's mistake at LinkExchange and started the new team with intense culture training as soon as a new member arrives, mostly in Chinese to begin with, but increasingly in English.

Thanks to the help of many individuals in both Las Vegas and Kentucky, as well as the senior members of the China team, it is heartening to see that, in a matter of just a few months, a group of highly motivated young people from all corners of China are now knitted into one big family, breathing and living the Ten Core Values. Many are grateful that they have made their best friends in Zappos. Some indicated that they have spread the Zappos Culture to their own family and circle of friends with amazing results. All of them feel that the Zappos Culture is the best part of their Zappos experiences so far. I am especially moved by the many new ways of elaborating and practicing the Zappos Culture that the team has developed and is continuously developing. And I'm happy to see that the essence of this evolution is documented in a bilingual blog created by the team to serve the team. Despite my many years of immersion in it, I'm now learning something new every day about Zappos Culture from this beloved team. Everyone in it is a gem!

ROBERT S.
employee since 2009

To me, culture is values. I truly appreciate the culture here at Zappos. As a new employee, I have come to work in an environment that really values culture with great comfort and pride. I come from a very diverse background and it's great to see that expressed in the workplace here. I value coming to work and I value doing my job. I love the feeling of warmth, comfort, and love when I come to work every day. I love coming to work with people who are not only co-workers but also family.

ROBIN C.
employee since 2007

This is my third Culture Book entry (wow, time flies!) and I always feel as if Zappos is an evolving, dynamic company. That being said, it doesn't ever lose its close-knit atmosphere, and that is something I really appreciate! You don't find the closeness at a lot of other companies that you find here. It's something I noticed on the first day I walked in and it's something I am very thankful for.

ROGER D.
employee since 2005

Wow! It's hard to believe that it's already been FIVE years for me here. I can honestly say that this has not only been the longest I've held a job, but it's been without a doubt the most life-changing one I've ever had.

Summarizing what the Zappos Culture means to me is almost a daunting task — especially when constrained to only a few short paragraphs. I'm going to address what affects me the most about the culture here. While one might argue that our Ten Core Values help define our culture, they don't describe it. Although we have ten documented Core Values, we're given the freedom to internalize them all in our own way. The culture here is one that encourages individuality in a team environment. While I guess the hope is that every employee here will come to embody each of the values, it's completely understood that we'll naturally gravitate more towards certain ones depending on our own personalities. An overall expectation would be that none of us be directly opposed to any of the values.

As I initially stated, working here has been a LIFE-CHANGING experience for me. I've grown to appreciate life in general much more. While walking around the grocery store, I no longer stare at the floor, but instead seek to make eye contact and smile at perfect strangers. I guess I do this in the hope that the smile on my face will bring one to theirs (delivering happiness). When faced with a seemingly insurmountable challenge, I no longer back down and walk away. Challenges are now simply opportunities to step back and rethink situations and to come up with creative and out-of-the-box solutions. The list of changes could go on and on.

When I first sat down to ponder on what I'd write about this year, I started to think about what it was like for me "pre-Zappos." This caused me to relive some not-so-pleasant memories, but also led me to realize just how far I've come as a person. Because of the culture at Zappos, the changes in my life outside of work are a DIRECT result of the work I do in the office.

ROSA R.
employee since 2008

Yo nunca había trabajado en una compañía como esta. Estoy muy contenta a cerca de la cultura de Zappos. Yo no sabía de qué se trataba, hasta que le ofrecieron una clase de cultura a mi departamento. Después de atender esa clase, fue que aprendí lo que es. Ahora ya comprendido el por qué ahí decoraciones en la oficina y desfiles. Me encanta el poder expresarme, el tener la habilidad de ser uno mismo, crecer y aprender más. También aprendí la importancia de ser humilde, seguir siendo amable y no cambiar tu forma de ser.

ROSALIND S.
employee since 2005

I'm still here!!!! Every year I look forward to writing a new entry for our Zappos Culture Book!!! I have experienced nothing but growth from 2005 to 2010 and a lifetime of memories. J The Zappos Culture is more than I could ever put into words. It is something you definitely have to experience yourself.

What we have here at Zappos, is culture from every individual person who works here meshed together and shared with everyone we come in contact with. We are led by example daily through complete empowerment of each other exemplified by F.A.T. (Fred, Alfred & Tony), which makes me know that I work for the greatest company in the world!!!

Zappos has brought about a movement in the workforce industry!!!! I see television shows like "Undercover Boss" and it makes me smile inside knowing that Tony has been concerned about what all of us go through in our positions since day one. Tony you are AWESOME!!!! You have sat with me at the front desk greeted guest, signing them in and they had no idea who you were. They would sit on the couch and were here to meet with you, and you so humbly introduced yourself to them and they were amazed!!! I know this because their eyes almost popped out.

I work for the HelpDesk Team and I have fabulous managers, Dave T. & Keith G. I have to give a shout out to everyone on my team because without them I would never accomplish my daily task. Josie, Dorsey, Julie, Zack, Renna, Anne, Missy, Andrea, Mary & Kaila, I love you ALL!!!! And, I could never forget Facilities and the entire Zappos Family!!!!

I thank God every day for blessing me with everyone and everything that has to do with Zappos. :)

What does the Zappos Culture mean to me?

Zappos culture is more than I can put into words.

Zappos culture is you, me, the present and the future.

Zappos culture is as natural as breathing........ now exhale J when you experience it, you can't live without it!!!!

Blessings.

ROSANNA V.
employee since 2007

It amazes me to think that after two years of being at Zappos, I'm still fascinated by how we, as employees, cultivate happiness. I am unable to put into words what I think everyone should experience for themselves, because our culture here at Zappos is truly a life-changing experience that will make you want to move mountains. I truly hope that when you read my passage, as well as everyone else's in this book, you can come fulfill your curiosity and eventually contribute your own.

SAM G.
employee since 2009

For me, Zappos Culture is a family atmosphere where we treat everyone within and outside the Company as family members. By treating everyone like family, the culture allows us to WOW our customers, vendors, and employees because we truly care about our family.

SANDRA G.
employee since 2008

Zappos is not judged by how much it loves its employees, customers and vendors, but by how much it is loved by its employees, customers and vendors. There is no place like Zappos!

SARAH N.
employee since 2009

Many companies have mission statements that they fail to live by. Zappos goes above and beyond with Ten Core Values that are embraced and executed across the entire company. Zappos provides so many unique opportunities by allowing us to be ourselves and be creative in everything we do. It encourages each of us to make positive changes and accepts our uniqueness. It is a privilege to work with such an amazingly talented group of people that care so much about their each other. There is no place like Zappos!

SCOTT S.
employee since 2008

The Zappos Culture and company has truly enriched my life. Even beyond that, I feel that every employee has the opportunity to give the same back to Zappos. I hope to continue to enrich and be enriched by and with Zappos as we continue to evolve. I love Zappos, yes I do, I love Zappos, how about you?!

SEAN K.
employee since 2006

Zappos Culture Book 2010! Another year, another culture entry. In previous years, my entries have been long, this year, I'm going to attempt short and sweet. The Zappos Culture allows us to create opportunities and pursue our passions. Having opportunities to do things you are passionate about is more common in entrepreneurship than in corporate America, but is something that is encouraged here at Zappos. Zappos delivers happiness in pursuing passions. How else can one organize monthly golf events and work on developing the golf vertical for Zappos, all while doing my primary job responsibilities? Zappos has empowered me to be the self-proclaimed Chief Golf Officer!

SHAWN K.
employee since 2009

The thing about Zappos that never fails to amaze me is how everyone treats each other. I was raised by great parents; they taught me what it meant to help others, and to be kind and humble. In my eyes, this company is like a parent for most Zapponians, but it goes further, building on all the good things they learned growing up. To sum it all up, Zappos is like a big family, never happy to see people go, always happy to see new faces. When you look in the dictionary, one of the definitions of family appears as: "a group of people who are generally not blood relations but who share common attitudes, interests, or goals and, frequently, live together. Example: Many hippie communes of the sixties regarded themselves as families." So I guess we're all just hippies. Best of all, we get work done while still having fun, and our productivity doesn't suffer; rather, it prospers from the environment we build around us.

TIM K.
employee since 2008

Every day I wake up and feel blessed to be able to come to work at Zappos. It is a place that you feel you belong for just being you, where your individuality is respected and, better yet, encouraged. Sometimes it just seems too good to be true that I am able to work at such an awesome company with so many great friends.

VANESSA L.
employee since 2007

"There is nothing in the universe like Zappos Culture." Chris Peake — 2009 Director of Performance.

Out of the many memorable phrases Chris has said, this one has stuck with me the longest. I would take credit for saying this because it truly affected me and I think it's brilliant... But honesty is the name of the game here! (And he runs faster than me and could take me out).

I haven't traveled the universe. I've only been to ten US states, Mexico, and a very fun three-hour excursion to Canada. I know in my heart I don't need to travel the universe to know that Zappos Culture is unique, special, and unlike anything many (if not all) of us have ever experienced.

I know this for these reasons –

1. Zappos encourages me and gives me tools to become the BEST me I can be.
2. I found myself here. I found my voice, I found my calling, I found my passion.
3. The relationships and bonds I have here are as close to family ties as I have ever known.

I believe emotions are best expressed through stories and I would like to share one of the biggest "Aha!" moments I've had. I go to boxing class. I wrap my hands and put on big gloves that make me feel like a Million Dollar Baby. One day, one of the instructors had us doing push-ups (as usual), but this time he made us all count together, out loud, as we went up to 30. Normally, we count to ourselves and it feels like a personal battle to get to 30. When we all counted out loud and as one, it felt like we were in it together. It was something I had to think about doing and took a little more energy to yell the numbers out after each push-up. I noticed it made it easier to reach the goal! I left feeling more connected to the class than ever before.

This is Zappos Culture to me. Is it something we have to think about? Yes. Does it take energy to protect it and build it? Yes. Does it give all of us the feeling that "We're in this together?" Yes. Is our culture the backbone of Zappos? A resounding YES! Our culture's worth cannot be put into a dollar figure and is even hard to put into words.

If I ever travel the universe, I'll get back to you and let you know if Chris Peake is still correct. I have a feeling he is.

VICTORIA B.
employee since 2007

I'm going on my third year at Zappos and I'm still having fun. I don't know of too many other companies where employees can say that after a couple of years employment. What's the difference? The culture of allowing everyone to be their best self while propelling the company to be its best. Go Team Zappos!

WILLIAM A.
employee since 2007

I have been with Zappos for two years and it has been a good job to have. It has been the best place to work for out of all the places I have worked. The people here make you want to come and be part of the culture.

Well it is time to go fix something, as that is what I do.

ZACHARY Z.
employee since 2008

To me, our Zappos Culture means being myself and embracing my identity. It means growing in ways I never expected. When I think about the person I was prior to working at Zappos, versus now, I find it amazing! Our culture allows us to be ourselves and everyone really connects with everyone else in a more family sort of way. I've never felt that way working anywhere else. Since the day I started working for Zappos, I feel that although our family has changed and grown, the family spirit and culture remains the same, and that, to me, is quite epic!

ZACK D
employee since 2006

Zappos has been my family for four years now. It seems like yesterday when I first started in shipping/receiving. Keith G. bought me aboard as a temp from Manpower. Rosalind S. was my trainer/mentor and she was awesome! We did more with less back in those days and had some memorable times — I wouldn't change a thing.

Life has a funny way of repeating itself. Fast forward to four years later, here I am, back on Keith's team with Rosalind as my supervisor. I am truly blessed to have great leadership, starting from the top, and working its way down to my peers. When I first came to Zappos I was looking for a company with good benefits, being that I'm out here in Las Vegas by myself. I would never have envisioned working for one of Forbes' "100 best companies to work for." Nor would I have ever, in my wildest dreams, have thought I'd find a new family amongst my co-workers.

EASTER

No blood in EASTER

that's chocolate

not blood

(shame on you for thinking otherwise)

Peeps

this year's winner of our annual Peeps contest

when it comes to Peeps
we don't peep around

SEX in the ci

reeps

ZAPPOS PEEP

Pe

FALL

Welcome to the
FALL
FESTIVAL
Zappos
.com

POWERED by SERVICE™

FEST

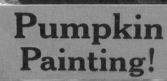

Pumpkin Painting!

Face Painting!

Zappos

BAKE-OFF CHALLENGE

Zappos.com

POWERED by SERVICE™

Apple

Pumpkin

Chocolate

WO

OODSTOCK

DETERMINED ADVENTUROUS FAMILY PASSIONATE EMBRACE POSITIVE CREATE LEARNING HONES z//!™

development

UMBLE COMMUNICATION DRIVE TEAM RELATIONSHIP OPEN-MINDED CHANGE WOW GROWTH WEIRDNESS OPEN SPIRIT FUN SERVICE DELIVER

AARON M.
employee since 2008

The Zappos Culture is one of empowerment and dedication. It's often said that working at Zappos is not about work/life balance, it's a lifestyle. I couldn't agree more. Some may take that as a bad thing; if so, Zappos probably isn't the right fit for them. A lot is expected of you. There is no 9 to 5. There is no downtime. There is no separation.

However, having this involvement and this dedication only allows for people to take real ownership in their roles and the company. When Zappos succeeds, we all succeed... Not necessarily in the financial sense, but in the self-satisfaction sense. This is what drives us. We want to see something larger than ourselves succeed and be great. I feel fortunate to be a part of it.

ABBY B.
employee since 2007

Zappos Culture means so much to me. It means working together to achieve goals. It means being more than just an employee. It means friendships. It means spending time with people you care about. It means parties. It means happiness. It means doing what you can for the bigger picture. It means that everyone is just as important as the next person. It means benefits (not just in the financial sense). It means creativity. It means spirit. But most importantly it means being able to be an individual.

ALEX M
employee since 2008

A few years ago, I toiled away at a stressful, menial job, for little pay, hardly any benefits, and as for a company culture, now that I think about it, I do not think one even existed. I was fresh out of school, the job was in my field, and I needed the experience.

Thankfully, Zappos came knocking shortly after and, as the cliché goes, the rest is history. (And yes, I did help myself to a generous amount of office supplies before leaving.)

In any case, I do not mean to rehash negative experiences, but only to use this anecdote as a way to exalt just how differently Zappos operates than the rest of Corporate America. Leadership likes to encapsulate our Core Values by talking about Delivering Happiness for everyone involved, and notice I did not use quotations because I honestly feel that would trivialize the veracity of that particular statement.

I guess I'm just trying to say that no matter how hectic my job at Zappos may get, I have a difficult time complaining because we have such awesome perks and benefits. We have an open-minded, inclusive Culture that says it's okay to wear a chicken suit to work. We enjoy free insurance, free lunch and snacks, we have Zollars, employee recognition bonuses, awesome discounts on products and, most importantly, we have a leadership that works hard to make sure that the company's successes are shared by everyone. This, to me, is amazing.

AMANDA E.
employee since 2007

I can sum it up in three words: Zappos is awesome.

AMANDA W.
employee since 2007

Life provides you with several doors. While some doors represent opportunities, there are also those doors that represent a downfall. One thing that Zappos has taught me is that there will always be an opportunity behind one of those doors... One just needs not to get discouraged, and to keep searching. Opportunity awaits!

AMBER O.
employee since 2005

There's no denying the impact Zappos has, not only on its employees, but also on the community around it. We've practically become a household name, bringing happiness every time somebody mentions us... and I know somewhere in the middle of all the madness, I help make a difference. Ever since I started back in 2005, I knew this place was some kind of wonderful. (Totally cliché, but true!) I'm so grateful for everybody I've met and the experiences I've had here. I'm happy to say that I'm part of the Zappos family and look forward to what comes next. =)

AMY V.
employee since 2007

Zappos is by far the best company I've ever worked for. I am very grateful to work with such amazing people. It's exciting to be a part of a company that is committed to continuously growing, improving and finding more ways to deliver happiness.

ANDREA L.
employee since 2007

When I tell people about my job, they either don't believe that I work for such a great company, or ask if Zappos is hiring. It feels good when you can brag about a team-building event like going to the movie theater, paid ticket, paid concession, oh yeah ... and you're still on the clock. Or when you show friends and family jumping photos and funny videos, knowing that other companies just don't treat employees like that... Some people are convinced that we just have too much fun. :) And yes, we do have a lot of fun, but the work is equally balancing.

Working in the video department is very rewarding. I would have never thought a year ago that I would not only be making videos but also star in them as well, even to the point where someone in a local restaurant would recognize me. This was especially nice because, not only did she purchase the boots, she also loved the quality of the photos, video, the presentation of the site, and that she got them the very next day. She was so happy with the whole experience.

It has been an amazing experience watching our team grow from three people to 16 in just a hair over one year. The changes from the first day to today can seem overwhelming, but the change has been smooth, and the department is improving.

I love working for Zappos, I'm proud of where I work and what I do every day. This place has become just as much a part of my life as my family.

ANDREW K.
employee since 2009

Hello, Zappos Culture Book. Let me begin with a three-part section of why I enjoy Zappos.

Numero uno. The fine folks that hold it down at KY are the ISH. They kill people with kindness and by that I mean that they are just fan-truckin-tastic. I enjoy coming to work with all these people everyday. Coming right out of college, I never expected to find a job like this. I feel so lucky to work for and with an awesome company such as this one. This beats my old job, which was a bikini oiler for elderly female models.

Now, I said this was going to be a three-part section. Well, I lied.

To sum it up, the culture at Zappos is unmatched. Thanks for the great opportunity and peace, love and chicken grease. One love, one world. Be easy, lemon stezzy. A.K. out!

ANGELA C.
employee since 2006

Zappos Culture is what allows me to be myself and to do what I love among people who love doing the same thing.

ANGELA K.
employee since 2007

Ever since I walked through the door at Zappos, I fell in love with it. I love my job and the culture. The people at Zappos are great. This is the best job I have ever had.

ANGELA M.
employee since 2005

During my five-year adventure here at Zappos I have experienced and learned more than most people do by the time they reach retirement age! The culture here at Zappos is one of the reasons why I have been here for over five years and have no desire to work anywhere else. Just knowing that some of my ideas are being used here at the FC on a daily basis proves that Zappos LISTENS to their employees and that is a great culture!

ANJI C.
employee since 2005

Zappos Culture is like a hypercube. You can take any one point and see that it connects to many people throughout our company, partners, and community. We are multidimensional and constantly moving with our Ten Core Values as key components of the rotating cube. I think this flexible structure and passion for human principles is what sets us apart from other company cultures. It is also what I treasure the most about Zappos.

ANNE P.
employee since 2008

The Zappos Culture is all about creating a community within your workplace. I think for most people, these are two separate areas of their life, but here at Zappos, people want to feel involved... not just with their job, but with those they work with and meet here. Zappos encourages each of us to reach out to both our neighbors and to everyone in every department. This kind of encouragement will not only lead to a stronger company, but to better people who live happier lives.

ANONYMOUS

To me, building a positive team and family spirit is the most important aspect of our culture because if we have that, all of our other values fall into place. I've learned from working at other companies that when people don't bond with their co-workers, they are less open and honest with each other, less likely to work as a team to achieve a common goal, and less likely to care about their work in general. It's a great feeling to know that I'm coming to work with friends every day at Zappos.

ANONYMOUS

Zappos is home away from home. I've just celebrated my fifth anniversary and it gets better every year. Culture like you have never seen it. Great people, great job. Can't wait to see what the future holds.

ANONYMOUS

For a dork like me, working at Zappos means I'm finally a part of the cool crowd.

APRIL S.
employee since 2007

Zappos has changed my life. I first started at Zappos two years ago. Although it has been only two years, I feel as though I am a completely different person now than I was then. I was shy and reserved. Due to past job experiences where people were pessimistic and hated their jobs overall, I avoided conversations and social situations that combined my personal life and work.

The first week I was at Zappos, I realized that people here held themselves differently. They were a family. They trusted and cared for one another and loved coming to work. I instantly fell in love with my job and my co-workers. Coming to work every day was an adventure, where being sick and staying home meant missing out on all the fun. All of my friends here have been by my side when I bought a home, when I got engaged and soon, when I get married. The friendships that I have made here will be with me forever.

I hope that each of you realizes how special you are to me, and how you have made my life better, brighter and more beautiful. All the great times we have had are hallmarked in my mind: the Holiday Party, Bowling League nights, Tap class, Cheerleading practice, The Polar Bear Plunge, Harry Potter Night, Java Joint, and numerous others! I hope to continue to make more friends and welcome more smiling faces into my family. Here's to seeing what the future will bring.

APRIL S.
employee since 2008

Zappos means to me, family, love, and string cheese fridays!

ASHRAF S.
employee since 2005

If you really want to know what the Zappos Culture is all about, I believe you don't have to look any further than yourself. Do you like being happy? Do you like feeling independent, yet still being able to work as a team? Do you like taking risks that involve real costs and rewards that are just as real? Do you enjoy working hard, but want to have it balanced by others things that are important to you?

If so, then you know what the Zappos Culture is all about. It's about things you already know and want for yourself. Zappos is simply there to help you nurture your own goals and face your own challenges.

BOCCHICHIO H
employee since 2007

I personally enjoy working for Zappos.com because the Core Values are what my life is about. When I was in the hospital after a horrible car wreck in 2008, my HR department was there for me and that tells you a lot about the core value of "Building a Positive Team and Family spirit." They also sent flowers to my mom's funeral and checked on my healing! If it wasn't for that them, I wouldn't think that I had an awesome job and felt LOVED. I want to come back because I felt the family spirit from my HR team. I was pushing for fast healing and recovery to return to work!!! Not only that, my CEO, my team and our Zappos Culture have shown me the true meaning of family spirit. Thanks a million!!!!!!!!!!!!!

BROOKE L.
employee since 2006

Everyone dreams of working for a company where you are not only respected as an employee, but also celebrated. A company where waking up for work in the morning is less of a chore and more of a treat. A company where your thoughts, ideas, opinions and creativity are valued, appreciated and cultivated into something larger. The difference between me and everyone else is that I've found that company.

I could not be happier than I am right now. I have an amazing job on an incredible team, doing what I've always dreamed of doing. Zappos is nothing short of amazing and I am blessed for each day that I get to come to work and use my creativity in an environment where it is nourished and applauded.

CAMERON T.
employee since 2006

My life in 2009 through the eyes of the Zappos Ten Core Values, the mini version, please read very, very, fast.

I introduced my high school classmates to Zappos.com. They were WOWed and loved receiving the 20% coupons. I have Embraced and Driven change in the positive growth of my department. We are now a department of 70+ people and are adding a video team to boot. Cool! Spent the day with Santa Claus and his elf, had Cupid deliver me a Valentine and got pinched by a leprechaun. That's fun and a little weird. I became Adventurous, Creative and Open-minded as I pursued and achieved my position as a senior photographer — an accomplishment I am very proud of. Yes, I know I am not being humble. I Pursued Growth and Learning and the Pipeline is awesome! Each and every day, I worked on Being Open and Honest in my relationships, a process that will continue through 2010, 2011, 2012... Had some pretty fun team-building experiences. Spent a lot of time getting to know my fellow team members out in the warehouse. Hi Greg, Sue, Julie, Suzanne, Lesley. Always finding ways to do more with less, amazing how something as simple as a styrofoam coffee cup can be turned into a photo prop that works! I am passionate and determined about Zappos and my job. I love Zappos! Enough said. Now breathe.

CHANELE H.
employee since 2007

I went to the dentist last month and when the dental hygienist found out I work at Zappos she excitedly told me a story about how she ordered a pair of boots, received the boots the next day, and then received a handwritten 'thank you' card in the mail. That's the Zappos Culture! I'm more excited/proud to be a part of this crazy company after three years than I was the day I got hired. It's gotten to the point where my family is now so ridiculously excited about Zappos that you'd think they work here. I honestly think my grandma loves this place more than I do. 2009 was a wild ride and I'm glad that I was a part of it. I'm looking forward to many more years full of fun and weirdness! Thank you, Tony and Alfred!

CHRISTINA K.
employee since 2010

The company culture was one of my main decision factors when I came to Zappos earlier this year. With that said, I've been lucky enough to experience other "cool workplaces" before, where weirdos are appreciated and a work/party balance is very important. I expected Zappos to be similar to what I'm used to, just on a larger scale.

After six weeks of being actually immersed in the day-to-day Zappos life, I'm learning that I don't HAVE TO be a weirdo nor a hardcore partier to be appreciated here, because everyone is different and people are valued the way they are. It feels great to know that I don't have to change myself to make friends and become successful at work. And this is allowing me to finally enjoy coming into work. It works way better than a beer fridge in the office, which, by the way, would be nice to add to the Zappos perks.

CHRISTINA M.
employee since 2006

Zappos Culture, to me, is caring about my team as if they were my family. It's hard work, dance-offs, tastykakes, jello cake, team buildings, laughing, crying, costumes, contests, and debating. I am going on my fourth year at Zappos, and couldn't feel more blessed, happier, and proud to have this company, and all the people who I work with in my life at this time. Zappos Culture still rocks and keeps getting better and better. WORD.

CHRISTOPHER R.
employee since 2007

One of our Ten Core Values, "Create Fun and a Little Weirdness," is probably the best part of the Zappos Culture, because it makes work enjoyable. Team building is always a fun experience and it also builds a positive team and family spirit. Two birds with one stone!

CLAY D.
employee since 2006

Our company culture is key to the many successes Zappos enjoys. Not only does it provide the foundation for delivering best-in-class customer service, but it also fosters an internal work environment that makes us uniquely functional. The Ten Core Values we all share provide a bridge between each group. With the core values in place, we all have something in common. Therefore, each of us feels comfortable approaching someone in another department, no matter how little we know about that person or department. This is why it's vital to be a "culture fit" when working at Zappos.

DAN C.
employee since 2005

This is my fifth Culture Book entry here at Zappos, and for me, 2010 is the representation of "Pursue Growth and Learning." We're currently gearing up for our second wave of massive hiring and so this particular Core Value stands out; I am teaching others the same way I was taught, preparing them to lead in the way that I have led, and helping them to embody the Core Values in the way that I have tried to embody them.

All of this came about because Zappos cares enough about its employees to continually educate them. I am especially thankful for the opportunities to absorb all of the leadership information I can. I have attended classes that I never would have heard about had it not been for Zappos. I have earned a certificate in Management Development, read great books like "The 5 Dysfunctions of a Team," and "The Tipping Point," and been inspired to take what I have learned one step further by stepping up and teaching others. For all that Zappos has given me, I hope to return the favor tenfold.

DAN H.
employee since 2009

I never thought I would have a job where constantly pranking my coworkers would be encouraged. The Zappos Culture puts everybody in a good mood and helps us to crank out some very high-quality work. I moved from North Carolina to Kentucky to start a new life with Zappos, and I think it might have been the best decision I have ever made!!

DANA B.
employee since 2005

Zappos has opened my eyes to endless possibilities, a vision I didn't know existed, and an experience that is unforgettable. The Zappos Culture is made visibly unique by three simple words: Ten Core Values. Ten incredible ideas that define us, represent who we are as a company, and forever change our perception of what a company should be. Our culture makes Zappos feels like a family, a community, and a "home away from home." It's truly amazing, and I am so thankful for the personal and professional growth that I have received.

DANIELLE T.
employee since 2007

I feel the same way about Zappos that I did almost three years ago when I started — grateful. Grateful that Zappos saw something in me that I didn't see in myself when they hired me and grateful that I have the ability to continue to work here. I work hard every day and definitely feel overloaded and stressed at certain points, but I spend my time here with wonderful people who continue to amaze me with their kindness, enthusiasm and creativity, so all that hard work has its rewards. I still enjoy coming to work every day and writing descriptions for jeans, jeans, and more jeans. :) I laugh all day long and I'm certain that not many people can say that about their workday. Thank you Zappos!

DARRIN S.
employee since 2004

One of the best bits of advice I've ever received was, "Surround yourself with people that make you want to be your best self".

My interpretation of "best self" is this:

– Purpose greater than one's own personal interests.
– Fear of stagnation.
– Relentless quest for the truth in decision making.
– A thrill for the unknown when the right answer is difficult to determine.
– Trust in the effort of others.
– Genuine desire to watch others succeed.

Zappos has a high concentration of people with these values and the Zappos Culture is a product of these people.

DEBORAH A.
employee since 2008

It would take too long to say all the things that I would like say so I will do it in one word, "WOW." This is the best place to work. Thank you, Tony and Alfred.

DENA M.
employee since 2006

The time to write these Culture Book entries seems to sneak up faster and faster as the years go on and when I think about it, that must be a good thing. As the saying goes "Time flies when you're having fun!" So that must be what is happening, and each year just gets better and better.

I know I have only been here for a little over three years, but when I think back on past years, Zappos as a whole seems very different, yet still very much the same. I am sorry to keep using these clichés, but like a fine wine, Zappos seems to get better and better with age... still keeping a focus on its core (the culture and customer service) but continually striving to be better. It just always keeps me excited for what is yet to come and it has been so much hard work and fun to be a part of it for as long as I have.

DEREK F.
employee since 2008

After years of the same old rat race, I thought that being happy with your job was just a pipe dream. Little did I know things were about to change. Two years ago, a great company called Zappos. set their sights on me and changed my life forever. Being happy at work is no longer a dream and I can honestly say that I love my job and I am excited about it. I never felt that way before; it was always, "Man, I can't stand this," or "Why do I have to do this?". Now it's, "I can't wait to start that project," or "I am so pumped to see that awesome brand's next line," and sometimes even "What time is the happy hour?!" These days, there is little left of that old me who wasn't happy, because now I can scream, "I'm happy" and truly mean it. Thanks Zappos!

DIANA R.
employee since 2009

What I love about the Zappos Culture is that there is always a friendly face to greet you. Let's face it... work is work. But when you are surrounded by people who are passionate about their jobs, their company and its culture, it lifts your spirits and makes working fun!

EDDIELYNN T.
employee since 2007

I LOVE Zappos. I've been here now for three years and it's been the most memorable work experience ever. I actually love going to work. I enjoy my team very much and I do consider them my family. It means a lot to me, especially when you have no family around. I've never come across a group of people of whom I can actually say that. I think the culture of Zappos is what separates us and makes our company unique in every way. The culture of this company is what makes me love our workplace and makes it enjoyable to come to work every day. I didn't know there was such thing as culture until I started here at Zappos and it is amazing.

ELMER K.
employee since 2007

Zappos is a great place to work. It provides a family atmosphere and the free lunches are a nice benefit.

EMILY T.
employee since 2009

I started at Zappos six months ago and the environment here is radically different than at any other workplace I've been exposed to. At Zappos, it really is about the Ten Core Values. The core values align all of us and drive the decisions we make personally and professionally. Understanding and living the values makes success even sweeter — it's something that we've cultivated together and that's just as valuable as gross sales or profit.

ERICA S.
employee since 2009

Coming to Zappos gave me a new sense of purpose and belonging at a time when I needed it most. Having just experienced a doubt-inducing layoff, and given the state of the economy at the time, I worried about being able to stay in my fledgling career. When I saw an opening at Zappos in their content dept., it seemed too good to be true, just as Zappos telling me how excited they were to hire me did! I went from feeling like the last kid picked for kickball to feeling accepted, appreciated, and supported. I come to the office every day grateful to work with a family of friends that inspire me to work harder and become better, both professionally and personally.

ERIK L.
employee since 2007

The main thing that strikes me about Zappos Culture is just how much the people here really care for each other. At other places, people might be friendly to each other, but there isn't a deep sense of family and belonging that permeates the atmosphere the way there is here. There are some people I work with here who I count among my closest friends, people who I feel I can come to with any problems I have, not just professionally, but personally as well. Even the management and leadership at Zappos cares about the employees here — we're not just numbers or cogs in a machine.

A lot of people talk about the need for a work/life balance. Zappos has made itself a big part of my life besides being where I work, thanks to the strong culture we have here. I'm glad to have it and I hope that it never goes away.

ERIN R.
employee since 2004

The Zappos Culture is like no other! I just recently hit my five-year anniversary at Zappos and I can honestly say I hope to hit many, many more anniversaries.

Here is what I've learned personally about Zappos Culture after five years:

People will celebrate anything here if it includes food. Sitting in a cluster of people every day will open you up to many opinions, personalities and commonalities. The people that are around you everyday probably know way more about you than your own family. Discussions around the water cooler are replaced with discussions around a cluster, an orb, a group of mannequins, or in a cage behind a photo studio. Team-building events outside of the building go a long way toward keeping spirits high. Zollars, LMS, WOW awards, couture shoots, JIRA, orbs, white balance, batches, pings, monkey slingshots and ZIMA are just a few words that you will say daily while working in our department. The people on your team will go above and beyond for you and make sure you have a great day even if you don't think you will. After five years of being part of the Zappos Culture, I feel proud to be here and experience this. I can't wait to see where the company and culture takes us for the next five years.

GERALD K.
employee since 2007

As a person who doesn't like attempting to define things, I would like to say that I do enjoy the atmosphere and productive influence Zappos has, both on my work and personal life. I've always described myself as a realist. To some people, a realist is easily described as a "negative" person. Through the open and honest nature of our Zappos Culture, I have and am learning that there is more than one way to say the same thing. I appreciate this, and I must confess that being made aware of this and working towards changing it (even being given help by coworkers on HOW to work on this), I have already reaped the rewards of this effort many times over. The open and honest communication alone in this company has helped me personally, and that is just one quality this company values. As I become more acquainted with the other values, I'm sure those too will have the same positive influence on my life. rock on!

GRANT S.
employee since 2010

I've been with Zappos for three weeks now, and it's pretty cool. Everybody works hard so there is no unneeded stress that a normal workplace usually provides. Zappos is very appreciative of its employees and never hesitates to hear their suggestions. Even though Zappos is a huge corporation they never forget about the little guys that make it work.

HANNAH E.
employee since 2006

Our culture here at Zappos is our most precious and unique commodity. It's what makes people want to be a part of this growing family. When people find out I work for Zappos, they often mention how cool it must be to work for a company deemed one of the BEST places to work by "Fortune Magazine." And to be honest, it is pretty darn cool, but better yet, it's really comforting to know that you're part of something bigger than just another "corporation." Here at Zappos, we're not just some nameless, faceless employees who are measured merely by their dollar output. We're each seen as true individuals and we're encouraged to flourish and grow to our full potential. I would have to say that out of all the fun perks of working here, the one I cherish the most is the avenues and tools we are all given to grow and learn.

JACKIE M.
employee since 2007

Whenever I mention Zappos to anyone, they instantly say "Wow, that's a really great place to work." I am fortunate and really proud to work here. I view Zappos as more than just a 9-to-5 job. Never in my wildest dreams did I ever think I would end up in Las Vegas, but I'm glad that I did. I ended up at Zappos and built relationships that will last a lifetime along the way. It's been an awesome three years and I can't wait to see what the future holds.

JAMES M.
employee since 2008

Thanks be to the Zappos Culture for allowing me to have a place to work where I can be myself and enjoy every day. I am able to show up, do my thing, then go home and have a happy life.

JASON C.
employee since 2007

There are tours of the Zappos office every day for people wanting to see what it is like here. Many of the people who tour comment how they would love to work here. A few say they don't know how any work ever gets done; it looks like everyone is having too much fun here.

I think that is one of the things that makes our culture special. Everyone comes to work each day wanting to work hard and do a great job, while still being able to have fun. That's because of the great environment that we have and the people we work with. Because Zappos is such a diverse company and allows each individual to express his or her own unique personality, you truly feel as if you have the opportunity to show who you are and what you can bring to the company.

JASON M.
employee since 2008

Dear Zappos,

I'm rad.
You're rad.
Let's hug!

Love,
Jason M.

JAY D.
employee since 2007

What does the Zappos Culture mean to me? It's whatever I make of it! Whether that's creating a fun, carefree environment for me and my peers or reps — so that they too can experience what a fantastic place this is — or acknowledging my fellow co-workers as I pass them in the halls. Sometimes I feel guilty for calling it work, because it's more of than just a job for me, it's become more of a livelihood. I've grown accustomed to extending this train of thought to places outside of work as well. For me, my interpretation of Zappos' culture is gaining and earning the respect of others while remaining humble throughout. And in this day age, how often can we admit that whatever we've learned in the job place is easily applied outside of it? Zappos has truly been an inspirational place for me!

JAY D.
employee since 2007

What does the Zappos Culture mean to me? It's whatever I make of it! Whether that's creating a fun, carefree environment for me and my peers or reps — so that they too can experience what a fantastic place this is — or acknowledging my fellow co-workers as I pass them in the halls. Sometimes I feel guilty for calling it work, because it's more of than just a job for me, it's become more of a livelihood. I've grown accustomed to extending this train of thought to places outside of work as well. For me, my interpretation of Zappos' culture is gaining and earning the respect of others while remaining humble throughout. And in this day age, how often can we admit that whatever we've learned in the job place is easily applied outside of it? Zappos has truly been an inspirational place for me!

JENNIE W.
employee since 2009

The Zappos culture had an impact on me before I had even stepped into the lobby as an official employee. I applied for the Content department three times before I was finally hired, always believing that I would one day be a Zapponian. I even used the word "destiny" in my last interview!

I first saw a job opening on Craig's List almost two years ago and wanted to find out everything about the company. I read every article I could find on the internet, but the most helpful material was on our own Zappos.com site. The blogs showed me not just a workplace but also a community, and that community looked — and later on, felt — inviting, exciting, and thriving! I wasn't particularly fussed about what my actual job would be; I just knew I had to be in this building in some capacity. My husband asked me if I thought I had found my dream job, and I had difficulty answering that question because I don't think of my work and involvement with Zappos as a "job."

I have found my dream "environment." Zappos Culture creates an environment where I can work, learn, laugh, play, and grow. I had previously been a high school English teacher for seven years, and the classroom, full of young people, can actually be a very isolating place. One's four walls can feel limiting and exclusive. The gratification and fulfillment I receive through interacting with talented, thoughtful, and engaging colleagues effectively remove the "walls" that typical work environments create.

Zappos Culture means never having to troll Craig's List for a job again. :)

JENNIFER H.
employee since 2003

Zappos Culture means family, friends and teamwork pulling together to make this company the best it can be. Wherever I go, I'm always comparing our culture to everyone else's. Looking back, in all the years I have been here, seeing all the changes along the way, the one thing that has remained the same is our culture.

'The goal is greater than the struggle.' We are a T.E.A.M (Together Each Achieves More).

JESSICA L.
employee since 2006

The Zappos Culture is all about Customer Service and WOWING others. Whether it's someone on your team, someone in Kentucky or a customer, it's about thinking "How can I make their day a little better?" It's about doing the right thing because it's the right thing to do. It's people genuinely wanting to do better each day, both personally and professionally.

Other companies may say they have a culture, but it's a matter of whether or not the culture is alive and breathing or if it's stagnant and dead. Here at Zappos, it's evident that the culture is alive and you can see it multiple times a day. It's up to each one of us to keep it alive and spread it around to others. It's always exciting, always new and always growing. No two days are the same around here. It's all about "work hard, play hard." Through parades, petting zoos, vendor parties and head-shaving contests, I like the fact that upper management has a sense of humor and likes to have fun.

JOANNA C.
employee since 2008

The Zappos Culture is what makes me scissor kick out of bed every morning. I spent most of my life feeling like a pinball, just bouncing around from one job to the next with no real direction or goal. When I came to Zappos, I felt as though I had found my home. I started at the Help Desk and was fully immersed in our culture! What an amazing opportunity!

My dream has always been to write for a living. By coming to Zappos, I am living my dream. I get to write content for cute shoes! I'm also part of an amazing team of people that I have learned so much from, and who have helped me to achieve my goals. I could not have planned this better; in fact, if I had tried to plan this, it wouldn't have worked out.

My background in the service industry gave me the foundation that I needed to come rock out in the Zappos world. This is my home. And I truly hope that this is the last company I ever work for!

JOE S.
employee since 2006

I have been with Zappos.com for four years now and I can honestly say that this is the best job I have ever had. The culture that has developed really makes a difference. Every department works to make sure everyone is happy and if they are not, the find a way to make then happy.

It can be something as simple as bringing in some cookies for the team, or something as big as a team outing to the local skating rink. It all adds up and just makes it a pleasure to come to work.

I am so excited to see what the future is going to bring to Zappos. With our growth expected to triple over the next few years, it will be awesome to see how our culture grows with it. Thanks!

JOHN F.
employee since 2004

Zappos Culture means never having to work within "the box." That box, which inflicts rules upon us, wipes us clean of ideas. This same box makes you loathe coming to work. It is this very same box that makes you look back on your life and realize you've gotten nowhere but older.

This "box" doesn't exist at Zappos. Ideas free flow at Zappos. Creativity has a place at Zappos. Trying new things is the norm at Zappos. There are so many ideas, thoughts and energies at Zappos you couldn't build a box big enough and strong enough to contain them. So, if you have a box, I would say throw it away — but that would be reckless. Recycle your box, visit Zappos and see a world without "the box."

JONATHAN B.
employee since 2006

The Zappos Culture, to me, means having faith in what they say and what they do. Zappos has grown so much in the past few years; it's amazing to look back and see the changes from where I originally started here to the position I am in today. It also means being thankful and realizing that I work for a truly great, generous and caring company. Zappos follows through with what they say and goes the extra mile with their employees — something that, for my part, is truly appreciated.

JONATHAN H.
employee since 2007

Zappos is magic. Where else can so many employees from all different backgrounds come together to work hard, play hard, and have fun doing it? The Zappos Culture creates a workplace that is fun, challenging, exciting, fast-paced, and makes me feel appreciated. I enjoy coming to work every day. I have a career I love and am surrounded by unique and interesting co-workers who always blow me away with their creativity and helpfulness.

The culture makes you feel like you are part of a family. I love the way Zappos does business. Communication is open and honest. Employees can be themselves, dress the way they like and decorate their desks. We have poetry readings, parades, karaoke, and tea parties, fashion shows, and many other fun and exciting things. What's not to love?

JORDAN S.
employee since 2008

I have learned so much since I have been at Zappos. I work with some amazing people, who are extremely good at what they do. And every day, I come in with an open mind, hoping to learn something from them. I feel like I've really grown up since I've been here. This place has challenged me, both personally and professionally, and continues to do so every day

JOSHUA P.
employee since 2005

WOW! I have made it through five years in the warehouse. I look back and say to myself, "What an exciting journey!" I have learned a lot and also taught a lot (so it seems) through ideas and thoughts. I thank everyone that has come into my life through my working here, not only the ones here in the KY Warehouse but also those that I have chatted with at the LV Call Center. We solely depend on the men and women that come to work every day to give WOW to our customers. Working behind the scenes and on the front line at the warehouse has brought out the best of me through the great Zappos Culture we share amongst ourselves. So, while they all sleep and to those that are watching, let's keep giving the WOW that we deliver on a daily basis.

KENNETH L.
employee since 2007

I've described a lot of different things in my time at Zappos. I've written about shoes, hats, handbags, sunglasses, snowboards, insoles, and even a fancy couture boot or two. Yet even after writing about all that stuff, I find it hard to describe our culture. It's just such an integral part of the Zappos experience that finding the words to do it justice is no easy task. The atmosphere, the like-minded people, the overall sense of community... well, that's best experienced firsthand. So let's just keep it simple: The culture here at Zappos is awesome. I couldn't imagine working here without it.

KEVIN M.
employee since 2006

This year I would like to take this opportunity to thank everyone in the Content Department for all their hard work and dedication. It has been another great journey and I couldn't have enjoyed it without this awesome group of individuals. Looking back on the changes that transpired this year, I can say that it took a lot of hard work and the positive attitudes of so many to get to where we are today.

It has been a blessing to work with so many incredible people here at Zappos. I can't say enough about this group. They are my co-workers, my friends, and most of all my family. Every single one of you rock in my book and I look forward to what 2010 will bring!

KRISTA A.
employee since 2007

Zappos is a genuine company, which surrounds itself with genuine people. I love coming to work, I haven't dreaded the drive into the office since I have worked here (which is almost three years). We have an amazing team in Direct Marketing and everyone contributes and works as hard as the next person. I think if I won the lottery I'd still be driving in every morning, just to see my co-workers and see what's for lunch!

KRISTOPHER K.
employee since 2006

What separates Zappos from every other company? You actually WANT to go above and beyond.

KYLE S.
employee since 2007

You know how when you're around a group of people and you think you should be mindful of what you say, not that it would be inappropriate, but rather, that your view and opinions would be judged or scrutinized? Well, this does not reign true in Zappos Culture. Our employees are diverse and compelling people that have a chance to be individuals in the workplace while maintaining common goals, truly a rarity in any organization.

LACY G.
employee since 2007

The Zappos Culture, to me, is simply the small things. Conversations with co-workers, snacks, volunteer opportunities. Knowing that there is a warehouse full of people to call your family. Speaking freely and being asked my opinion in surveys.

Knowing that this is the last place I want to work.

LAURIE W.
employee since 2005

Two days after I write this will be my fifth anniversary at Zappos. This will be my longest relationship ever. ;)

I feel more than lucky to have been with such an amazing family for so long. Working with Zappos has changed the way I see everything.

LIANNA S.
employee since 2010

OK, so I am really new — I'm the new UX person for 6pm.com. I've been here since January 19, but started CLT this past Monday. I was actually standing three feet away from you at the All Hands meeting but you looked busy so I didn't say hello. But I will do so the next time I get the chance.

My first taste of Zappos Culture, actually, was during my interview. Zappos flew me in from Atlanta for a day and I proceeded to meet with about 20 people in eight hours. I'm sure if it were at any other company, I would have run away screaming. Instead, I was so enamored with the environment here, I was pumped full of adrenaline all the way through my red-eye flight back to Atlanta.

Not gonna lie. I felt pretty special — not only did I meet with all these people, they all came to lunch, spent time with me and got to know me (I think one question asked was "Can you drink??") And I wasn't even hired yet! At my old company I never had lunch with my boss, EVER... it was like this unspoken caste system. In the three weeks since I've been here, I've been to my boss's house, seen my boss's boss at Steel Panther, been on a boat cruise (booze cruise) with the whole Tech team, played poker with the entire 6pm team, and had lunch with almost every member of both the UX and 6pm.com teams. To be honest, the shots are a bit much for me, but when in Rome...

The best thing, to me, however, is something very simple that I think a lot of people take for granted. The fact that I can wear JEANS and HATS every day. You have no idea how much that opens up your wardrobe.

Thanks for this awesome new thing.

LINDA H.
employee since 2005

Zappos is like my second family. It's my home away from home! I enjoy coming to work every day and this is because of the family atmosphere.

LISA M.
employee since 2007

There is so much to say about Zappos. Honestly, I could go on and on about how amazing this place is and how glad I am to work here. But I feel I would never find the right words. The Zappos Culture is why we continue to be so amazing and why we continue to amaze our customers and each other. If our culture didn't exist we wouldn't have made it as far as we have.

I strive to embody the Core Values, but I am not perfect. Our culture is so solid because of all of us that strive for that perfection. I am truly glad I found Zappos when I did and I am glad to still be here. Here is to the future, wherever it leads us.

LYNN E.
employee since 2005

I have been with Zappos now for five years. It just keeps getting better and better. The Ten Core Values are great guidelines to follow to become part of the culture that is Zappos. If you can incorporate them into your daily routine, you will have become a fellow Zapponian. The culture here is like no other I have experienced. It gives everyone common goals to work toward to become one big, happy family. I am proud to say that I work for Zappos and that the culture here has become a way of life for me.

MAGDALENA M.
employee since 2008

Coming to work is more than just clocking in and clocking out for the sake of a paycheck. Your co-workers are your friends and a second family. You feel so taken care of that it inspires you to give back and then some. You are constantly reminded of how fortunate you are to work for such a unique and special company. At the end of the day when your feet and back hurt it makes everything okay...you have contributed to a cause that truly understands the importance of taking care of your fellow man.

MATT B.
employee since 1999

"Amazing, unpredictable opportunities for personal and professional growth." This is how I would sum up what the Zappos Culture means to me.

Don't get me wrong — I really love and appreciate all of the day-to-day perks of working here that contribute to our culture. The overall relaxed, fun work environment is one enormous benefit. The sense of community, the vast library, the free food and, of course, the parties are some of the other countless benefits I try not to take for granted. But were it not for the frequent and unpredictable opportunities to learn and grow on the job, to take on a new responsibility, to learn from my co-workers, to be exposed to the various workshops, speakers and personalities made available to us each and every day, the Zappos Culture would not be nearly as impactful on my life.

Since I have worked here most of my adult life, these experiences have played a huge role in molding me into the person I am today. I feel unbelievably lucky to have been a part of all the growth opportunities the Zappos Culture has afforded me, and will no doubt continue to offer me.

MATTHEW S.
employee since 2009

I knew this was the place for me when my manager's primary consideration, when figuring out where to mount the new LCD TV for monitoring data, was not to disrupt the trajectory of our office football games.

Unreal. And SO awesome.

MATTHEW W.
employee since 2006

I usually write a half a page but I will limit myself to a few sentences this time. The friends and new acquaintances I've made at this company have become as important to me as doing a good job in work. I hope to hang on to that should I ever leave the company. I hope I am here for a long time to come, and I hope Zappos continues its appreciation of its fine employees.

MANON B.
employee since 2009

I <3 Zappos! Here's why...

I've been employed at Zappos for just shy of a year now. Before working here, I was dealing with one of the toughest struggles in my life, losing my dad. That process alone revealed to me things I didn't even know about myself at the time. It became clear to me that on the heels of something very painful and life-changing, I would have to join a company that not only allowed me to be exactly and authentically who I was, but also encouraged positive growth and forward movement. I knew of Zappos long before working here. In fact, my dad was one of my biggest cheerleaders when it came to attempting to pursue employment here. Since my time with Zappos, I have not only come to embrace a more positive outlook on life and its future possibilities, but I have found myself doing the most peculiar thing... something I hadn't seen myself, nor many around me do in quite a long time... smiling at work. It sounds like such a little thing, but it is actually prodigious in scope and effect. We don't all have the same job title here at Zappos; we don't all do the same tasks or go about them the same way; we may not even all agree with each other on the way things are done all the time; we are not (yet) a perfect utopia. But what are we? We're a group of people, vastly different and bizarrely similar in one way: we care about how what we do affects those around us, both internal and external customers alike. And we strive to make the effects we have on others uniquely positive. I am a better person for having worked here. There is no company I'd rather be a part of... and the way I see it, part of my continued pursuit of everyday joy includes that fact remaining a constant far into my future.

MELISSA L.
employee since 2008

The Zappos Culture is unlike anything else. It's incredible how Zappos managed to put together a culture so unique, so outgoing and so friendly that people not only want to come to work each day, but work is a big part of their social lives. Like it or not, at Zappos, you're family — like unicorns and nNarwhals. Yeah, I said it. Unicorns and nNarwhals are part of the same family., I have proof.

MICHAEL F.
employee since 2010

As a newbie who's been here at Zappos for less than five weeks, I have merely scratched the surface of the Zappos Culture. At first glance, it might seem overwhelming to many. I am not the most outgoing person and I was worried the extrovert nature of Zappos Culture would be overwhelming for me; surprisingly, It has not been that way at all. Participation in the "extracurricular activities" is optional and there is room and respect for all temperaments. I have never felt pressured or uncomfortable in my time here. I believe it is that freedom and open mindedness that keeps the people here smiling as much as they do!

MICHAEL J.
employee since 2007

On March 22, 2010, I will have been at Zappos for three years. So many changes have happened. The Outlets where I started are no longer there. The one in Kentucky is wonderful, but it was time for me to move to what I love to do. And now I am doing what I love to do, style clothing!!! I have accomplished a dream of mine. I get to style Vivienne Westwood apparel. I have very few fashion designers I look up to. She is one I look to for a fashion forward, avant-garde look. Now I get to style her apparel. I love every moment of being a Junior Stylist for Zappos.

MICHELE K.
employee since 2008

The Zappos Culture is very special. I have worked in many jobs in the past and nothing even compares to Zappos. Zappos culture is unique; everyone is encouraged to be themselves. One thing I think is very special here is that each of us has a voice that can be heard. We believe that good ideas can come from anyone. For instance, when we needed to make things more efficient in an area, we get feedback from anyone who wanted to share his or her ideas on how to make it more efficient. Most companies only allow the top head of command to make decisions and no one else has any input. To be able to have a voice and to be heard gives me a great feeling and boosts my sense of self-worth.

I feel very blessed and fortunate to work for such an amazing company. Like I said before there is no place that compares to Zappos. We work hard and play hard!!!! We have unbelievable benefits. The benefits seem endless sometimes. One of my favorite memorable benefits was the Employee Appreciation Day. It was a surprise to almost all the employees. The employees had two hours to play and I do mean PLAY!!! We even got paid for it!!! We had obstacle courses, shoe lace relay, a Zollar tent, a potato sack race, awesome catered food and so much more. The great thing about it was that all the managers and supervisors worked the areas for the employees. I worked in the Zollar tent, which was awesome. The TMs work so hard and it was great that we got to work for our TM's so they could have a great time. I love that we create many different fun activities that brings us all together as a team and family. I tell my friends and family about my job here and they all say the same thing: "I want to work there!!!" I believe our Ten Core Values is what makes us such a unique company. Zappos WOWs me every day!!!

MICHELLE T.
employee since 2007

Camaraderie... Luv... Family... Comforting... Understanding... Inspiration... Effervescent.

MIRANDA W.
employee since 2005

The culture at "6 p.m." is absolutely unique. Who would have thought two rows of completely different personalities would mesh so well together? Being on the team for seven or eight months now, I have come to the conclusion that this team is what I really call my family. Not only could I approach each individual about work, I know that if I ever needed them outside of work they would be asking me "Who, what, when, where, why, and how."

I'm excited and anxious to see where we can take this business with a team full of such passionate and determined individuals

NAJUM A.
employee since 2009

The Zappos Culture means a lot to me. When I first came here, I really didn't know what to expect. The next thing I know, people are talking about the culture left and right. It didn't take me long to figure out exactly what they meant about Zappos having an amazing culture. This company is not like any other I ever have known. This is the first place I have ever been where it is okay to have fun while you are at work! I feel that this is a huge part of our culture! I have worked at places where it started off fun, but in no time I was bored out of my mind and found myself planning to quit. Since starting at Zappos, I have not once even thought about leaving. I come to work every day and love every minute of it!

NAOMI M.
employee since 2004

WOW! It's been six years already. Time goes so fast when you love your job! I am so glad that I work for a company that can use the quote, "Work hard, play hard," because all the fun stuff we get to do is extra motivation that keeps me in the right mindset to say "I love my job." And you always know that if you step it up at times that we are busy, you will soon be rewarded with a fun trip to the forest, the movies, or possibly a longer lunch break to go eat with other co-workers.

I also love the fact that, whether you are a manager, supervisor, or team member, you feel like everyone is equal … so if you have something to talk about, you feel comfortable going to the necessary person to get things off your mind.

And I still love the great benefits. Thanks to everyone that makes this happen.

NAOMI S.
employee since 2008

We are so lucky to work for a company like Zappos where we can be who we are. It's relaxing to know you can go to work and just be yourself. Just being able to wear what I want is great. I always hated wearing the same uniform day in and day out at my last job. It's nice to meet all sorts of different people. Just wanting to say thanks to all who make this happen!

NATASHA S.
employee since 2007

Zappos Culture.
What does this mean to me? Hmm …

C – Cat

U – Unicycle

L – Love

T – Touch Screen

U – U R Amazing

R – Arachnophobia

E –Tender loving Care

I know none of this makes sense, but that's what I was going for.

Zappos encourages you to be yourself. No matter how weird you are; and that's how I intend to stay. This company wouldn't be so bright and vibrant without all of our Crazy personalities. So Thank you for being you, and Thanks for letting us be us! «+3

NATE L.
employee since 2008

Most institutions frown upon goofy, quirky personalities. A few merely tolerate it. Zappos embraces and cultivates it.

NED F.
employee since 2001

The Zappos culture to me means coming to work in my favorite pair of Chaco mandals, grabbing some popcorn as I walk through the lobby, coming to my desk and turning on the NPR, getting motivated by my daily Chuck Norris inspirational message (today I found out that Chuck Norris has the ability to tickle himself), interacting with other like-minded Zapponians, working on projects and coordinating with other people in achieving our daily goals for the Department, watching Aaron M. put pico de gallo in his morning oatmeal (now, that's weird!), saying "Hi" to the tours coming around the office, bringing back a rubios mahi mahi burrito back to the office for lunch, going home and doing it all over again the next day. The culture at Suite 100, 2280 Corporate Circle is part office/zoo/circus/science lab, and it's all ours and nobody else's!

NICK P.
employee since 2006

Lately I've been thinking a lot about the company culture here at Zappos. I've had a few very bad customer service experiences at other companies in the past months and every time it's happened, one thought has popped into my head. Why? Why would these companies treat their customers this way? Our company culture and our attitude toward our customers have become so engrained in me it's like an involuntary reflex at this point. I simply assume every company will do the right thing in any given situation with their customers because that's what WE do. When it doesn't happen I'm just shocked and confused. It really drives the point home that what we're doing here is truly a good thing and goes beyond just running a business, we're treating people they way they should be treated.

PATRICE C.
employee since 2008

Within the Zappos family there are so many different personalities and styles, which is exactly what makes our culture unique. I love the open display of creativity and individuality because you actually get to know real people at work.

PHILIP S.
employee since 2006

Our Zappos Culture is the one thing that separates us from the rest. It embraces who you are and encourages you to be yourself. Everyone who works at Zappos contributes a little of themselves into our culture and makes Zappos what it is; the greatest place to work. While other companies try to mold you into their ideal employee, our family molds Zappos into what it is today. I'm proud to be a part of such a unique culture and hope I can contribute more of myself in the future.

RAFAEL M.
employee since 2008

As I am about to finish my second year at Zappos and I can only say that I am in a great place in my life, in the very broad sense of the word "place." This town is a fun town to live in; I like the house that my wife and I rent, but above all, the place where I work is great!

Zappos Culture generates a creative environment that allows you to grow as much as you want to. Once you are in, there seems to be very few limitations to accomplish what you want from for yourself and your team. What else can you ask from a job?

RAINA A.
employee since 2007

Zappos is a fun place to work! It's all about the people here at Zappos. Without each and every unique individual, our office would be pretty boring and drab. I think we all make work a less daunting task, and turn it into a positive and fun environment. I like being excited about coming to work in the morning. That is something that I've never felt at any of the other places I've worked for. My team also makes me feel right at home. We're like a make-shift family of fun and weird hard working people, and I love it! The camaraderie on the 6pm team is absolutely amazing!

Thanks :)

ROBERT A.
employee since 2005

Change. The word conjures up numerous meanings: moving away from the status quo, shaking things up, happiness and sadness, etc.

Change is never easy, yet it is integral to life itself. Every day, we grow and learn based on our environment and experiences. We make mistakes and learn what not to do next time. We celebrate achievements and successes, and encourage others to raise the bar higher. However, as mentioned earlier, sometimes it's not as easy as we think. We wonder how this will benefit us (both the collective and individual). What's going to happen? Why can't things remain as they are?

What most people don't realize is that change happens, and it will always happen, regardless of whether it's celebrated or denounced. All we can do is be the best that we can be with our jobs, families, relationships, etc., and move forward to the future one step at a time.

ROBERT A.
employee since 2007

Zappos Culture is an environment where everyone can be themselves, enjoy their work and grow as a person. It's amazing to see an office filled with people working hard as well as having fun. When visiting Zappos, it's like visiting another planet! Everyday you'll see people smiling, laughing, saying hello, and welcoming guests.

ROBERT B.
employee since 2010

I just started working for the company a couple of weeks ago, but I can already tell I'll be here for a long time! I didn't know a corporation that cared this much about its work force existed in America. The benefits, the people, the entire environment is unlike any other place I have worked. It's like I'm waiting for the catch, but the truth is there is no catch. Zappos is a great place to work!

SAMANTHA S.
employee since 2009

I came to Zappos at a low time for me personally. There were not a lot of jobs in my field of choice and I had experienced two layoffs in two years. I was very skeptical about working in a call center, but decided to give it a try since I had heard so many good things about Zappos. The Zappos Culture is unlike that of any other company I have worked at before. This is a company where I truly feel that I can be myself and let my individuality shine through. Zappos employees are truly from every walk of life and every day we take time to create fun and a little weirdness.

This is one of the few companies I've worked for where I wanted to be weird and let my crazy side shine through. At my previous jobs, the employees just threw on a fake smile and "played the game," so to speak. At Zappos I can truly say everyone seems genuinely happy to be here and wants to thrive and grow personally and professionally. I laugh hard at work every day, even when I may not be in the best mood, because the happiness and laughter are so contagious. My life has improved significantly since working here.

SARA M.
employee since 2008

Zappos culture means being able to come to work as myself and not as a separate work persona. It opens up communication by allowing real language and not risking the loss of meaning by subjecting it to a corporate translation.

SARA W.
employee since 2010

I have always hated interviews. And by hate, I mean HATE. I feel completely uncomfortable, my mind goes blank, and my personality disappears. It's a curse. However, the second I sat down with my future manager and co-workers at Zappos, I knew this was the place I needed to be. I felt completely at ease with everyone and the wacky, off-the-wall questions just made me more relaxed. I didn't feel uncomfortable or unprepared, and I was able to just be myself. When Zappos came back and said they thought I would fit in too, I knew it was meant to be! From the minute I started, I felt like part of the team, without first-day-of-school jitters or getting-to-know-you awkwardness. It seems like I have known everyone for a lot longer than three weeks. Even as a newbie, I am loving Zappos!!!

SEAN C.
employee since 2007

Zappos is my second home where I just happen to work.

SHARON I.
employee since 2007

Zappos continually WOWs me. I feel very lucky to be a part of the Zappos Culture. The employees are the most helpful, caring people I have ever worked around. Management goes over and above to make sure the work environment continues to reflect the core values. We are encouraged to take classes and read books to promote growth and learning. Zappos has many great benefits and programs to help their employees in many areas, both professional and personal. I do not mind going to work, which is a great feeling. Thanks for being such a great company.

SONNET T.
employee since 2010

A ZONNET BY SONNET

For years I worked in frustration,
Hauling gear in the snow and rain.
There's not much fun at a news station —
It's enough to drive one insane.

To Zappos I came — they're much more humane.
With health care, lunches, candy, and snacks,
It's such a change — I couldn't complain.
I'll cash in my Zollars to buy some backpacks.

I feel like I can relax
My co-workers are jolly,
not looking to stab backs.
Zappos friends make time for folly.

I've only been here for a few weeks,
but I'm sure liking these freaks and geeks.

STACEY E.
employee since 2007

Recently, our User Experience Director asked our team to share the top three things that really get us excited to come into work each day. It was a great exercise in simply stopping for a moment and reflecting on the past year. With that said, I thought it would be fun to share mine with the world.

My top-three-most-excitable-Zappos-work-related-things are:

#1– I have a very strong feeling of being challenged in different capacities, almost daily.

#2 – It doesn't come often, but I work hard for the days when I feel really great about my work at Zappos. They are well worth the personal celebration that evening.

#3 – I truly enjoy learning from my Zappos peers on a nearly second-by-second basis (side note: this is not an exaggeration).

STACY E.
employee since 2009

I started working here at Zappos just about three months ago.

I came from beautiful Colorado Springs, Colorado. When I moved I didn't quite know what to expect from Kentucky. All of my family, my husband and even my cats are still at home in Colorado. I thought I would feel lost or alone in my new home here. Quite the opposite. I have a family here at Zappos. Everyone has treated me so well and been open to all my weirdness! I love that we are a team and look after one another. I love that there isn't that thing hanging around this place... you know the thing... the "I really don't want to do that; I will just let the next shift take care of it." No, that isn't allowed here. We look after one another because we are our own work family. After all, we do spend more time here than we do at home. It's amazing I am a Zapponian and proud of it! I miss my family at home but I am so happy I have my Zappos family here.

Zappos truly lives up to its work hard/play hard soul. When we are working, we are working hard!! And when we are playing... Well, you get the idea! Thanks for listening to my little piece of this Zappos Culture.

I love my work family and I am proud to work for a company that the road rises up behind.

Wooooooooo hooooooooooo!!!

STEPHANIE H.
employee since 2006

So, what does the Zappos Culture mean to me? Well, it means that I have an actual name and not just an employee number like so many other places I have worked. I get to work with family and not just co-workers. I love the fact that Zappos encourages me to be myself and they like me for it. That is probably why I enjoy coming into work everyday!

STEPHANIE S.
employee since 2005

Zappos Culture means equal opportunity for everyone. I have worked here for five years and I can honesty say, I have never felt discriminated against, as I have felt in previous jobs. If you have a goal, everyone here is willing to help you achieve it. Zappos also offers us a variety of classes, both personal and professional. I feel Zappos has made me a better person.

STEVEN T.
employee since 2006

It's been a good three and a half years for me so far here at Zappos. I never thought that I would end up working at such an amazing place. The culture here is phenomenal, the benefits are outstanding, and the people here are one of a kind. I could never trade in my time here at Zappos for anything, as it has been and will continue to be an awesome experience. Thanks for everything!

TARA J.
employee since 2007

Zappos Culture = family. I'm an East Coast transplant and I miss my home and family very much. My team at Zappos has become my second family and that means more to me than anything. I know that everyone here truly cares about me and what goes on in my life, and that makes being away from my real family that much easier.

THOMAS C.
employee since 2009

Zappos offered me my first job after graduating from college. I spent months applying all around the country in a crushing loop of applications and rejections. I was desperate for work and was willing to take any position, whatever form it came in, so a call center really didn't seem so bad compared to some of the other places that I was trying. As hungry for a job as I was, I never expected to find a new family of people that I care for and who could bring me to tears with their generosity and genuinely given friendship. I value my diploma for graduating from Zappos training as much as I value my college degree, if not more so.

TIFFANY G.
employee since 2008

The Zappos Culture stems from the relationships that are built here on a daily basis. It's taking a coworker out for a drink when he or she has had a bad day. It's getting things accomplished while having a good time. It's perpetrating a funny email chain. It's saying "Hi," to someone in the hallways. It's the 20 or more hugs I get every day. It's all these tiny little connections that build and grow on themselves. Before you know it, these amazing relationships manifest. It's kind of cool, actually.

TIM S.
employee since 2009

Working at Zappos is not a job, it is a culture. Putting all employees through a four-week training class, regardless of pay or job title, really reinforces the fact that everyone here is on the same team. After only being here a couple of months, it is pretty cool to see how people are encouraged to start something they are passionate about, whether it be a parade or a big project that impacts their job. I look forward to getting to know more people and living more of the Zappos Culture.

TOM E.
employee since 2009

On a daily basis, I'm reminded of the one-of-a-kind culture exhibited at Zappos. However, it's not until I travel and talk to other professionals outside of the Zappos world that I truly realize how rare and special our culture is. I feel privileged to be part of this happy family and look forward to our continued success!

TRACY P.
employee since 2007

Zappos Culture means happiness, fun and family to me. I'm closer to my work family than most of my family at home. My Zappos family helps me through all my problems and gives me shoulders to cry on. They care of me as if I were their family too. We have fun together outside of work as well as at work. I love my job and my friends. I always want to be at Zappos and enjoy the culture we have built.

VANESSA S.
employee since 2005

I knew from my first day at Zappos that I was in for the ride of my life. It was AMAZING to realize that I was finally a part of a company that put so much back into their employees. With so many opportunities available to me, I knew that Zappos is where I wanted to be. Zappos is the Johnny Depp of companies, the elusive unicorn, the epitome of endless possibilities.

Through the friends I've made, the friends I've lost, the people that have come and gone, I know that Zappos is "it" for me. It's the company that people talk about, that I brag about, the place that has given me so many opportunities that one couldn't even fathom elsewhere. Most importantly, it is the place that helped me grow into the person that I am today.

To me, Zappos is more than just a job. It's a home away from home. Every time I step through the front doors, I know I'll be greeted with countless smiles, open arms, and plentiful laughs. I don't tell people that I work every day. I tell them I'm living my life doing what I love.

VICTOR O.
employee since 2008

Zappos Culture, to me, is about creating an atmosphere to work in that revolves around family and acceptance. Something that has amazed me ever since I started working here is the diversity within my department. People come not only from different places and backgrounds, but also they have very different personalities and views. Although there are so many differences among us, there has always been an atmosphere of acceptance and appreciation for each other. I have never worked anywhere else where individuality has been embraced and encouraged to the degree that Zappos does.

ZELIA K.
employee since 2007

I'm very grateful to have a good job and work with wonderful people. They truly are my family. There are times when we disagree but I always know that I can depend on them. I appreciate my boss, Tony, he's done a great job at making this place a great place to work.

Zelia K.

COMMUNICATION   WEIRDNESS   DELIVER

RELATIONSHIP

ADVENTUROUS   SERVICE

HUMBLE

DETERMINED   FAM

EMBRACE

OPEN-MINDED   PASSIONATE

OPEN   DRIVE

FUN   POSITIVE

LY   HONEST   CREATE

GROWTH   CHANGE

LEARNING   SPIRIT   TEAM

WOW

AMELIA S.
employee since 2009

For this entry, I was asked to write what Zappos Culture means to me. "Culture" is one of those problematic terms that refers to many things, both tangible (the shirts, the smiles, and the parades) and the intangible (the feeling of not hating my job, the benefits, and the personal empowerment). When you walk into our building, you see the culture, and you breathe the culture. It is intoxicating. I have my bad days like everyone else. But, more often than not, I am in a contented mood and I am smiling for no other reason than that it feels right. And I think this is the best part of our culture: I know that I belong here because everything feels so natural and comfortable. I just can't imagine being anywhere else.

DONAVON R.
employee since 2007

Three years ago I was beginning my career with Zappos. Honestly, I can't believe that I am still here. Getting on the Zappos Train was a short-term solution to a problem; I had recently been laid off and I needed a job to pay the bills. I really had no intentions of staying here long-term. My recruiter actually noticed this during the interview process and called me out on it. "We want to offer you the position but we don't think you want the job" is what he said to me. My reply: "I really don't want it." So why did I take the job? What's probably more important is, why did they invite me into the family?

I was drawn to Zappos' focus on Core Values! I knew that I was going to be stretched and challenged in ways that I had never been before. I knew that I would learn lessons that I needed to learn and that I would truly grow in my time here. To say that I have done so would be a disgustingly HUGE overstatement on my part. I am not the same person I was three years ago, and for that I am extremely grateful to the leadership here at Zappos.

I now have a better understanding of business and the way that business should be done. I have a better grasp of what leadership is all about and the importance of that role in today's society. More importantly, I have learned who I am. I have been encouraged and challenged to break out of my shell and go after my full potential! I am not there yet but I am on my way, more and more every day.

To think that the very element that drew me into Zappos is the very element that I am sharing with other companies and businesses is mind-blowing and humbling! I can't believe that I have been given the opportunity to help other companies become centered on their core values in order to create an environment that impacts their employees the way that I have been impacted by Zappos.

JONATHAN W.
employee since 2008

Wow. That's really all I can say to sum up the past two years. I came to Zappos (like many others, I believe) because I needed a job with benefits.

For months after training (in early 2008) I was waiting for the veil to be lifted, to see the reality of this new job and new (to me) company. It was never lifted. It had never been there in the first place. The past two years, I have learned that a company can be completely open and honest and you can really make lasting friendships with coworkers. I am not very good with names, but I know many, many names here at Zappos. I loved the Zappos experience so much that I pretty much made my wife apply. I have seen her grow in the last year, so that's just another great thing about Zappos, with growth and learning being encouraged, people can really step outside of the box and surprise themselves and others. We are one big supportive family here.

As a Culture Guide with Zappos Insights, I now have the distinct honor of showing the culture off on a daily basis. People are hungry for change, and many don't believe that there is hope for their situation. I love seeing people who start a tour with folded arms and stern faces turn 180 degrees by the end of the tour. Many of the most excited and enthusiastic visitors are the ones who were sent by their companies to see what we are doing, but had not really thought that it was really possible. I have the challenge of keeping my presentation humble, which is the hardest value all-around. I think that the daily reminder for me is going past Tony's desk, a cube that is the same size as anyone else's, and is right in the middle of everything downstairs. To watch someone who has really accomplished something big act like just one of the gang (which isn't even an act, it's really who he is!), without an inflated sense of self, now that is the perfect example.

I hope that on the Insights team, I can make a difference for people in their day-to-day work lives. I get to inspire and assist in making work a better place for everyone, how cool is that? Gotta go, we're plenty busy "Making 'fun' of work!"

MATTHEW W.
employee since 2007

I have been with the Zappos family for three years and it still feels like my first day at work. The people here are just so infectious... you can't help but to be happy when you step into those front doors (Thanks Rosalind!). I look forward to making more friendships and enjoying another great year with this wonderful family here at Zappos.

MIGUEL P.
employee since 2008

The Zappos Culture is fast and we do what it takes to make an idea come alive or get the job done. We work smart and know how to celebrate. Many times there are unknowns or no processes in place because were playing with new technology, but we figure things out and build it as we grow, fine-tune it along the way, and always try our best to make things better. Through our experience, we learn how to "embrace and drive change."

In our work environment, employees are empowered to make things happen. Everyone is a contributor. In the early days, our company focus was to provide the best selection of shoes. Then we evolved to providing the best customer service, and now we are on a mission to deliver happiness.

In order for Zappos to evolve over the last decade, many of us have been driven and continued to make the experience better for our customers. This has all happened because we learn how to deal with change and embrace it openly.

PAM C.
employee since 2006

Okay, what do I say that I didn't say last year, or the year before that or the year before that?

I've been with Zappos for three years now and it has been an amazing adventure every year! I started with the Merchandising team and I'm now with Zappos Insights, a team that didn't exist until a little over a year ago. What does that tell you? Progression? Growth? It can mean a lot of things. To me, it means that I am lucky to be with a company that nurtures us to grow in any way possible and to be part of something big that we can't take for granted.

As you read this Culture Book, I ask you to do one thing. Keep an open mind and see the possibilities. Look at your life now and look at how it can be in the future with a culture that motivates you and your employees to be happy.

It's all about happiness (and great customer service) at Zappos. And the main ingredient to that is the culture — where we are "Constantly Using Leadership To Uplift Remarkable Employees".

ROBERT R.
employee since 2009

Zappos Culture is simply the art and science of creating a world we want to live in.

I remember when I first read the Culture Book ... Abbie M. talked about how happy her mother was that she had a family here in Zappos. Abbie then wrote, "I find myself not taking off my work badge until I'm home, because I want to make sure it's known – just in case I stop anywhere – that I work for the best company in the world!"

Ever since reading that, I've known that I wanted to wear the Zappos badge.

Since then, both my personal and professional life have taken off. I'm accomplishing in months what I thought would take years. The culture is so focused on service and on people that by simply being here I have felt myself become a better person, worker, boyfriend, son, brother and friend. And I feel passionate about sharing what a values-based culture can do for every company in the world.

Hallo

ween Golf

mixing a couple traditions never hurt anyone

and for the record, wearing
a helmet improves your score
by an average of three strokes

JOY JOY

HAPPY HAPPY

ZOLIDAYS

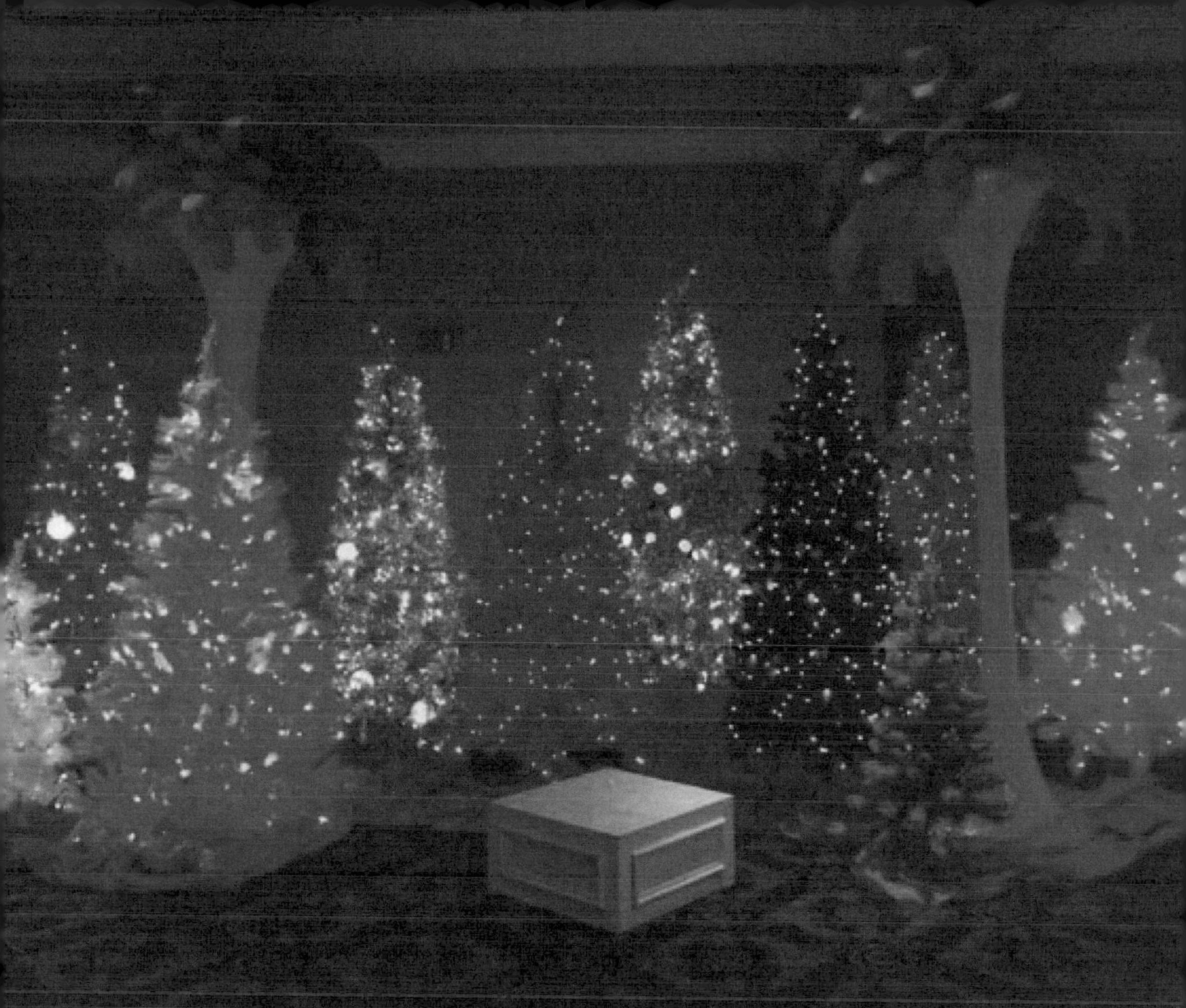

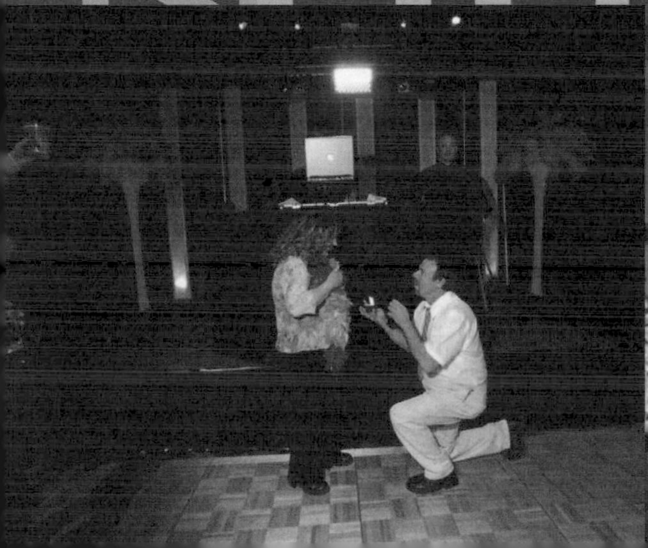

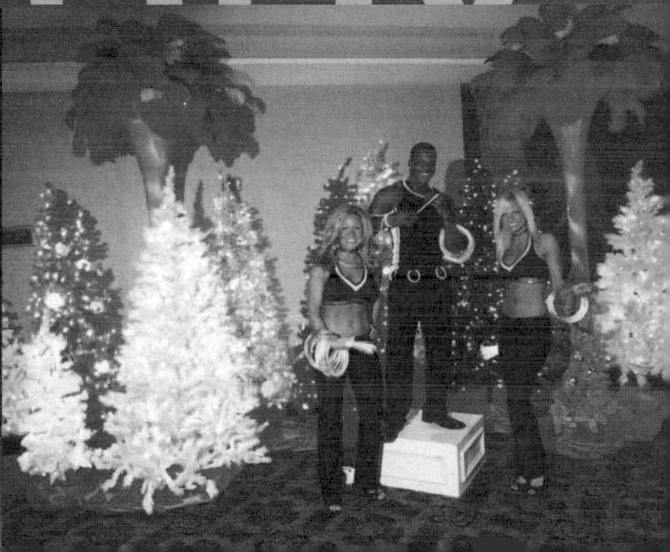

LIVESTRONG DAY

LIVESTRONG

Proceeds Benefit the
Lance Armstrong
Foundation

What is LIVESTRONG Day?

STRONG

LIVESTRONG CHANGING

LIVES EVERY DAY

C

AD

HUM

FAMILY

RELATIONSHIP

DETERMINED

EN-MINDED **WOW**
OPEN FUN
HONEST CREATE
GROWTH SPIRIT CHANGE
ENTUROUS TEAM COMMUNICATION
LE POSITIVE
LEARNING DELIVER SERVICE
EMBRACE
DRIVE WEIRDNESS
PASSIONATE

ASHLEY M.
employee since 2007

A friend recently told me that she thinks of me whenever she sees stories about Zappos ... which is often. She asked me "Did you have any idea that Zappos was this great when you were applying to work there?" That served as yet another reminder of how lucky I was to find Zappos. I have a job that I enjoy at a company I'm proud to work for, working with people that I really like.

HILLARY L.
employee since 2006

The Zappos Culture is knowing that you will be lifted up by your Zappos friends and family when you fall down.

CARON O.
employee since 2007

One of the many things I love about Zappos Culture is that we always take the positive road! We had a lot of big changes this past year... and through it all, we always remained positive! I love that! Somehow Zappos has a way of making something big and scary not so big and scary after all! Thank you!

JASON M.
employee since 2009

Every time I hear the word Zappos I can't help but think of the theme song from The Jeffersons. It's such a cheery tune, which fits our company personality. We are always aiming for "movin' on up..." to the next level of service and the next level of performance. If someone asked me what Zappos' address is, I think I'd reply "The Deluxe apartment in the sky!"

MOXA G.
employee since 2009

The thing I like best about the Zappos Culture is that it allows each of us to be individuals, while still being able to unite us all as one. The most significant thing I have gained from the Zappos Culture is the importance of being passionate about what I am doing no matter how small or insignificant it may seem, as well as the importance of sharing that passion with the people around me.

MICHELLE F.
employee since 2007

The Zappos Culture truly embraces and embodies core value number seven "Build a Positive Team and Family Spirit." It is always so great to experience time and time again instances of your fellow co-workers really feeling more and more like a family. It is always great to know that you have the support of your teammates and that they will so willingly lend a helping hand anytime you may need it. I am truly happy to be able to work with such great people every day. It makes for such a positive work environment where you absolutely enjoy coming into work every single day and being surrounded by true family.

ROWENA D.
employee since 2006

Working at Zappos is a fun career and lifestyle filled with opportunities as big or small as you want to make them. It's like working with a bunch of great friends that support, challenge and care about you.

SARAH Z.
employee since 2009

I am impressed by how Zappos simultaneously builds its employees' work ethic and personal character. Zappos does this by allowing its employees to grow professionally while also encouraging them to utilize their own individual strengths. For instance, I am challenged on a daily basis by the many different responsibilities and projects I take on outside of my normal job description, while my character grows because I am encouraged to think outside the box and find ways to do my job more efficiently and effectively. In sum, Zappos has taught me that keeping your individuality at work is extremely important to finding happiness in a job.

STEPHANIE S.
employee since 2006

The Zappos Culture ... it's fun and silly, you can't compare it to any other company, it has some great benefits, yes, but it's so much more than that. It's a family.

The past year has been one of the most difficult years for me... and I'm not sure I could have made it without Zappos and its culture. I've worked for Zappos for almost four years, and I look back at how it has changed my life and made me a better person. Not many companies would hire someone without any college education, like myself. But Zappos did.

When I had my son, it was another Zappos employee that was with me in the hospital. After I had my son, it was a Zappos employee's mother who stepped in to watch him while I worked. When I need a free babysitter, items for my baby, or someone to rely on, it's always a Zappos employee who helps...

So, from a single mom to all Zappos employees, "Thank you for making Zappos my home!" This culture really is one of a kind.

ADVENTUR

FAMILY   HUMBL
RELATIONSHIP

DETERMINED   EM

DRIVE
WEIRDNESS

CREATE

HONEST

OPEN-MINDED

GROWTH

TEAM

OPEN POSITIVE

US

LEARNING

DELIVER

COMMUNICATION

SERVICE

SPIRIT

FUN

WOW

BRACE CHANGE

PASSIONATE

FREDRICK H.
employee since 2009

Zappos Culture is unlike any other! Going to "work" is fun, enjoyable, yet productive! I leave work tired, often dirty, but fulfilled and happy — an odd combo, heh? It's a relief to walk around and see your work family, laughing, playing and SMILING, all while doing their job of WOWing customers! That is what Zappos is about. We are encouraged to work hard, play hard and I love it! Rock on Zappos!!!

SUE M.
employee since 2008

Our Culture and the Ten Core Values that created it are the touch points for everything we do. We interact with each other, with our customers, and with our communities through the lens of our culture. Unlike other companies, we don't just post these ideas on the wall, we live and breathe them every day. I believe that our complete investment in our culture gives us a unique freedom to create new ways to grow our business and have fun doing it!

WEIRDNESS

HONEST

CREATE

COMMUNICATION

OPEN-MINDED

POSITIVE

OPEN

GROWTH

FUN

VE

VENTUROUS

TEAM

DELIVER

WOW

SPIRIT

RELATIONSHIP

Y

DETERMINED

SERVICE

LEARNING

EMBRACE

CHANGE

HUMBLE

PASSIONATE

ZAP

some of you might've already met our half human, half magical Customer Loyalty Team (CLT) members...the Zappets!

PETS

what you might not know is that they each have twins that also work at Zappos.

meet Giovanna, Abraar, Megan and Lauren (don't worry, we have problems telling them apart too)!

CORPORATE

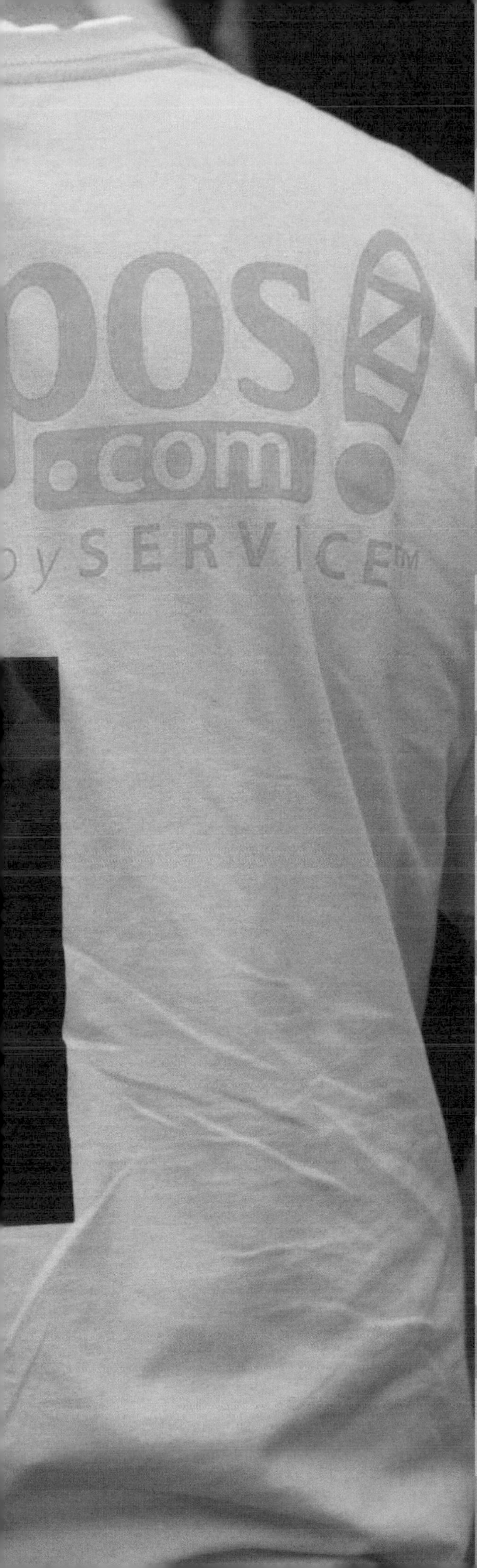

CHALLENGE

what's a Corporate Challenge?

when companies throw down the gauntlet

and compete in grueling physical tests

of eating, drinking and having fun

no, really, that's what it is

HEY
HEY HEY
MONK

WE'RE THE MONKEYS

EY ROW

taking a toss down memory lane...

when Tony used to sell pizzas from his dorm at Harvard

then Alfred would buy a whole and sell them off by the slice at a markup

(which explains why Alfred became the CFO of Zappos)

now that they're no longer college students,

pizza profits went to the LIVESTRONG foundation

PIZZA DAY

HUMBLE CREATE GROWTH ADVENTUROUS HONEST

TEAM OPEN FAMILY SERVICE

WOW SPIRIT

COMMUNICATION OPEN-MINDED EMBRACE DELIVER FUN

RELATIONSHIP DRIVE CHANGE LEARNING WEIRDNESS POSITIVE PASSIONATE DETERMINED

AJAY R.
employee since 2009

The Zappos secret sauce: Work hard, work smart, have fun... Shower. Repeat.

ALEC F.
employee since 2009

It's been just over a year since I moved to the USA from London, and it's coming up on my first-year anniversary at Zappos. Although my family is in Vegas, it was never my plan to stay here; I was figuring I'd look to build my new life in a cosmopolitan city like Seattle or San Francisco. How does one even really do that? It's not so hard to understand — it's that reckless impulse I've followed several times in life to run away and start over. It's seldom that easy. I wasn't totally blind, though. I've worked all kinds of places and done many different jobs. I never learned how to view my job as just a job; it's never about money or title. What seems to matter to me (to my disbenefit more than a few times) is the who and the what. It doesn't make searching for jobs a pleasant thing. Then I found out about this local company with an unusual name, pored through its YouTube and blog videos, laughed with faint bemusement and thought, "Is this place for real?" I saw they had a role that sounded more or less perfect for me and applied. Fast forward to my interview and on my tour I started to see that Zappos is what it claims to be. Halfway through the day, I figured out that this is where I would LOVE to be. I remember asking someone if it was possible to want a job too much? The answer was no. Fast forward a few weeks to my induction class and we're being welcomed to the last job we'll ever have. I'm not a cynical person but I reserved my thoughts on the proposition.

Fast forward to today as I'm writing this. I'm very happy. I've got a great job at a company that is unique, precisely because it has so many wonderful people to work with, many of whom have become my good friends. After a hard few years, I've found a place where I feel I belong, in the last place I would have thought to look. Somewhere that lets me truly be myself. Many things continue to change at Zappos, and every such change implicates and interrogates its culture. One constant I do see is that Zappos gives its employees the ability to explore their personal and professional growth every single day, and for that I feel extremely lucky. This is the why and the where. I still miss home from time to time, but I remember responding that yes, if there was a job that was worth moving 5,000 miles to have, maybe this could be it.

ALEX K.
employee since 2005

From the outside, the Zappos Culture looks like parades, posters, confetti and happy hours. But to me, it's much more than that; it's the mutual respect, the friendships and the smiling faces. Everybody is working towards the same goals with equal effort and focus. We are inspired by each other's creativity and intelligence to continually improve ourselves and those we come into contact with.

ARUN R.
employee since 2009

The Zappos Culture is essentially a set of shared values and beliefs that inform the way we approach life and the many decisions we make on a day-to-day basis. These values truly shape how I think and approach my work, where I don't accept the "standard" or "best practice" solution if it doesn't fit with our values and beliefs. At the core, what's different about our culture is that the shared values and beliefs are genuinely shared and not just the CEO or the executive team's beliefs/values. These shared values and beliefs result in alignment that few companies of this scale can achieve and decisions are rapidly made at any level without the need for top-down mandates. The empowerment, openness, passion and speed of execution that result from our shared values (as opposed to top-down mandates) makes this an incredible place to work. Having been exposed to many companies with varying cultures, I have a deep appreciation for the Zappos Culture and feel privileged to be part of it.

BENJAMIN F.
employee since 2010

Hello, hello, hello. All I can say is WOW, it is great working here. I have only been here for a month and I feel like I am coming home rather than starting something new. The environment and people are so... what's the word?... encompassing... yeah, that's a good one! There is an air of acceptance and comfort here that just lets creativity flow. I love it. I have already been to several company-sponsored events, all of which were great, especially Sean Stephenson, (a great motivational speaker).

Zappos is definitely focused on promoting personal growth and life/work balance and I second, third and fourth that. I am also a firm believer in feeding the mind, body and soul, especially the body (considering I take snack breaks like smokers take smoke breaks) and Zappos is there to support me each step of the way. Zappos and the Ten Core Values here definitely coincide with how I want to live my life. I am lucky we got together. We chose each other!!! (Sniff, sniff!). Thanks to everyone who works here at Zappos and makes Zappos such a great place.

BRANDON M.
employee since 2009

Zappos Culture, to me, means the freedom to grow in all directions... the challenge of learning something new every day... the excitement of meeting new people, and building friendships.

It's an entity that's always there, pushing me to be a better person.

BRIAN C.
employee since 2008

Creative Undertones Lovingly Tended Unto Rewarding Experiences.

BRYCE M.
employee since 2009

I have never met such a great group of friends as I have at Zappos... people I look forward to seeing again, even after the longest of workdays. The Zappos Culture is not brought in by people when they arrive. Instead it is something that we grow into through the influences of the wonderful people here. Every one of us has a part in shaping the culture, but even more than that, the culture shapes us.

CRYSTAL C.
employee since 2008

you: zurl, eagle?
zurl: eagle is http://tinyurl.com/eeeagle

DAVID R.
employee since 2008

The Zappos Culture allows employees the freedom of expression in actions, dress code and personality. At the same time, we work hard and sold over $1 billion in merchandise in 2009!

DEAN C.
employee since 2009

When you think about it, 40-plus hours a week is a big chunk of your life you spend just producing income so you can support yourself and your family. I think today the perception is that those 40-plus hours should be all work and only about the money.

At Zappos, I have come to enjoy my 40-plus hours a week I spend here because it is about so much more than money. Of course we work extremely hard, but we spend each day with people we enjoy being around, laughing at the constant goofiness that ensues.

DENLY J.
employee since 2009

Yikes, this is difficult...

What does it mean to me? Zappos is a company of individuals, not employees. You can have a laugh and be goofy with no one looking at you as if you've lost the plot. It's happy smiley faces, at least most of the time, which is infectious in a good way :). Enjoy!

DYLAN B.
employee since 2008

I've been at Zappos now for a year and a half. My skills as a professional web developer have improved in this company so much you'd think I've been working here for five years. With so much work put in to the culture it really allows information to flow between people. We don't feel pressured to keep our noses down working constantly. Sometimes just discussing programming and theory can do more for the company than trying and failing to accomplish something. I'm excited to keep learning here at Zappos, and to also pass on what I've learned as we continue to grow.

ED L.
employee since 2005

The first time I got excited about Zappos was when I got a call from Recruiting. I was on a trip in the Bay Area with my family when HR called me in for an interview. I was excited mostly because my grandfather was a shoemaker who made and sold shoes as I grew up, so it brought me great excitement to work for "a company who happens to sell shoes." It has been over four years since that day and I wish this journey never ends. It has brought me joy and honor to be part of something like Zappos. Thank you for letting me a part of all this and I wish us much more success for many years to come.

A shoemaker's grandson.

GEOFF B.
employee since 2008

To me, the Zappos Culture is about being open and true to yourself. Whether you are more on the outgoing or quiet side, there's one thing we all share — the utmost respect for our fellow coworkers. Personally, I feel this is one of the reasons why the company keeps such a tight-knit culture.

HINA J.
employee since 2008

One can win admiration and respect from another with a smile and humility. One of the important lessons of life learned from a great company (culture) called "Zappos."

IAN M.
employee since 2008

As a student of politics and history, my understanding of the world's pre-Wilsonian Fourteen Points geo-political climate and the prevalent viewpoints of that era have traditionally influenced my impression of culture.

From what I gather, the idea of culture has shifted greatly over the 90-some-odd years since that time, almost doing a complete turnaround; where there was formerly imposition, there is now a great deal of appropriation. Fortunately, this company has made the conscious decision to categorically reject both of these approaches to culture, opting instead for what one might describe as an isolated, or perhaps contained, organic approach. Although I could not find any historical evidence that supports this cultural system, the recent empirical evidence is quite strong and I feel confident that it will be successful.

JAMIE W.
employee since 2007

For me, the Zappos Culture is all about working hard, but having fun while you're at it.

JEFF N.
employee since 2008

Zappos Culture, to me, is simply that we are what we claim to be. We value our customers, so we treat them like they are something valuable — not just another person. We claim to cherish our employees, so we give trust and freedom that helps them prove they are worthy to be cherished. So many companies make claims to do these things but then fail to deliver when faced with tough times or potential profits. Zappos is not a company that strives to service people, it is a company that is built on servicing people. If Zappos were to stop doing that, it would cease to exist — and that is what our culture means to me.

JEN W.
employee since 2009

Being fairly new to the Zappos Culture and family, I've had the chance to experience what it is that makes Zappos so special. I love that while we work hard, we play hard as well. I love that my co-workers also happen to be my friends. I love that we are encouraged to be ourselves and to never stop learning. I love that I actually have a voice and am able to express my creative ideas freely. I love the freedom and trust that the company bestows upon its employees. I love that I never dread coming into work each day. I'm extremely grateful to be a part of such an amazing company and look forward to seeing what the future holds for Zappos.

JOHN B.

I have only been at Zappos for a short period of time, but even in my brief employment I have already seen and experienced things that I would never have seen at any other place I have ever worked. Here are some for your consideration:

1) A company that really cares about their customers. This is engrained in all we do and all of the decisions we make.

2) A close group of people who are so happy when being around each other that they schedule activities and trips with each other outside of work. These are not sporadic events, they happen many times each week.

3) A work environment where you are encouraged to be yourself at work. As for myself, I am not an overly outgoing, zany, or whacky person. Even though I am not this way, I find it refreshing that people who are this way are allowed to express themselves. This makes the work day fun, exciting, and unpredictable.

JOHN F.
employee since 2007

After being at Zappos for a few years, and having had the opportunity to meet lots of people through tours, conferences, business meetings, parties, etc... it has become very apparent to me that Zappos is truly a unique company. The Culture of Zappos is really, in essence, the heartbeat of the company. People cannot say enough about how inspired, motivated, touched, and just overwhelmed they are after seeing Zappos and our culture. There have been times when this culture was challenged, perhaps by someone trying to achieve more without considering the impact on the culture, and the company has suffered. We have always been able to recover, grow stronger, and learn from these mistakes. As Zappos enters a new era of growth, we will see more and more challenges to the culture. It is up to us, the employees of Zappos, to make sure that we don't let that culture take a back seat, and risk losing what makes our company such an awesome place to us, and everyone else.

JOHN H.
employee since 2008

Zappos is a group of friends that you want to hang out with. You are free to be yourself and live your life. I love working here and look forward to every day.

JOHN P.
employee since 2008

All truth is in the eye of the beholder. Some is commonplace, some is rarely known, but only that which is sought after will guide you.

KEVIN C.
employee since 2008

Zappos is really my home from home. Being here is really like being part of one big happy extended family. We live and breathe for each other, share the successes, take it on the chin collectively when we occasionally fall down and then we all learn together for next time and do it better. Different people, different styles, all coming together and in unison to make this company great — these are the recipe ingredients for Zappos' success. I am just proud to be making my small contribution and be part of the overall family cooking team!

KULWINDER S.
employee since 2009

I love working at Zappos because this place is way different from other companies where I have worked before. Zapponians are the best, always happy and trying to make everyone around them happy. Being here, I have experienced that "Happiness is very contagious." One of the things I like about the Zappos Culture that it lets you be who you are and that contributes greatly in bringing the best out of everybody. There is always something fun and weird going around that helps bond people together. I like the parties and fun activities; they help us break away from work and have some enjoyment. It is a great learning experience and I am happy to be a part of the Zappos family. I like the WOW philosophy and exercise it every chance I get to make people happy and special. The response I always get from people is WOW. My response? "I am proud to work in a Company that delivers "WOW.""

LAUREN A.
employee since 2007

Zappos Culture 2009 in four parts:

One:
Snowboarding/falling down all over Big Bear and walking around the streets in the dark; entering the Matrix; drawing pictures on placemats; wayward nerf warfare; new foods (Dim Sum! Crawfish! Pho! Bi Bim Bap!); hiking through Zion/camping under the stars; banging the crap out of some rock band drums. I can't even begin to think about Zappos Culture without thinking of the incredible people who catapulted my year from moments into memories. Culture begins and ends with them.

Two:
Here is a 2009 playlist made up of nine songs that did not actually come out in 2009:

Orange Juice - Rip it Up
Daft Punk - Face to Face
The Jesus Lizard - Boilermaker
Mirah - The Garden
Uncle Tupelo - The Long Cut
The Flaming Lips - Yoshimi Battles The Pink Robots Pt. 1
Grouper - Heavy Water/I'd Rather Be Sleeping
Suicide - Ghost Rider
SonGodSuns - Minors Into Fire

Three:
Here are two conversations I had at work today:
Co-worker 1: Give me a signal.
Co-worker 1: Like scratching your elbow as we pass in the hall.
Me: I will lick my elbow if he says anything bad.
Co-worker 1: Can you really do that?
Co-worker 1: Congratulations on tricking me into trying to lick my elbow
Me: YES

Co-worker 2: Why would you throw that with your left hand?
Me: Because I'm left-handed?
Co-worker 2: Yeah, whatever.
Co-worker 2: You're left-handed.

Four:
In conclusion: I started working at Zappos over two years ago, and I'm pretty proud of the ways I've grown and changed in that timeframe. But the person I've become contains so much of the Zappos Culture, so much of the people around me, that I can't separate myself from it and I can't imagine who I'd be today without it. So I'm submitting examples from my life this year instead of just telling everyone, because it's really something you need to see for yourself.

LYNN W.
employee since 2008

Zappos lets me be me. I can wear what I like. I can try new things with my job. My team is like family. They are always there when needed. Zappos is wonderful and I love working here!

MARK M.
employee since 2008

Zappos looks pretty crazy from the outside. Parades, outings, donut eating contests, karaoke, etc. Day to day, though, working at Zappos is a lot more like working at a normal company than you might think. The thing that sets Zappos apart is the group of people that work here. Zappos has attracted an amazing group of people who really make work enjoyable. I love all of the fun perks Zappos has to offer, but the part I enjoy most about the job is working with all of these great people.

MATTHEW G.
employee since 2007

The culture at Zappos has united so many talented, smart, quirky, and intuitive people in a Petri dish of sorts. We will either derive the formula necessary to take Zappos to a new level or incubate some sort of hyper-mutating Dev Plague that will end life as we know it... OK, probably both.

MATTHEW R.
employee since 2006

I never know what to write for my culture essay, because so much has already been said and there's nothing I can say that would be original.

So... Zappos is different, in a good way. Interpret that as you will :)

RACHEL M.
employee since 2008

When I think about Zappos Culture, I think about the amazing friends and family I've got here at work. Never have I had such fun at work and even on my worst days, someone always makes me laugh.

RYAN A.
employee since 2007

nerf guns, booze cruise, bowling, pizza, cranium, bagels, (food) by RayMorgan, eff, gasss, pizza, beer, hack-a-thon, punch and pie, clapping for everything, cow bell, fork you, shat, night-shift subs, tipple-phips, parades, poop, 9.9/10, #matrix, burn, big-time burn, indian burn, newburn, flipping the bird, twitter, flickr, pippi, team-building, eeeeeagle, #cweissjokes, chicken dance, pepperoni pizza, triple ess, cj's, hotspots, hot deploys, toilet bowls, lATER pHIL, the lord's chips, luchadores, zamundah, good toast, poo-bios, banned in canada, hhs, ginger bat, creepy, ninjas, dopplegangers, tiger-face, DinaV, scrum, standup, duck butt, nerds, drink, rinse, repeat.

RYAN Q.
employee since 2008

I have high hopes for this year. I think our culture will be put to a real test with everything that's evolving around our business and our goals. I'm surrounded by amazing people, some of the most brilliant and insane professionals I've ever worked with. I'll be making many cookies this year.

ZiP

SEAN M.
employee since 2005

I recall walking into a store at Christmas about 12 years ago where a volunteer for the Salvation Army was standing near the door, ringing his hand bell, as they normally do to attract attention. This volunteer was not just randomly ringing his bell; he was attempting to play "Jingle Bells" on a single monotone bell. If you've never experienced "Jingle Bells" played via a monotone hand bell, I don't recommend adding it to any sort of "Top ten things to do before I die list." It was awful. Absolutely horrible. It made me want to go running head first into the nearby wall just to take away the pain. The bell ringer's accuracy was good. He played perfectly to the rhythm as I would expect to hear Jingle Bells, and each note from the bell was perfectly in tune to the note the bell was designed for. The problem was that there was neither depth nor complexity. His performance really took the passion and cheer out of a song that represents one of the most cheerful songs for the holiday season.

That bell ringer could have had 100 additional volunteers out there with him all playing Jingle Bells in unison on the same pitched bell, but that would not make it any better to listen to. In fact, it would just be a louder version of what one person was doing before. I would have found the experience much more bearable if he were able to find at least one or two more bells with different pitches to swing around. The more bells he could have added, the more enjoyable I likely would have found his performance. With 100 people all playing different bells, I might have sat out in front and listened for a while instead of having a desire to ram my cranium into brick.

Zappos was not even in business when I experienced the monotone Jingle Bells, but I believe it helps describe why the Zappos Culture is so amazing.

There has been a lot of focus in the media on the hiring process at Zappos, including the rigorous interviews and employee training classes, but the culture just starts there. The real culture is created after the hiring and training. It is a result of the company allowing the different voices of Zappos employees to be heard. If all Zappos employees were forced to think and say the same things, we might be technically aligned, but we wouldn't be a very exciting company to work for, and I don't believe our customers would care to connect with us. We would essentially be 1400 employees playing Jingle Bells on 1400 of the exact same bells. Symphonies are engaging, 1400 of the same monotone bells are not.

The Zappos Culture represents the depth and complexity created from the individual personality of each of our employees. It is the passion created by allowing each individual employee to take strides to do the job the best way they can, even if it may be a little different than the person next to them. The Zappos Culture is a symphony of personalities that really cannot be described; it must be experienced.

SHELDON S.
employee since 2007

The top five things I like about the Zappos Culture:

1) Working with great people.

2) Awesome benefits.

3) Getting sloppy drunk with co-workers — no one cares!

4) Company parties are always fun (see #3).

5) We are always improving.

SOTHEAVY O.
employee since 2007

With a new overlord (Amazon), there's a lot more pressure to increase our throughput. Tension is higher, stress levels are increasing, and the longer work hours await, but that hasn't decreased the amount of fun and laughter occurring in the department. From random sound bites blasting in the room to flying foam projectiles, we still know how to have a good time and put a smile on everyone's faces. This alone makes coming to work every day worth it.

STEPHEN H.
employee since 2005

I love our culture. I recently moved from one part of the company to another (as I have done a couple times during my career at Zappos) and find that everyone embraces the Ten Core Values in their own quirky ways, regardless of what they do here, or what building they work in. I was going to write more but I was just hit by a foam dart fired from across the room and must now retaliate.

STEVEN L.
employee since 2009

I've been at Zappos for over six months now, so you think I'd be getting used to it, but it still amazes and (dare I say it?) WOWs me that everyone here is so genuine. You may find molded nerf guns, hard work and wacky fun elsewhere if you're really lucky, but you won't find a better bunch of people or a better culture anywhere.

SUSAN A.
employee since 2007

Wow, it has been almost three years for me now and I can't believe how fast time has gone! I work with such amazing and motivational people. I appreciate that I can consider them not only wonderful co-workers, but also friends outside of the office. Everyone here works very hard and has fun while they are doing it. It is cool to be part of a company that really cares about its employees. Most companies create a mission statement when they start the company, and maybe they update it a few times, but they don't really strive towards a clear and concrete goal. I love that Zappos created the Ten Core Values years back and truly expects employees to work by those values. I am so thankful to have such caring, thoughtful, and entertaining co-workers. There's never a dull moment!

WILLIAM W.
employee since 2007

Our culture is a mosaic that makes up the picture that is Zappos. Each of us is a tile, bringing our own unique tint and color to one part or another. No one tile is a complete picture, only when we step back and take in the company and its culture as a whole can we truly appreciate the concepts we comprise.

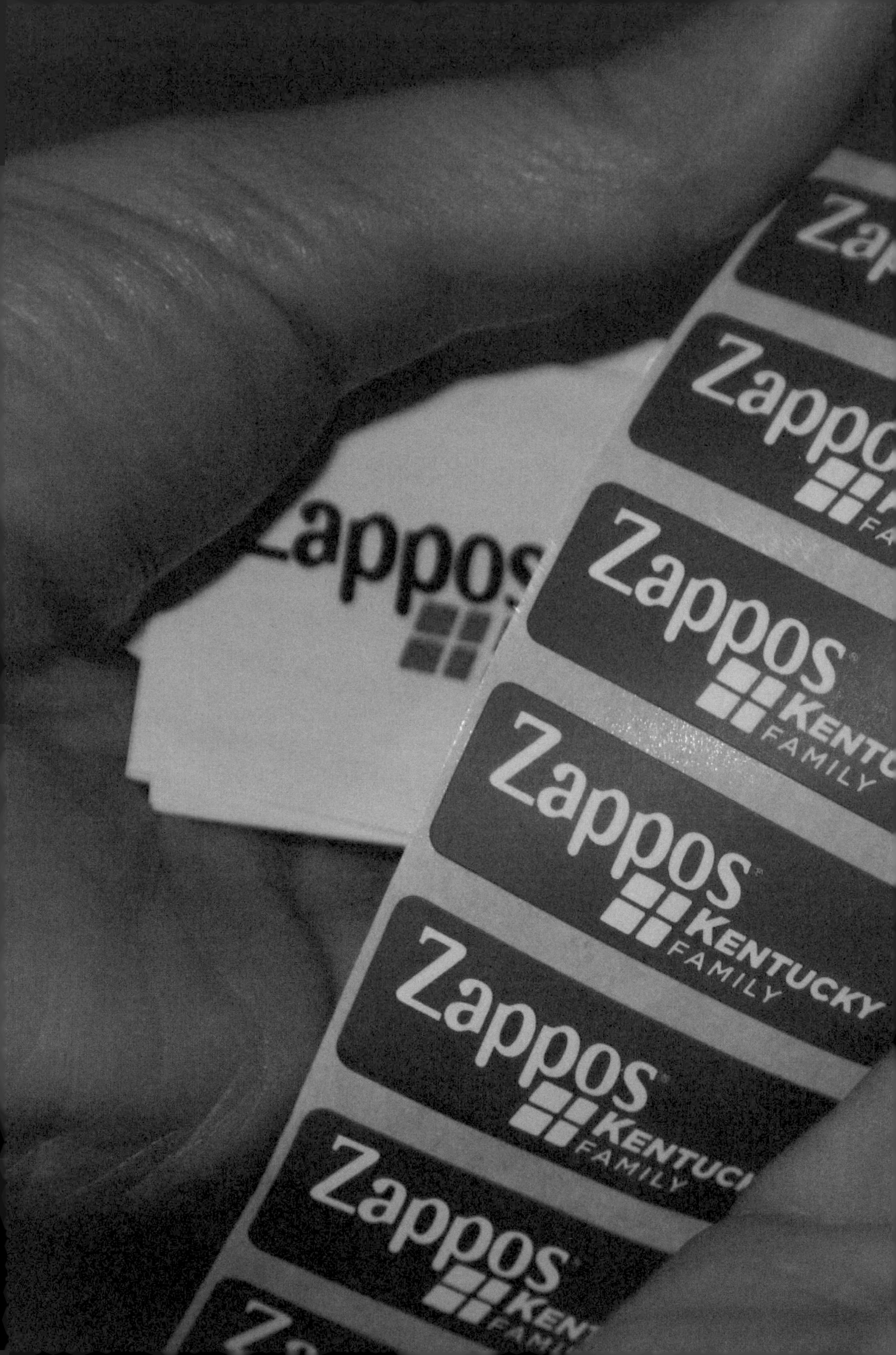
Zappos
Zappos
KENTUCKY
FAMILY

Fulfillment Centers

a shoe lover's dream closet

zappos customers sometimes place
an order one night, find it on their doorstep
the very next morning and ask "how?"

short answer: our fulfillment centers
yes, this is where the magic happens :)

PICNICS

LUAU

KYstyle

Employee APPRECIATION Day

FIESTA!

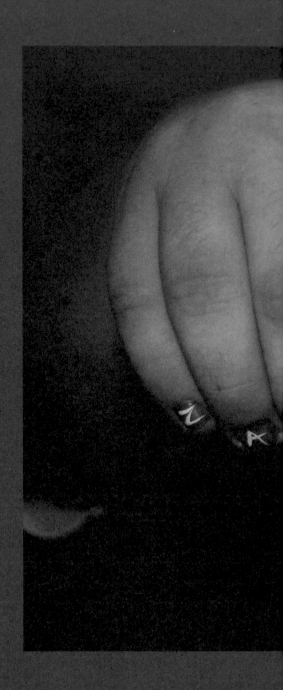

Spirit
KYstyle

SERVICE DETERMINED PA GROWTH

SPIRIT

DELIVER FUN

OPEN

TEAM

WOW

HUMBLE

CREATE FAMILY POSITIVE CHANGE OPEN-MINDED

EMBRACE COMMUNICATION WEIRDNESS LEARNING

DRIVE RELATIONSHIP

IONATE

HONEST

AARON F.
employee since 2007

Before I came to Zappos, I kind of floated along not knowing where my life was headed, bouncing from job to job. I was constantly tardy to work, if I even showed up. I came into Zappos thinking it was going to be just another job, but then I met the love of my life. She had worked here for a while before I started, and she showed me what a great place it could be if I lived the culture. Not only did she better me as an employee, but as a person too. I will always thank her for how she has helped me, and gave me the extra push to advance within the company. It it weren't for the culture at Zappos, I would probably be at another dead-end job today.

AMBER L.
employee since 2003

Zappos has been more than just a job for me. The one thing the sets us apart more than anything else is our culture. I still get weird looks when I tell my family and friends that I have 123 Zappos shirts in my closet, or get served a lunch at no cost to me every single day that I work. Not to mention the other 543 extraordinary benefits that Zappos offers! The atmosphere encourages me to pursue growth and learning outside of my daily work activities and sometimes even pays the cost associated with me doing so. I have dedicated myself to doing what I can to help the company grow and actually feel that Zappos returns the favor. As always... I LOVE MY JOB! Bet you can't count on one hand how many people you know who can say the same (unless they work at Zappos!)

AMBER F.
employee since 2010

The Zappos Culture is different from that of any other company that I have been a part of. It's about being yourself, and a little weird, so that you can be more happy and productive at work. When I wake up in the morning, I don't have an initial dread about going to work, like I had when I worked for other companies. I am excited and happy to go to work at a place like this.

AMY B.
employee since 2009

I love the culture here at Zappos. What company gives so much? Zappos, that's what! Keep it up!

ANDREA "ANDI" P.
employee since 2007

Here are a few of the things I have to remind myself of after three years as a Zapponian:

– In the real world, I can't walk up to a Diet Coke machine and press the button without putting money in.

– In the real world, I have to worry about taking my lunch or having money to buy it.

– In the real world, people don't usually have fun at work.

– In the real world, I used to have to wear business suits and heels every day.

– In the real world, creativity and innovation aren't always welcome.

– In the real world, you sometimes hear "no" more often than "sure, why not?"

– In the real world, titles matter.

– In the real world, my work was just a job and not a passion.

After three years of happiness at work, it's hard to remember that it wasn't always this way for me, and that makes me want to do everything I can to ensure that our culture grows and thrives as much as the company... and that I never rejoin the real world.

ANDREW M.
employee since 2008

Zappos rocks! I'm very fortunate to work at such a great company!

ANGELA H.
employee since 2005

Zappos is unlike any other place where I have worked. The atmosphere is great and the people are even better. I have built some great relationships here. Zappos goes above and beyond to make the team feel appreciated, with so many extra benefits and events… I have worked here for five years and I hope that this is just the beginning!

ANNETTE S.
employee since 2006

Zappos has one of the best cultures around… people here are just like family. We are all a team that works together to accomplish our goals. Everyone works together to WOW our customers, and it works! We embrace all changes and it doesn't affect our work at all, it seems to make us strive harder at what we do. It's amazing that a company so big seems to accomplish so much in such a short time. Everyone is so positive all the time and always happy.

I am proud to be a part of Zappos' big family, it will soon be four years since I started and I hope this will be the last job I ever have. Time sure flies when we enjoy what we do! Thanks, Zappos for coming into my life! WOW! what a ride it has been and continues to be.

ANONYMOUS

The feeling that the Zappos Culture brings kind of sneaks up on you. Many of us come to Zappos as we would similar jobs here in the greater Louisville area. Other than Fords, we don't make many things here in Louisville, but we pack and ship EVERYTHING, thanks to the UPS world headquarters here. At Christmas, I see many of the same faces I worked with years ago as a seasonal/temp hire in other warehouses. I would often work two of those jobs until one laid me off, something better came along, etc. Zappos Culture catches up with you one day when you see your face on Site Manager. It's your anniversary, another year at Zappos! And you are not looking for work. That may sound like a simple observation, but trust me, it is a wonderful feeling. Keep up the great job, Zappos.

ANTHONY V.
employee since 2004

I also wanted to take a second to thank you for asking us to write this. It's a great way to reflect on what the culture at Zappos has taught me over the last year… and this year, I learned a lot!

APRIL H.
employee since 2007

I've had to learn in a roundabout way that the Zappos Culture" is all about caring and sharing! Without our family culture here at the FC, there is only work. We are more about just work. There's a loving culture here, more so then at anywhere else I've ever worked. I think other companies could learn a thing or three from us!

AUDREA H.
employee since 2007

I sometimes smile on the way to work when I see the Zappos logo on our highway marker signs, since I know that's where I'm going for the day! It's fun to know you're going to a place that feels just like your living room at home. It's comforting to have friends and family (some companies call them co-workers) at work. The Zappos Culture, to me, is a FEELING of love and appreciation of me. It's not a "type" of culture that you can categorize. It's more of a feeling/vibe you get just being around everyone here. We are not a cult, we don't have Monday "Kool-Aid" drinking sessions, (lol) (even though people think we do!) I feel appreciated and know my position in the company is as important as Tony's position. Zappos really cares about people and their well-being as humans. I'm Super, Duper, Duper, Lucky to work for Zappos!

BARBARA T.
employee since 2007

I have been at Zappos for over two years. I enjoy my work and people I work with. I am a part-time worker, which works out great for me. Our free lunches are a great bonus.

BERT H.
employee since 2005

The Zappos Culture isn't just Ten Core Values that are written down and not acted upon. It isn't something that comes up when it's convenient and fits an individual's personal agenda. I attribute this to our Executive Team for making our culture a focal point within the organization. Companies that I have worked for in the past have had tunnel vision on efficiencies and the bottom line. They failed to realize the positive correlation between a great company culture and a successful business.

This is absolutely the best place I have worked and it's due to the fact that I enjoy the people I work with. I don't see them just as co-workers. I see them as extended family. With that being said, my favorite Core Value is No. 7 – "Build a positive team and family spirit."

BOBBI K.
employee since 2009

I've been at Zappos only a little over one year. But I absolutely love it, just as I did from day one! This is the only job I've ever had where I don't mind getting up to go to work! It's fun, weird and not too hard! We do a lot of laughing while getting our work done. I would tell everyone and anyone... "This is the best place to work!" I love Zappos!

BRENDA B.
employee since 2008

Well, now it's this time of year to re-examine what Zappos means to me.
Zappos = Family

I never knew how true that that statement was until I ran into an ex-coworker at a Zappos function. Now... usually it would not be that big a deal and I might have said "Hello," and asked a question or two and then passed on my way. However, when I saw this co-worker, I felt like I had seen a family member that I had lost touch with for years and I was SOOOO excited to see him!!

I REALLY feel like the people that I work with here (in the past/present/and future) at Zappos on a daily basis are TRULY family. I KNOW that the people I have met here will be with me always, and what other word can you use for people like that? You guessed it... FAMILY!!

I pity the fool that doesn't have a GREAT day!!

CANDI B.
employee since 2009

I love Zappos for so many reasons. Of course, the free food and health insurance are at the top! I also like how I can come to work and feel like I'm just visiting some friends and we all happen to be working at the same time. Zappos really does great things for the people who work there. You never know what will happen from day to day... there's always something going on to make our "work" day fun and different.

CHRIS K.
employee since 2007

Zappos is the last job I want to have. I love Zappos — it has been very good to me. Zappos, you make today's dreams come true. Woohoo!

CRYSTAL B.
employee since 2005

The Zappos Culture, to me, means, absolutely loving the place where I work. It means I look forward to coming in to work every day, to being around others who enjoy being here, and that I want to make the company as successful as it can possibly be. I like to watch for all the new and upcoming additions to Zappos. I want the customers to be as pleased as possibly possible, just as I am. At Zappos, people can be themselves, relax, have fun, eat good food (free), have great benefits, go to parties, have dress-up days (Fridays are PJ's Day), yet be serious about the work, know what it takes to get the job done and have a successful day. Zappos treats us well and we, in return, help to make others happy. Thank you so much for allowing me to be a part of a wonderful company!!!

DARYL M.
employee since 2007

Zappos is awesome! This is truly the greatest place to work. Our culture here is unique and it has a life all its own. We are all one family working together to get the job done, WOWing our customers and having fun along the way.

DENNIS W.
employee since 2004

The essence of our Zappos Culture is the Ten Core Values. Very simple, yet very powerful. I find our culture and Core Values to be the fundamentals of my life inside and outside of these walls. They are good and honest ways to live and do business. That is what makes it so easy to live and to cultivate. I do at times struggle putting it into words, especially to people that don't work here. Originally, I thought it would be a passing phase we were going through, but that could not be further from the case. The culture here is so very unique and it's still going strong. It's kind of like the "force" in Star Wars. You can't touch it or see it, but it's there. I guess you can see it actually. We have some pretty awesome events and you can see everyone involved thoroughly enjoying it. It's truly a powerful force that keeps us working together, always trying to improve on what we did last week and last year. The willingness of everyone to go above and beyond is in every department that I have dealt with. It's easy for me to pick up the phone and call someone that I've never spoken to and start to build a relationship to get things done. Email is a handy tool, but I'd much rather speak to someone in person than send an email. Our culture makes that very easy. Simply put, it makes "working" easier.
I look forward to 2010 and how we can continue to grow our culture and help our newest partners understand it just a little bit better.
Go Cards!!

DIANE P.
employee since 2007

ZAPPOS CULTURE is...

Believing that we are all products of our environment!?

So we give 110% every day to create an environment that reflects our values.

A simple concept really creating an awesome place to work!

DONNA R.
employee since 2008

I started working at Zappos about two years ago and I have to say it is the best company I have ever worked for. The Ten Core Values that Zappos lives by make it feel like being with friends and family all day. It is the best place to go to every day. Thanks, Zappos.

DONNA W.
employee since 2008

ZAPPOS, DEC. 23RD ANY YEAR:

'Twas the night before Christmas and all through Zappos, not a creature was stirring except a few wackos.

I was in my nighty, Paw in the Raw,
"We want to VTO", but the Boss say "Naw, Naw."
Then up on the conveyor we heard such a clatter,
we raised our heads to see what was the matter.

What to our wondering eyes should appear,
but more damn shoes to pack without any beer.
The leads run around, well "snap, snap," whilst some just want a nap.

Time is near and what do we hear?
"Print and Apply is down!", but have no fear,
maintenance is here.

Soon, things are rolling, the last truck is loading.
We want to get these things out before St. Nick,
so come on, UPS, deliver lickedy split.

The Customer is WOWed and we wear a smile.
We'll get to read, just for awhile.

So on Christmas morning, while opening your gifts, we are proud to know there'll be no tiffs.
From all of us to all of you, here's a big "MERRY CHRISTMAS," and we'll see you again real soon.

This place is the best place to work! WE ALL ROCK! Thanks to "F.A.T."!

EDWARD B.
employee since 2007

I love working at Zappos because of all the great people I work with. Even the leads, and managers are nice and helpful. I like the great benefits, as well as the free lunches, snacks, and sodas. I will have been here for three years in March. Hopefully, I will be here for a long time.

ERIN B.
employee since 2007

Zappos has become my world in the past two and a half years. The people aren't just people anymore, they are my family... my job isn't just a job, it's a way of life. I take the things that Zappos has given me and apply them to my everyday life. The culture, the Ten Core Values, the Zapponian way of life. :) I have always wondered where I would be in my "grown up" years and even though I still don't know the answer to that, it's good to know that I will never fill out another job application!!!! I have found a home here and I hope it will not end anytime soon!!! I love my people, I love my bosses, I LLLOOVVEE the SHOES, all in all I LOVE ZAPPOS!! Thanks for everything!!!!

Till next year... Keep rockin', Zappos :)

p.s. And YES, Rick Dye is still a DIE HARD CARD!!!!!! GO CARDS!!!!

FELIX L.
employee since 2009

Zappos-KY: My weekend and holiday morning haven where I can write code!

GRACE H.
employee since 2007

I feel so fortunate to be working for Zappos. This is by far the best place I have ever worked.

GREG D.
employee since 2008

I've been at Zappos for about two years now, and there is nowhere else I wanna work. I love the people and THE HOLIDAY PARTIES!! (yahhhhhh)

GREGORY P.
employee since 2007

It means even an old guy like me (I'm 61) who is set in his ways can learn to relax and have fun at work and that it just isn't "Come to work, collect a pay check, and go home."

I drive 80 miles from Lexington every day to get here and people ask me why. It's because I'm enjoying what I do. Most don't understand, but in time they will. I'm just thankful I have a job.

HELEN C.
employee since 2009

I am WOWed by Zappos culture, values and mission! I feel that I am a true Zapponian. I have found the place where I belong! My true home away from home. Zappos is my extended FAMILY. A company/family that truly excepts all of our unique differences as people!! Not only is Zappos accepting, they encourage and welcome our differences! I am not all that strange in appearance, until you give me the opportunity to help create P.J. Friday's at the Fulfillment Center. (Nothing bad can happen on P.J. Friday.)

I have made a duct tape outfit, dressed up for Woodstock and created our own dress up days and potlucks to promote company culture within our departments. I Love Zappos! I want to create a new job at Zappos that totally fits my personality and helps me shine as the Culture Creator for the Fulfillment Center! I would love to make a FC Fun Calendar and totally get out there, I want to encourage and create Fun and Weirdness in the FC again!

I am like the Wal-mart greeter of Zappos FC. I love coming into work and being able to be me! I love being friendly to everyone I see and maybe cheer them up along the way! I love our Core Values and all that we stand for as a company. I look forward to coming to work every day to deliver WOW! So, thank you for the great employee appreciation that makes WORKING enjoyable!

I enjoy all of our benefits – the free medical, dental and vision insurance, the short and long term disabilities, the free life and dismemberment insurance, the free lunches and vending machines, the opportunity to be me and be encouraged to do so, the free t-shirts, the Zollar store, and of course, THE BONUS check at the end of the year. I could go on and on! So once again on behalf of me and my children, THANK YOU and God bless!!!

ISAAC S.
employee since 2005

"Become who you are." — Friedrich Nietzsche Zappos gives us the opportunity to be the type of person we are.

JAMIE S.
employee since 2005

Culture is a term that has different meanings. And for Zappos that statement says it all. We have our definition of Culture like nobody else. At our Home away from Home, we all share common values and goals. Everyone contains great practices and caring attitudes. But each and every person makes our culture, all the diversity and friendship. After four Culture Book entries, I feel sometimes I say the same things, but they are things that can't be said enough. People, from top to bottom of the company, made it what it is… my other family… a place where I have the ability to have a conversation with anyone about anything on my mind. What can I say? Zappos is Culture and Culture is Zappos. I need it, I want it and I love it.

JASON H.
employee since 2005

I have only worked here for a short time, but this is one of the best places that I could possibly ask to work… a place where we care about our team members… where the team members come first and the goal for a manager is to make their team time here at work enjoyable. Also, that same great focus and fun we enjoy with our team is also shared with our customers. Everyone in this company has such a drive and focus on taking care of the customer and making sure that they are getting great service. It is great to know that there are companies out there like this one, and I am very fortunate enough to be a part of one. Zappos is the greatest place ever!!!

JENNIFER D.
employee since 2009

Most people are lucky if they can find a job that doesn't suck... a job that they can drag themselves out of bed for and stand to be at for eight hours or more a day without going insane or losing their souls. Well, those of us who work at Zappos are more than lucky. We work for a company that knows how to rock and how to have fun. I am so happy I work at Zappos — this is a job that I want to, can't wait to come into each day. It's a place I want to spend time at, with people I want to be around. I am finally a part of a company that "gets it" — their core values and belief in having fun are more than just lip service. The company lives and breathes its culture everyday. I'm so glad to be here, helping build that culture, and being part of it.

JOANN W.
employee since 2010

In the short time that I have been working at Zappos, I have come to realize the potential of this company and all the people who work here. Our culture is unlike any other company! On a daily basis, I am surrounded by

Zany coworkers who create an

Awesome atmosphere. We love to

Party and are

Powered by our Core Values. There is a lot of

Out of the box thinking which, of course, leads us on the path of

Success!

I love Zappos!

JOSEFINA R.
employee since 2007

Hola me llamo Josie Ramirez.

Yo soy parte de la familia zapponian desde noviembre 2007. Y es una de las mejores cosas que me pudo pasar. Por que es una verdadera familia. No siento que es un trabajo. Espero que Zappos siga creciendo pero su cultura siga igual.

JOSEPH O.
employee since 2008

AWESOME! <--- That's the word of the year, fellas! I have met some great people here and picked up the best group of friends I could ask for along the way. There's never a dull moment and there is always a smile on someone's face. Don't go changin' it!

JOSHUA C.
employee since 2009

The Zappos Culture is the driving force behind the excellent customer service that we strive to provide to our customers. By Zappos showing us, the employees, that we do matter and our roles — no matter what they may be — are vital to the company's success. It makes us want to give 110% because we know we are a part of something bigger. Not only does Zappos provide the best customer service around, it also gives back to the community. I am proud to be a member of the Zappos IT team and look forward to being here for a long time.

JUDITH C.
employee since 2006

I have been at Zappos for four years as of next month and it's by far the best job I have ever had. The benefits are awesome. I am a picker and I love my job! I tell everybody Zappos is a great place to work. I plan to stay here until I retire. Thank you for Zappos!

JULIE E.
employee since 2007

Best place to work at! I love my job and the people I work with; we're more like a family than an employee here. Thank you so much for letting me be a team member at Zappos.

JULIE V.
employee since 2007

SpongeBob SquarePants said it best when he described the word Fun.

F is for friends who do stuff together.

U is for you and me.

N is for anywhere or anytime at all down here in the deep blue sea.

F is for frolic through all the flowers.

U is for ukulele.

N is for nose picking, sharing gum and sand kicking here with my best buddy.

JUSTIN F.
employee since 2010

Zappos Culture to me seems like starting a new life. Other companies I have worked for in the past were always strictly work and that was it, but here, it's different. You still work hard and get the job done, but you also have fun at the same time and that's how it should be. The environment here at Zappos is great and hopefully I will be a part of the team for a long time.

JUSTIN W.
employee since 2007

The Zappos Culture, to me, means accepting all employees' unique traits and qualities and, as a business, infusing those special traits into a team environment to make us unique. This drives exceptional performance, not just from individuals, but from every group. It means that we can all be very different, but collectively focused on the same goal of WOWing internal and external customers. It means setting aside preconceived ideas about how people should look and act and instead focus solely on enjoying the daily adventures, with the end result of being the best customer-focused company in the world.

I humbly submit that we are very good at what we do, because we do it together, all focused on the same goal.

KARI P.
employee since 2009

Seven months ago I decided to venture out and try something new, so I got a job at Zappos. And just recently I decided to embrace and drive change and join our new KY Pipeline team. I keep telling people that coming to Zappos was one of the best decisions I ever made. I really do mean that. I love working here and I love my job. Everything I had heard and read about Zappos really was true. One of my favorite things about working at the KY Fulfillment Center is to see how willing everyone is to help each other out. It's a family spirit for sure! So many people have been willing to help me when I've had questions or have needed to get something done. I can trust people to really be there. And it's a super fun place to work! I mean, where else can you do karaoke, dress up crazy and play games... all while you are at work?! Being a part of this culture has changed the way I view a lot of things. I love Zappos. I really do!

KATIE F.
employee since 2008

Zappos is the best place to work. I love my job!!! How many people do you know that can say "I love my job?!" Zappos rocks my world!!!

KENNETH H.
employee since 2008

When I came to Zappos, I figured it would be like any other job. I was wrong. The benefits and culture of this company has impressed me. Keep doing what you do best (WOW people)!

KENNETH P.
employee since 2008

I have only been with Zappos a short time, but in that time I have come to like the way things have gone. The co-workers I have become friends with are super, the managers are great, it's a different kind of company.

KIMBERLY S.
employee since 2007

Zappos is an awesome place to work!!! I went from being a stay-at-home mom to working here, and everyone has made me feel right at home from the start, just like family! Zappos takes care of its employees… they treat us like family, not just employees. The benefits are GREAT, catered lunches and free vending machines, where else can you get all that? Nowhere! The people here are wonderful! I hope to be working here for a long time!

KRISTIE R.
employee since 2007

It's an honor to work for a company that encourages you to be yourself! I'm very fortunate to have the opportunity to work with such a great HR team. As a group, we are as different as night and day, but we fit together like pieces of a puzzle. I actually enjoy coming to work every day to be with my extended Zappos family. Zappos doesn't just preach the core values and unique culture, we LIVE it… weather we're singing karaoke in the warehouse, decorating cookies, having a pirate themed scavenger hunt, a duck tape clothing contest, to the most extravagant Holiday Party and Summer Picnic. And what a HUGE honor to be named one of the "Best Places to Work in Kentucky" and ranking #15 on the "Fortune 100 Best Places to Work" list! WOW!

KYLE G.
employee since 2006

Zappos is Awesome!! From daily fun and new activities to seasonal parties, this place really knows how to show its employees a good time. Along with providing a fair and balanced working environment, they reward us for things such as hitting over rate, doing something safe or correcting something that maybe a safety hazard… one employee can even reward another for something great they have done. After being here four years, I've seen a lot of things come and go, but one thing still remains the same… the Zappos Culture.

KYLE K.
employee since 2007

It's hard to describe the Zappos environment. It's like a narwhal riding a unicorn — except the narwhal has chain-saw hands and the unicorn has laser eyes, but the unicorn is actually half grizzly bear — and they both ride around on a magic carpet made of bacon and pizza rolls. They spend their days battling evil wizards and their robotic ferret minions. That's how awesome the Zappos Culture is.

KYLE M.
employee since 2008

If you ask me, Zappos is awesome. I've been here for two years and it's honestly the best place I've ever worked. I mean where else are you going to find a job that caters in lunch every day, as if the free insurance isn't enough! When I tell my friends and family about all the fun and exciting things they do for us here, they are always so jealous.

LEANN W.
employee since 2005

Zappos culture is coming to work enjoying what I do and who I do it with. On top of that, we have great benefits. So with that said, I would like to thank everyone that makes this happen.

LEE S.
employee since 2005

What does Zappos Culture mean to me? Well the culture is diverse — very diverse. You might be working and learning Spanish from your other worker next to you. I love how we work as a team towards success, because in here, there is no solo act to follow, only one team. I find this place to be diverse, but close enough for a farmer and a city slicker to work side by side to get the job done.

MARY D.
employee since 2008

I have worked at Zappos for two years; this job is my second family! I love everything from HR to my team members. We all have a special bond, working side-by-side everyday. I hope Zappos is my last job; I am 50 this year and just love it. Is not just a job. I love coming in every day because something good is always happening. Zappos really does care for their employees and when you have a problem you can go and talk to anyone. We WOW people every day, but Zappos WOWs us too. I worked at Earthgrains in Georgia, for 13 years and they did not have a culture, all about numbers and products going out the door. Thanks for this opportunity.

MARY J.
employee since 2007

Zappos is truly the best place I have ever worked. There's free food, great benefits, terrific parties and the chance to work for — and with — pleasant people.

And our culture provides us with an extra ... job security. When other employers are floundering, Zappos flourishes! Thanks to everyone at Zappos for providing the WOW factor.

MATTHEW D.
employee since 2009

The Zappos Culture is an overall experience that no other organization that I have ever worked for has even come close to offering! The environment and atmosphere — created when a company values its employees to the extent that Zappos does, is truly incredible! Here's to another year of WOW!

MATTHEW G.
employee since 2009

Zappos, Zappos, ZAPPOS!!!! What a time I have had here, and so many more good times to come. I am constantly confused when I think of what this company does for its employees. There is no better place to work and I don't see anything getting the upper hand on happiness. May we strive and grow for years to come.

MATTHEW M.
employee since 2010

I'm in my first year at Zappos. This is by far the best job I have ever had. I have never been at a job where all the people are in good moods day after day. I plan on many more years and great times at Zappos. Some of my best memories at Zappos are from KIVA, working for the best manager and lead. They make it so easy to come into work every day. Also, all the Kentucky and Louisville fans, together at lunch watching the basketball games on the big screen... Kentucky winning and Louisville losing. GO CATS!!! Zappos is moving up the charts every year on the top 100 best places to work in the United States of America, and honestly, I really don't see why it isn't #1.

MICHAEL D.
employee since 2007

Zappos has been a good place to work. Though the work can sometimes be tiring and the days long when you are on overtime, the day can still be nice because of the people I work with here. My coworkers are friendly and fun to work with most of the time. Plus you have to like the many benefits we have here. To me, the good benefits and good fellow employees equals a good job to have… so I am happy to be here !

NOAH J.
employee since 2009

When I think about Zappos Culture, I think of a workplace where people are striving to improve themselves and those around them, not just in their work, but in their lives as well. It's a place where fun at work is viewed positively, where people wonder what's going on if you're not smiling, and where no one is satisfied with being just good enough. I haven't been here long, but I look forward to growing with Zappos and all the great people who work here.

NORRIS S.
employee since 2008

I began working at Zappos two years ago. There always seems to be something going on to make you enjoy working here, whether it be the holiday party after New Year's, the zoo, parking, or an event right here. All the benefits, food and beverages could make you look back at your last job and say, "Wow — Zappos is the best." I never ever had a better job. I can't help but be thankful that I work for a company that cares so much about me.

NOUR E.
employee since 2005

I have been part of the Zappos family for more than five years now. I have found a home here and I enjoy coming to work every day. Working for a company that adopts the philosophy of fun and weirdness and lets you be yourself is astonishing. I have witnessed Zappos growing and getting bigger, yet its main goal remains the same: to keep the Zappos Culture alive.

Thank you, Zappos!

PAM D.
employee since 2007

Hello, my name is Pam and I am a Zapponian! This has been the best job for me. I work part-time, come in at 9:00 a.m., work for two hours, go to lunch, work another two and a half hours, and go home. We have free vending machines, free lunches, T-shirts, and parties. What's not to love? All this, plus awesome team members and team leaders to work with. On top of all this, we get a huge discount!!!! Yippeeeeee!

PATRICK B.
employee since 2009

Zappos Culture is a thing of beauty. It's a melting pot of people wrapped up in a little green and purple dotted bow. The culture is what defines Zappos. It's about service, pride, weirdness, and WOW.

REATHA M.
employee since 2007

I have been with Zappos for two and a half years. It has been a very busy, sometimes hectic, but interesting time. It is amazing, though, when I stop and think of all the people who have come and gone, whose paths have crossed mine and, I believe, left an essence of themselves behind. Zappos is all about culture, and the people are one aspect of the culture that makes up Zappos. It has truly been a blessing and a privilege to work for Zappos.

RITA W.
employee since 2007

I would like to thank everyone who has helped me. I really like my job. I like working with everyone and appreciate the opportunity to meet and work with different people. It is really a nice place to work. I like the people and enjoy working with them. Thanks again.

ROXANNE Z.
employee since 2005

Zappos has a very unique culture. From my experience, after working here for five years, I don't think any company can come close to having the same culture as we do at Zappos. I can never have enough of the parades, tours and the fun events here that each department throws. The fun never gets old. I believe these events are what set Zappos Culture aside and make it different from the others.

SANDRA S.
employee since 2005

Changes, Changes, Changes, are always going on at Zappos. Some are great and others are not, but when you're happy at your job, it's hard to like all changes. I have been doing the same thing for pretty much five years. My friends and I are glad to have such good jobs. Zappos, thanks for all you do for your employees.

SARA BETH B.
employee since 2010

Culture: shared beliefs and values of group: the beliefs, customs, practices, and social behavior of a particular nation or people.

Zappos Culture: essence of all Zapponians; lifestyle of caring for others, sharing joy, inspiring the world, and wearing great shoes; giving back to all and savoring everything. Fun, excitement, wackiness, and goodness all wrapped up in one.

SARAH J.
employee since 2005

Today is going to be a great day! How can I be so sure? I just walked through the doors at Zappos. It is a pure joy to be able to work somewhere that you feel good about. I have never once avoided the question "So where do you work?" I raise my head high and proudly announce "At Zappos!" Then I try to contain my smile when people not only know what Zappos is but gush about how much they love it. I hope that I never have to work anywhere else!

SHEILA J.
employee since 2007

About two and half years ago I worked in THE worst warehouse ever. It was dark, smelly and the people were just in a bad mood all the time. You could tell that I was not the only one who hated that job. Then a friend told me about this great place to work called Zappos and told me to go fill out an application. Two days later I had an interview and was hired. Little did I know that this would be the greatest job I've ever had. Instantly I felt welcome. The people are so great here, just like a family. I feel very lucky and tell everyone I can about this place and how well we all are taken care of. NO job I have ever heard of gives employees the things that we get here. FREE food, FREE vending, AWESOME insurance, just to name a few. BUT the greatest thing is the LIFELONG friendships I have been so lucky to have found. THANK YOU ZAPPOS.

WITH LOVE and GRATITUDE

STEFANIE W.
employee since 2008

You might think that after two years, the novelty of working at Zappos would have worn off. Not even close! It's so much more than a job. I used to correct people that said they "loved their jobs." You can't love an inanimate object, right? You like a job, not love it. I'm eating those words now. I love the work, the people, the Ten Core Values, the Culture and, most of all, the opportunities! It means so much to me that I can pretty much create my own path. My bosses are very supportive and encourage me to take it to the next level. Our culture is unparalleled and I LOVE it!!

STEPHANIE S.
employee since 2007

Zappos is more than just a job. It's a family. I know that most people don't understand what we all mean when we say this, but I'd really like to take the time to explain it a little bit. Before I had this job, I was a very unhappy person. I bounced around from job to job and was dealing with personal struggles in my home life. The day I started here is the day everything began to change. I found myself surrounded by people who were not just co-workers, but friends that became my family. They helped me through some really tough times and without them I don't know where I would be. I have spent the last three years here because of these people. I cannot see my life without Zappos and am excited to see what the years to come will bring us all!

STEVE T.
employee since 2004

Zappos Culture is a way of life for me and my family. This includes the people I work with. I consider them my family also.

What more can I say!!!!!!!!!!!!!!!!!!!!!!! Zappos ROCKS !!!!!!!!!!!!!!!!!!!!!!!!!!!!!!!!!!!

SUSAN W.
employee since 2006

What does the Zappos Culture mean to me? WOW, that is a hard answer to sum up! I have been here just over three years and never could have imagined how much Zappos would become a part of my life. I mean, I have worked at some great places in the past, but never at a place that really impacted me. When I first started I heard people talking about "living" the culture and I would more than willingly participate in events, dress up, parade around being goofy but just didn't get what it meant to begin with. After about nine months, I noticed that I talked about what I did at Zappos a lot, pretty much in every conversation I had in and outside of work. Now, at the three-year mark, Zappos is fully blended into my life. Some of my best friends are at Zappos, my fondest and funniest memories come from Zappos and this is my home away from home. You get a ton of support in everything you do from deciding to run your first 5k to changing career paths. You are viewed as a valuable person at Zappos and people truly care about your happiness. What more could you ask for?

TEANN B.
employee since 2009

Even though I was just officially hired as a Zappos employee, I've been here since May 2008. Since then, I have to come to learn what being part of the Zappos family is all about. It is a lot of hard work, but we have fun doing it. There's always a surprise about your day and you never know what's next. You can be your own person here and not have to worry about anyone judging you. And of course, all the FREE stuff we get is pretty awesome as well!!!!!! I love being part of this weird and crazy family. It makes coming to work worthwhile.

TIFFANY S.
employee since 2006

I have worked at Zappos for almost four years now and I have to say it's the best company I have ever worked for. Any time I need anything, someone is always there, for a hand or just someone to talk to and understand where I am coming from. Without Zappos I don't know what I would do — they pay for my lunch and medical bills. Thank you Zappos for everything you have done for me.

TRAVIS R.
employee since 2008

What does the Zappos Culture mean to me? Well, it means coming in every day and enjoying what I do for a living. I have been here almost two years and have truly enjoyed every single day. I would say that very few people in the world could truly say this without owning their own company.

VANESSA D.
employee since 2007

I'm honored and thank my Lord for allowing me to work at such an awesome place — Zappos!!! It is so amazing how this company keeps selling thousands of products, and we still HEAR "WOW" from thousands of customers all over the USA!!! I enjoy reading customers' comments on our website; they inspire and encourage me, and acknowledge that my work is worthy and beneficial! Also, Zappos has taught me a lot and changed my actions, thoughts and words. The hard work is what has had the most impact on me. I didn't realize that hard work would teach me to be patient, think positive and control my attitude. I appreciate their respect and the fact that they let me do anything... my deafness doesn't matter. That is what Zappos Culture all about!!! :o)

YORDANKA C.
employee since 2006

HOLA, my name is Yordanka! Everybody knows me at Zappos because I'm a Cuban girl with a Russian's name. :) I feel so great working in this company. I have been here for the last three years, and I think this company is AMAZING! Especially because they give us the opportunity of "superation" with the amazing classes to improve ourselves. Besides that, my daughter, Angelina, wants to come to Zappos every day; she is a Zapponian and a PARTY fan. She said "Mama, I love my family and I love Zappos too!!!"

10

TEN YEAR

ANNIVERSARY
PARTY

Stanley the Giraffe
reflecting on life
and making new friends

2010

Vendor Party

climbing WALLS

AERIAL

acrobats

just the standard faire
at Zappos' annual
vendor party...

TAG
you're it

ADVENTU

RELA

COMMUNIC

WE

PAS

PARTNERS

DRIVE   TEAM

FUN   CREATE   POSITIVE

CHANGE   SERVICE

OUS

NSHIP   WOW   OPEN

ON   SPIRIT

NESS   GROWTH

LEARNING   OPEN-MINDED

NATE   DELIVER   HONEST   EMBRACE

DETERMINED   FAMILY

HUMBLE

PARTNERS

ALEX T.
UPS

As I enter my eighth year as your UPS representative, the Zappos Culture now means Delivering Happiness to Vendors as well as Employees and Customers. Tony has always touted culture as the number one priority because if you get that right, everything else will naturally fall into place. First, your company's unique, great culture delivers happy employees. I have seen many of my client companies' cultures but only Zappos empowers employees to deliver WOW through service. They are happy and enthusiastic; it shows with every internal and external customer interaction, during work and off-work hours.

Working at Zappos is more than just a job; it is a way of life — as validated by Fortune when it named Zappos one of the "100 Best Companies to Work For." There are not too many companies that acknowledge and appreciate the importance of a positive vendor relationship. You have done many things (for example, vendor appreciation parties) to cultivate it. Over these wonderful years, Zappos has treated me like a member of the family and I appreciate the culture. Based on my interactions with your other vendors, they all share this feeling. Working with Zappos is definitely a privilege and honor. As the physical and metaphoric conduit between you and your customers, UPS will continue to creatively provide the best service, so we can collectively WOW and deliver happiness one customer at a time.

When you have a dynamic culture that fosters happy employees and vendors working collaboratively together, you will deliver happiness to customers. Happy customers will (and they do) tell their friends, families, and business associates about their positive Zappos experiences, through word of mouth, Twitter, and other social media outlets., This leads to more business and brand growth. So, everything does naturally fall into place when you get the culture right.
Zappos got the culture right!

ANNA M.
LifeCare, Inc.

I've only been working with Zappos for a few months and I'm surprised at the impression the Zappos Culture has made on me in such a short time. It has been a great experience, as your model of "WOW" now has me pursuing that same value within my organization as we look to provide excellent customer service at every opportunity – both internally with my colleagues and externally with clients and their employees. I've been WOWed. Your sense of fun helped me realize there is more than one way to get something done and why shouldn't the journey be just as fun as reaching the destination? I can't wait to experience more!

AYELET & STEVE L.
Yaleet, Inc.

It is not often that we find another company whose culture and focus aligns so well with ours. Yaleet Inc., distributors of Naot Footwear, and Zappos come together in a unique meeting of two dynamic companies. We see a synergy of cultures between the "Yaleet experience" and the "Zappos experience." Both companies set high standards for themselves and consider themselves a "family." Zappos has become an extension of the Yaleet family. At Yaleet our employees are encouraged to share their knowledge, break barriers, and step beyond the ordinary. Every Zappos employee that we have ever come in contact with has shared this vision. Both companies share an unfailing commitment to integrity and make customer service a very high priority, while thriving in an atmosphere of trust and good humor. It is only when we walk into a Zappos' office that we may be surrounded by a parade of people singing or attacked by Nerf™ balls and laughter!

BILL A.
Earth Footwear

When working with Zappos, it is hard not to be a "believer." When you see how dedicated people are to service, their jobs and each other you can't help but "sign up." It is not a retailer/vendor relationship in the traditional sense. I genuinely feel part of the team. The daily flow of communication is part of the rhythm of my day. Because the staff includes so many great people who are genuine and hardworking, I just want to do everything I can to support their business. Also, despite the breakneck pace, the stress level never seems over the top . . .probably because a good party could (and likely will) break out at anytime.

CAMERON B.
King Fish Media, LLC

After two years as a Zappos business partner, everyone on the King Fish Media team feels truly included in the Zappos culture. We experience the energy and enthusiasm of the brand on a daily basis. Business collaboration takes patience, and making the effort to understand where both sides complement one another is paramount. Zappos took the time to listen, and to understand how to leverage our strengths against their own. It is hugely apparent that the people who work for and with Zappos love what they do, and we completely dig being a part of that spirit. What is consistently amazing is that when we share with friends and business partners that we work with Zappos, the reaction is always the same. People light up when we mention the Zappos name, and inevitably, they share with us their experience with the company. Whether it's relating a terrific customer service moment, or mentioning the fun, and vibrant company culture, it's obvious that Zappos exceeds at delivering happiness. Quite simply, no other business today can match the services generated by Zappos employees.

CHRIS W.
Premier Packaging

What does Zappos Culture mean to me?
Well … it means freedom! Freedom from the everyday way of doing business. Freedom from the neckties and khakis. Freedom from the stuffy conference rooms and meetings with blank stares and the same old blah-blah-blah. It means a great party every now and again … and a big smile every time you stand face-to-face with a Zappos employee. It is incredibly refreshing to work with the Zappos team at the KDC every day and to continually feel a part of the creative solution and the bigger picture rather than just being another supplier.
Thanks for being a great partner!!!

PARTNERS

DAN S.
IMG-College

Of course, our partnership with Zappos at the West Coast Conference (WCC) has its business goals and objectives for each entity. However, at the core of this partnership are the beliefs and values the WCC shares with Zappos, specifically, two of Zappos' Ten Core Values: to "WOW with service" and to "Do more with less." Both of these core values are exhibited by Zappos and the WCC in an important component of this partnership, the shoe drive and "Kidz Day" at the Zappos Men's and Women's Basketball Championships in Las Vegas.

The shoe collection, donation, and subsequent distribution, performed in conjunction with the Zappos/West Coast Conference Basketball Championships in Las Vegas resulted in more than 6,000 used and new shoes being distributed to the international non-profit organization, Soles for Souls, as well as to underprivileged youth in Las Vegas in 2009. We expect to blast past that total this in 2010, and "WOW" the Las Vegas community with our joint ability to serve.
The actual distribution to Las Vegas youth on the day of the final game in Las Vegas last year was particularly telling of Zappos' and the WCC's shared commitment to "Deliver WOW through Service." Zappos' employees, approximately 50 in number, along with WCC personnel, went above and beyond to make sure every child who came through the line was fitted and 'wowed' with their new shoes that had been donated by Zappos.

While the shoe drive certainly demonstrated both organizations' dedication to "Deliver WOW through Service', it also is just a small demonstration of both entities' commitment to "Do More with Less." Both Zappos.com and the WCC have built their brands and established a niche in their respective industries by doing more with less. This shoe drive, carried out by the WCC at all eight member institutions before culminating with the Las Vegas distribution, had minimal costs yet affected the lives of thousands.
This event is just a microcosm of the overall belief that there is no limit to what can be accomplished in any industry, no matter what resources are available. The West Coast Conference competes at the highest level of intercollegiate athletics with a budget that pales in comparison to the six BCS conferences, while Zappos has established itself as an industry leader, relying most heavily on its most valuable resources, people and hard work. In an era when the words "partnership," "core values," and "ideals" are thrown around rather loosely, Zappos and the West Coast Conference have developed a foundation for a relationship that tries to live the true meaning of these words, and where employees from every level of each organization are intimately involved.

DANNY M.
Deer Stags, Inc.

When asked this year to submit my thoughts on what the Zappos culture means to me, the question was phrased in the context of "family." My company, Deer Stags, is a family business where, at the end of the day, the entire point of our company is for our Deer Stags family to live happy, healthy, and fulfilling lives. It has been fascinating to watch Zappos evolve, and observe the way everyone in the company — from Las Vegas to Kentucky, and beyond — interacts with each other in their business and social lives, displaying the same passion, support, and values that I recognize from my own company. As a vendor, Zappos has very much become my extended business family. I travel all over the country, but when I'm in Las Vegas, I know I have a place to hang out, friends to spend time with, memory's to reminisce about. I feel at home. So I think "family" was an especially appropriate way to think about this question, because the Zappos culture is all about family, and Zappos itself IS a family!

DAVID C.
Intelligrated

Zappos … what an incredible company.? The Zappos Culture … WOW!?
It's smiling faces, friendships, family atmosphere, dedication, passionate service …
oh, and don't forget the parties.

All of these values make the customer loyalty and long-term partnerships so AWESOME!

EVAN F.
Feed Your Sole

What the Zappos Culture means, to me, is simply working with great people. The people at Zappos treat the vendors, the customers, and the other employees with respect. Zappos is a place where you want to spend time and are motivated to help the company do well any way you can. In my opinion, Zappos, above all others, cultivates tremendous relationships and consequently, that turns into a positive for the business by being fair, smart, kind and fun to be around. Business is never easy but there really isn't any reason to treat people poorly and not have fun with what we're doing. It certainly isn't rocket science and the Zappos Culture really encourages everyone to work together toward a successful common goal and enjoy the ride along the way.

HOBIE B.
Wolverine World Wide

We first worked with the Zappos team when they were still located in San Francisco. We had only been in business for less than two years and were still trying to build the brand and chart our course. When Zappos approached us about carrying our footwear, we were skeptical, to say the least. Why would someone want to buy a pair of Harley-Davidson boots online??? Wouldn't they want to try them on? Well ten years and thousands and thousands of happy Zappos/Harley-Davidson customers later, I guess it has worked out pretty well. Thanks to all the folks at Zappos for their support down through the years and best of luck in the future.

JASON W.
Ecco

What does the Zappos Culture mean to me? Knowing that from order to delivery and every step in between, goal #1 for everyone at Zappos is the dedication to exceeding customers' expectations. This is followed by goal #2 ... having the most possible fun in the process! This is what makes Zappos so special.

JULIE C.
Mullen

Wow – We're going to Zappos to see if we can do their advertising.

Wow – This is the coolest shuttle driver in the world.

Wow – That giant ball is made out of nametag stickers.

Wow – There's a measuring tape above the urinal.

Wow – I never had a guy with so many tattoos hold a door for me.

Wow – A girl with roller skates just went by our meeting.

Wow – I think I just saw Elvis eating cheese.

Wow – That's the biggest bottle of Grey Goose I ever saw.

Wow – Tony is buying us our 8th round of drinks.

Wow – We were just invited to be your advertising partner.

Wow – Zappos really does give great wow.

PARTNERS

KEITH B.
Commission Junction

To us, Zappos Culture is based on respect: respect for your customers, respect for your co-workers, and respect for your partners. We've had the pleasure of working with Zappos for ten years, and during that time we have always felt appreciated. Thanks Zappos for WOWing us with your partnership!"

Kel K.
Kel & partners

To me, the essence of the Zappos Culture is about doing whatever it takes to bring happiness to people. Bringing happiness has no bounds and never appears to be limited by finances, geography or conventional wisdom. For Zappos, the more unheard-of the approach used to do this, the better. Zappos employees are truly — not just through lip service — empowered and encouraged to bring as much happiness to people's lives as they can on a daily basis. It is all of these things that makes the Zappos Culture so exceptional and so infectious.

Ken P.
Twig Footwear

For better or worse, we live in a society where we are titles first and people second. I am a rep for Twig. Alesha is my buyer. Tara is a clerical. Erica is a Manager. Andy is a Divisional. And so it goes, until you get to Zappos.

At Zappos, we are treated as people first. This is a departure from any other business that I have ever had dealings with. I am respected as a person. I am treated like a person. I am dealt with as a person. Titles or associations are secondary at Zappos. We are names, not titles, at Zappos. It is truly the rare, exotic company that recognizes this. I consider it a privilege to be working with a company that understands the value of the individual.

MARCIE V.
Morgan Stanley

Whether it is touring headquarters, visiting the Kentucky warehouse (both pre- and post-Kiva) or working with a broad range of Zappos teams, we have always been impressed with how humble, open, candid and enthusiastic Zapponians are. What has impressed us the most is how every employee is driven to WOW his/her customers, vendors, and partners. Through the years, we have witnessed that Zappos is a truly customer-centric company and customer obsession is deeply embedded in your DNA and culture. The foundation of our business is also building relationships and trust with our clients and we are honored that we were able to earn the trust of Zappos. With each and every interaction, we focus on providing the best advice and maximizing the service we provide to our clients. Through our partnership with Zappos, we have been inspired and have been able to elevate our client-obsession by internalizing the Zappos WOW philosophy.

Thank you for integrating Morgan Stanley into the Zappos family and including us in milestone Zappos events such as your 10-year anniversary celebration, employee all-hands meeting, employee appreciation party and of course, working with you as you joined forces with Amazon.com. We are honored that we have had the unique opportunity to work with this truly unique company. We look forward to continuing our partnership. Cheers to another ten years of delivering happiness!

MELINDA W.
Microsoft

The opportunity to partner with Zappos over the last two years has consistently provided a source of sunshine for my team and me. The Zappos crew is genuine, down-to-earth, honest, incredibly hospitable, HAPPY and FUN. That speaks volumes about the Zappos Culture, and doesn't even touch on the amazing and valuable business they work on every day. It's such a unique and welcome experience for the tables to be turned around and for us to feel such appreciation from our advertising partners!

MICHAEL V.
Nets Basketball

Our perspective as a franchise has always been focused on setting ourselves apart from the pack, to be special and different. By executing our mantra of "More Than a Game,", we create experiences and relationships with our fans and partners that they will not find anywhere else. Zappos not only shares that same viewpoint, but leads the way in bringing it to life. Our experience with the Zappos Cculture this season has been remarkable and we look forward to continuing our relationship for years to come.

PETER K.
Amazon.com

During my 13 years of M&A experience, I have never seen a more unique and energetic culture than the one I observed at Zappos. During our due diligence and interactions, the entire Zappos team went out of their way to be open and honest (a Zappos Core Value). It was clear that management was genuinely concerned about the company's Ten Core Values, its employees, and the future of Zappos. I look forward to a very bright, shared future.

SANDY P.
Axis Promotions

Zapponian: A way of thinking, being, creating and working.
Zappos: The most refreshing, optimistic and opportunistic, and HAPPY workplace I am lucky enough to visit.

Very proud to be a partner and share in the world of Zappos.

SIMON W.
Yahoo!

I've had the pleasure with working Zappos as a partner for close to five years, and the first thought that comes to mind when I think about the Zappos Culture is passion. That's a quality that can't be taught, and one exuded by every person I've come in contact with at Zappos: they're passionate about the company, passionate about what they do, passionate about working hard, and – most importantly – passionate about having fun. The admirable culture at Zappos permeates everywhere, even to those they touch with their exceptional customer service. Basically, Zappos delivers happiness to consumers and to partners alike. It's truly been a pleasure experiencing the Zappos Culture first-hand. Best wishes for continued success!

PARTNERS

STEVE T.
IMG

When I first met with Zappos a few years ago, I was shocked by the way I was treated. Surprisingly, one staffer offered me an airport ride, followed by a bottle of water outside their office on a hot summer day in Vegas, snacks, complimentary books and more. I rarely receive this kind of treatment (sometimes on my birthday) and I thought, "This can't be true!?" However, having been back to Zappos numerous times, the staffers are so genuinely nice, accommodating and well mannered, it really makes you feel good.

I lead my life quite simply — I keep my wife happy, which allows our three kids to be happy, which creates a harmonious home environment, which in turn allows me to focus on work without worrying about personal distractions. It's analogous to the culture at Zappos, where if you keep the employees happy and engaged, everything else falls into place. When the employees are aligned on the same page and working toward the same goal of providing genuine world-class service, it helps, particularly in challenging situations. (For example, unlike most companies, at Zappos, employees will spend the time and effort to always "make things right!")

I've become more impressed with Zappos after every visit, and now, having had the privilege of working with Zappos on a couple of projects, I always chuckle to myself, after interacting with the team at Zappos, that this is a company I would love to work for. Which says a lot, coming from guy who works in his dream job of sports marketing.

WAYNE G.
IBM

FUN. That is what the Zappos culture means to me. But, just fun is not enough to keep Zappos growing at the rate it is. The culture of allowing individual expression and creativity at all levels is what makes Zappos stronger than the sum of its parts. Employees want to work harder. Customers want them to succeed and vendors love to do business with them. It's a culture of FUN that everyone wants to be a part of and that's what makes Zappos a success.

DRIVE TEAM
FUN CREATE POSITIVE
CHANGE SERVICE
ADVENTUROUS
WOW
RELATIONSHIP OPEN
COMMUNICATION SPIRIT
WEIRDNESS GROWTH
LEARNING OPEN-MINDED
PASSIONATE DELIVER HONEST EMBRACE
DETERMINED FAMILY
HUMBLE

DELIVERING HAPPIN

launch

DELIVERING Happiness

DELIVERING Happiness

welcome to

happy

HOUR

mayor Oscar B. Goodman
talks about Vegas, happiness
and show girls
(not necessarily in order of importance)

"just read #deliveringhappiness by
@zappos & it inspired me to make my
workplace more fun than it already is.
Is that possible? Yay for WOW."
            as tweeted by @tonyhawk

so what is DELIVE

BOOK SIGNING | 10 – 11PM
SIGNED BOOKS WITH A $33 DONATION TO LIVESTRONG

a MOVEM

that happens to have a BOOK

g News   Bloomberg

ENT
about HAPPINESS

a MOVEMENT

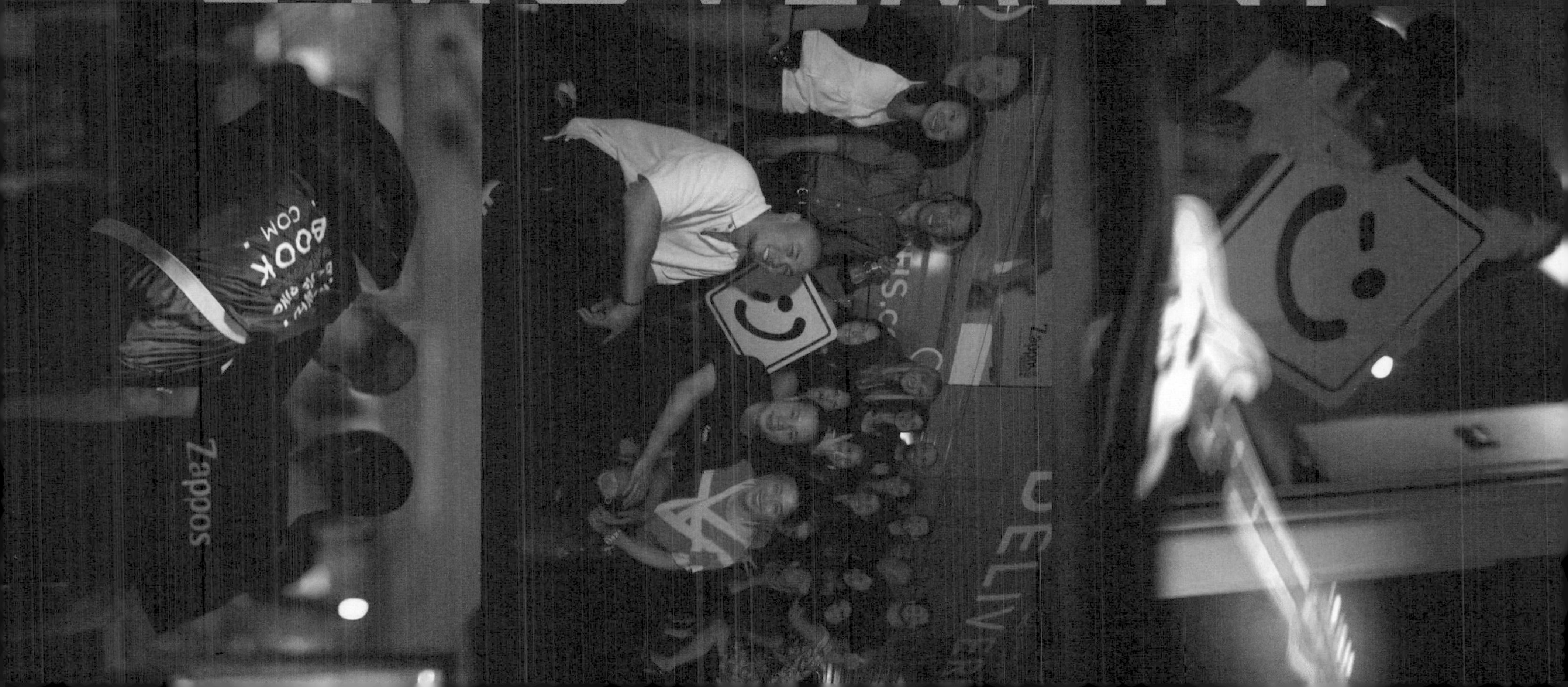

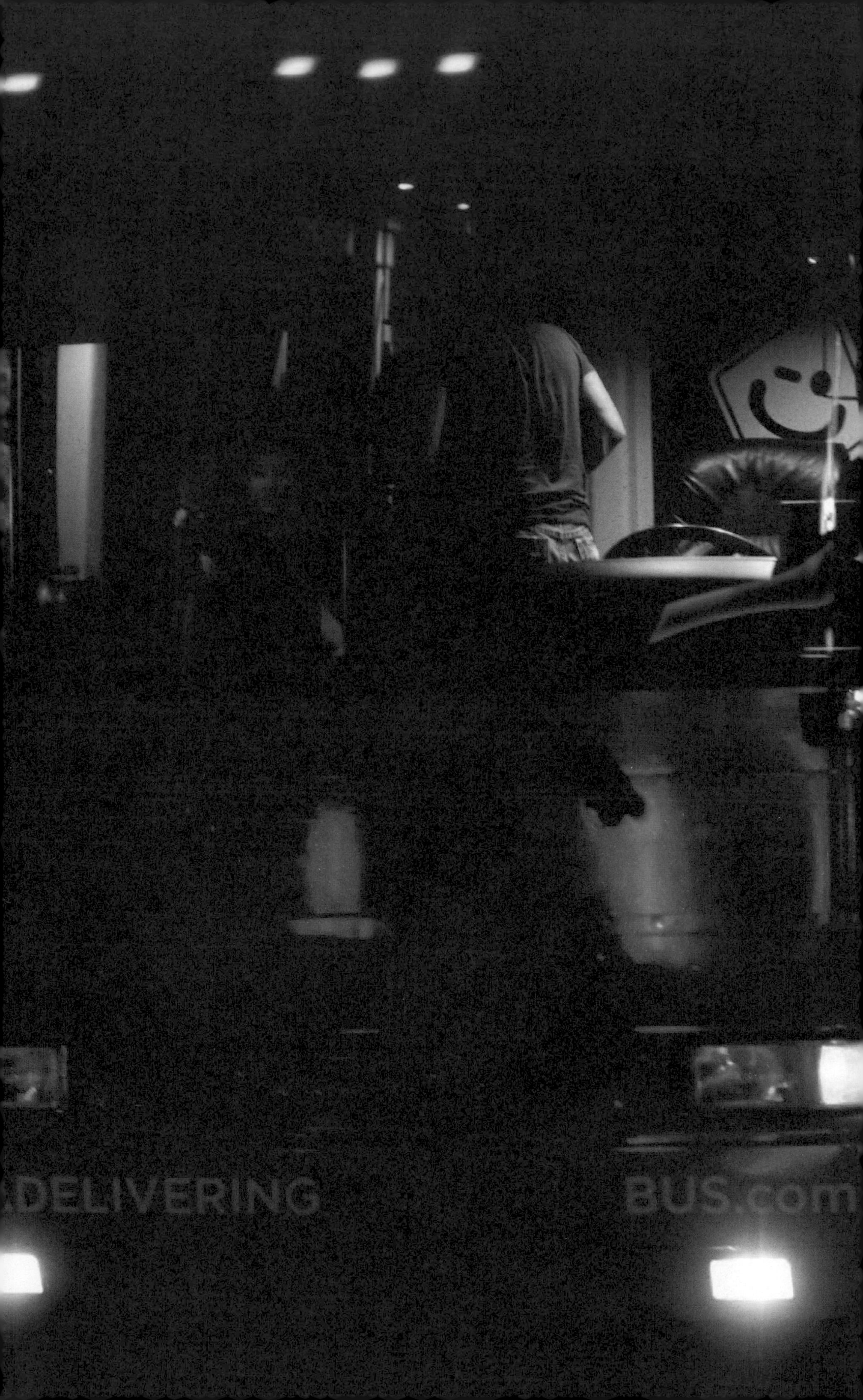

ADELIVERING
BUS.com

last

and by

no

means

least

it's time for some

CUSTO

OMER

appreciation

CUSTOMER

"Watermelon Vans. The happiest pair of shoes I own." – Dawn Walker

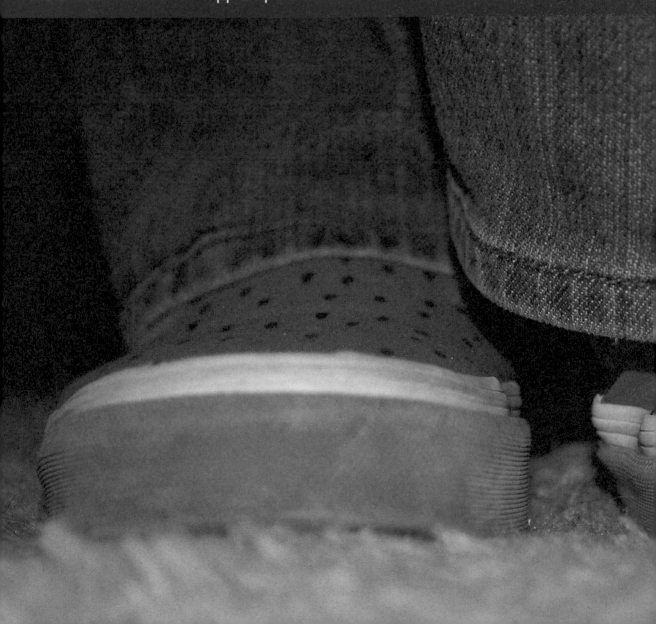

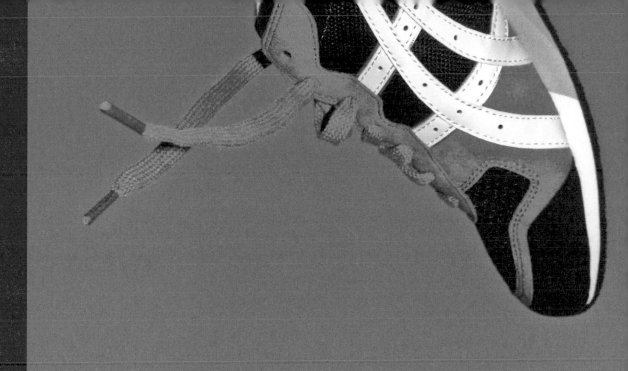

"I'm always so excited when getting a new pair I throw things in the air. At times they might even be the shoes themselves."
— Grady Herndon

"Sparkle Toes" (as my sweet little toddler calls them)
— Amber Wadey

appreciation

"As a South African I have never purchased anything from Zappos... yet, but I love the culture, and what Zappos has created. The book has been incredibly inspiring for me as a small business owner."

– Marcel Boast, reading the 2009 Culture Book

"We were so inspired by your Culture Book that we decided to create something similar. We have just begun the process, but in 2009 we launched an initiative called "In It To Win.""

– Jamie Guerrero, HR at Phillips Consumer Lifestyle

" The amount of happiness you have depends on the amount of freedom you have in your heart."

-Thich Nhat Hanh

photo
Khanr

Amy Mancini, the JHPTR
(J. Hilburn Partners that Rock)
and their Zappos-inspired Core Values

Core Values

1. **Belief in Slow and Steady**

2. **Embrace and Drive Change**

3. **Contribute Beyond Self-**
   through philanthropy
   and mentorship

4. **Obsess over the customer**

5. **Treat others as we'd like to
   be treated**

6. **Lead by Example
   and Innovation**

7. **Inspired by success of others**

8. **Share our successes openly**

CUSTOMER

rada

dova

National Parks, and nature in general, make me smile. A lot.

– Caity Engler

"Monarch butterflies. How do they survive a thousand mile trip over tall
mountain ranges? No one really knows. But they do it. Year after year.
It's awesome. Zappos core value #8 – do more with less."

– Rebecca Arney

APPRECIATION

"Random photos taken in the great state of Nevada. I almost passed out hiking up hills carrying that 12 foot longboard."

- Greg

another year passes
another year of living, breathing and being

ZAPPOS CULTURE

TILL
NEXT
YEAR

don't forget to keep life...

FUN

and a little weird

it's always so hard to say goodbye
so we won't

but Stanley has something to say though

BYE
BYE